Extraterritorial Dreams

Extraterritorial Dreams

EUROPEAN CITIZENSHIP, SEPHARDI JEWS, AND THE OTTOMAN TWENTIETH CENTURY

Sarah Abrevaya Stein

The University of Chicago Press   CHICAGO & LONDON

SARAH ABREVAYA STEIN is professor of history and Maurice Amado Chair in Sephardic Studies at the University of California, Los Angeles. A Guggenheim Fellow, she is the author of many books, including *Saharan Jews and the Fate of French Algeria*, also published by the University of Chicago Press.

The University of Chicago Press, Chicago 60637
The University of Chicago Press, Ltd., London
© 2016 by The University of Chicago
All rights reserved. Published 2016.
Printed in the United States of America

25 24 23 22 21 20 19 18 17 16   1 2 3 4 5

ISBN-13: 978-0-226-36819-1 (cloth)
ISBN-13: 978-0-226-36822-1 (paper)
ISBN-13: 978-0-226-36836-8 (e-book)
DOI: 10.7208/chicago/9780226368368.001.0001

Library of Congress Cataloging-in-Publication Data
Names: Stein, Sarah Abrevaya, author.
Title: Extraterritorial dreams : European citizenship, Sephardi Jews, and the Ottoman twentieth century / Sarah Abrevaya Stein.
Description: Chicago : University of Chicago Press, [2016] | ©2016 | Includes bibliographical references and index.
Identifiers: LCCN 2015043311 | ISBN 9780226368191 (cloth : alkaline paper) | ISBN 9780226368221 (paperback : alkaline paper) | ISBN 9780226368368 (e-book)
Subjects: LCSH: Jews—Turkey—History—20th century. | Sephardin—Turkey—History—20th century. | Jews—Europe—History— 20th Century. | Jews—Legal status, laws, etc.—History.
Classification: LCC DS135.T8 S75 2016 | DDC 940.3089/924056—dc23 LC record available at http://lccn.loc.gov/2015043311

To my grandparents, z"l,
Jay and Lorayne Stein
and
Victor and Sally Abbey (Abrevaya)
whose extraterritorial dreams I have followed across many borders,
and to the City of Angels.

Like most young Jewish men born in Turkey toward the end of the century, Vili dispar-
aged anything to do with Ottoman culture and thirsted for the West, finally becoming
"Italian" the way most Jews in Turkey did: by claiming ancestral ties with Leghorn, a
port city near Pisa where escaped Jews from Spain had settled in the sixteenth century. A
very distant Italian relative bearing the Spanish name of Pardo-Roques was conveniently
dug up in Leghorn—Vili was half Pardo-Roques himself, whereupon all living "cousins"
in Turkey immediately became Italian. . . . Uncle Vili knew how to convey that intangi-
ble though unmistakable feeling that he had lineage—a provenance so ancient and so
distinguished that it transcended such petty distinctions as birthplace, nationality, and
religion . . .

ANDRÉ ACIMAN, Out of Egypt

Dear Rebecca, we must have patience until God brings us all back together again in
good health, which is most the important thing. Let the children know everything. They
should write down on a piece of paper like the ones they used to have our dates of birth
as well as when they became French. As for you, if God brings you neither money nor
jewels do not be concerned. They take it all anyway.

LETTER BY BENSION HAIM YACO SOULAM TO REBECCA SOULAM
[NÉE BENSASSON], written from the Drancy internment camp, c. 1941–1942

If I reckon up the many forms I have filled out during these years, declarations on every
trip, tax declarations, foreign exchange certificates, border passes, entrance permits, departure permits, registrations on coming and on going; the many hours I have spent
in ante-rooms of consulates and officials, the many inspectors, friendly and unfriendly,
bored and overworked, before whom I have sat, the many examinations and interroga-
tions at frontiers I have been through, then I feel keenly how much human dignity has
been lost in this century . . . Human beings made to feel that they were objects and not
subjects, that nothing was their right but everything merely a favor by official grace. They
were codified, registered, numbered, stamped and even today I, as a case-hardened crea-
ture of an age of freedom and a citizen of the world-republic of my dreams, count every
impression of a rubber-stamp in my passport a stigma, every one of those hearings and
searches a humiliation. They are petty trifles, always merely trifles, I am well aware, trifles
in a day when human values sink more rapidly than those of currencies.

STEFEN ZWEIG, The World of Yesterday, 1943

CONTENTS

NOTE ON TRANSLATION AND
TRANSLITERATION

The complexity of being an extraterritorial subject or protector nation is often embodied in archival documents, which employ multiple spellings and versions of people and place names. In the interest of honoring my sources, I tend to employ proper names as they appear in archival originals, except in the instance of people or place names commonly employed in English-language scholarship, e.g., Edirne, Istanbul, Izmir, and Salonica. In transliterating Ladino, I employ the Aki Yerushalayim system, which represents the language phonetically. Hebrew transliterations accord to the system of the Library of Congress with diacritics removed and phonetic guidelines respected.

All translations are my own unless otherwise specified.

Introduction: Extraterritorial Dreams

In June 2015, Spain granted citizenship to qualified applicants able to demonstrate descent from Jews expelled from fifteenth-century Spain. The policy evokes another, passed a year earlier, which avails Portuguese citizenship to the descendants of Jews who fled the Inquisition and forced conversions of fifteenth-century Portugal. Both sets of actions pay tribute to their countries' multicultural legacies, although similar policies towards Muslims have not been implemented. Many Sephardi families in Turkey, Israel, and the United States (and beyond) have embraced the proposals, seeing Spanish or Portuguese citizenship as a shortcut to EU citizenship—a useful commodity regardless of whether the new citizen intends to dwell on Iberian soil.[1] To others, Spain's and Portugal's pursuit of Sephardi subjects appears crass, and the associated conditions, language and historical examinations, and fees imposed by the state distasteful.

All these actors, seemingly unknowingly, are reenacting a drama first staged five centuries ago, when, in accordance with a series of bilateral treaties between the European powers and the Ottoman leadership (known to the Ottomans as *ahdnameler* and to the Europeans as the capitulations or the capitulatory regime), the states of Europe began to register Ottoman-born, non-Muslim subjects—at first, almost entirely Christian translators—as protégés, or protected subjects. Then, as now, strategic motives underlay the development. For many centuries, as today, the European powers viewed the acquisition of Christian (as well as some Jewish) subjects as materially and symbolically advantageous, while the individuals involved perceived the acquisition of foreign protection as a canny investment and a hedge against an unstable world. The pursuit of Ottoman Jewish subjects, it seems, suggests the enduring salience of a centuries-old story, as well as a metric by which to measure and evaluate current events.

This book is not so much preoccupied with the history of the protégé as with the prismatic breaking apart of this status in the modern period, including its transmutation into various legal spectral forms. More specifically, it traces the experience of Ottoman Jewish women, men, and children—Jews of Ottoman birth or descent—who held, sought, or lost the protection of a European power in the late nineteenth and early twentieth centuries, when the capitulatory regime was giving way to the passport regime and the Ottoman Empire giving way to various successor states.[2] Some of these protégés remained in the place of their birth, partaking in a transition from empire to nation-state, protectorate, or mandate regime. Others carried their legal status to émigré settings or passed their legal identity to children or grandchildren born outside the empire who in turn carried protégé status through migrations of their own. These circumstances meant that a Jewish man or woman could exist, legally speaking, as a British protected subject dwelling in Shanghai who had inherited this legal status from a father who, despite having been born in Baghdad, obtained British protection from a consul in Bombay: or as a Portuguese protégé born in Istanbul who lived all of her adult life in Rio de Janeiro, never setting foot on Portuguese soil; or as a French protégé of Ottoman descent raised in Vienna who had dwelt neither in the Ottoman Empire nor in France; or as the Ottoman-born, Salonican-dwelling subject of the Greek state compelled to struggle with Hellenizing authorities to preserve Spanish papers acquired in 1912, when her war-torn city was no longer Ottoman but not yet Greek. These trajectories, all real, were "extraterritorial" insofar as they concerned people with a degree of exemption from local law due to their protection by a foreign power.[3] These stories are constitutive of what I am calling the Ottoman twentieth century, an era in which residual traces of a quintessentially Ottoman legal regime were palpable even after the empire was dismantled, and well outside its erstwhile boundaries.

In invoking "extraterritorial dreams," I conjure the reveries and traumas of a variety of actors who contended with extraterritoriality at a time when the value and future of this legal niche was profoundly uncertain. There were, in the first instance, Jewish women, men, and children born in the Ottoman Empire (and their children or grandchildren, who might have been born elsewhere) who held, sought, or lost the protection of a European state. Second, there were the many state representatives with whom these individuals dealt:

consuls and vice-consuls (some of whom were themselves Mediterranean or Middle Eastern Jews), ambassadors, auditors, legal counsels of state, foreign ministry representatives, local police—all of whom had the power to affirm or deny a request for paperwork or even annul or transform the paperwork issued by others. Many of these officials, as we shall see, harbored phantasmagorical ideas about the benefits protégé Ottoman Jews offered (or the threat they posed) to the state. Third, there was a class of people we might call active observers: Jews and non-Jews who lauded or criticized extraterritoriality from a variety of perspectives—legal, local, xenophobic, communitarian, nationalist, Zionist, socialist, imperialist.[4] Finally, there was a bevy of nongovernmental organizations invested in the fate of the protected subject. These organizations, which included a number of powerful Jewish philanthropies, appreciated that the fate of Jewish extraterritorials (like the fate of other holders of ambiguous legal status of the time, including the stateless, expelled, transferred, and exchanged) was of international concern. Reconstructing the multivocal conversation about extraterritoriality conducted between these parties (and understanding what this conversation teaches us about modern citizenship, Jews, and the relationship between the states of western and central Europe, on the one hand, and the Ottoman Empire and its successor states in Southeastern Europe and the Middle East, on the other) is the principal goal of this book.

Over the course of the late nineteenth and early twentieth centuries, as the number of Jewish protégés soared, emigration from the Ottoman Empire increased, and as the legal utility of protection became ever more ambiguous these myriad actors furiously debated the nature and future of extraterritoriality as a legal phenomenon. Among the questions they asked were: Was the protégé status, as one legal theorist put it, "out of accord with the system of the modern world"?[5] Ought this legal category to morph into citizenship? Or had the large numbers of Mediterranean, Middle Eastern, and Southeastern European protected persons become costly liabilities to the state—so much so that previously extended promises of protection be revoked (at least from the poor, who promised the state little financial return)? Conversely, could the scaling back of protection by the states that had the largest numbers of protégés in the eighteenth and early nineteenth centuries—namely, France, Great Britain, and Italy—provide an opportunity for other states with a strategic interest in the early twentieth-century Mediterranean—namely, Spain, Portugal, and Austro-Hungary?

This is a transnational, transregional, and transimperial story whose case studies take shape at the moments (sometimes banal, sometimes tense) at which empires, states, and individuals meet, compete, and collide. In the pages that follow we meet protected subjects whose histories wove through India, China, Great Britain, France, Spain, Portugal, Angola, Morocco, Algeria, Tunisia, Egypt, Palestine, Syria, Iraq, Turkey, Bulgaria, Greece, Italy, Austro-Hungary, Germany, Brazil, the United States, and the Ottoman Empire (which at times controlled certain of the aforementioned territories). Our focus is primarily upon histories of Jews; but in almost every instance, the relationship between Jewish protégés (and would-be protégés) and state authorities echoed with the history of other protégés, would-be protégés, and colonial subjects, be they Greek Orthodox, Armenian, Melkite, Maronite, Catholic, Muslim, Hindu, Buddhist, or Sikh. One can tease the thread of Jewish protégé history without losing sight of this larger tapestry; indeed, this exercise throws certain dimensions of European, Jewish, Ottoman (as well as Middle Eastern and Mediterranean), émigré, and legal history—in addition to their complex intersections—into sharp relief.

Notwithstanding the global reach of this book, local dynamics had a palpable impact on state attitudes and policies regarding Jewish protégés. Local dynamics also influenced individual Jewish protégés and seekers of protection, who made tactical choices based on their assessments of the interfering historical waves. Though "local," the dynamics that undergirded protégé relationships were not narrow, geographically speaking. On the contrary, these dynamics were shaped in all the urban centers of the Mediterranean and Middle East, from Tetouan to Alexandria, Cairo to Jerusalem, Beirut tō Baghdad, and Izmir to Istanbul; across the Sephardi diaspora, from Marseilles to Manchester, New York City to Rio de Janeiro, and Calcutta to Shanghai; and within the states of Europe and their colonies abroad. This transhemispheric history is also local insofar as the legal functionality of protection came to vary in the twentieth century over place and time, dependent upon whether one was a man or a woman; first-, second-, or third-generation protégé; poor or rich; aggressive in one's pursuit of papers or not. Sometimes protection was provisional, sometimes permanent. Sometimes it had an expiration date, and at other times its shelf life was unspecified and hinged on negotiation between a protégé and state representatives. At times, the state could annul a protégé status after declaring it "false."[6] At other times, the solidity of a given relationship of protection could be strategically challenged, stretched, or leveraged by the protégé himself. Jewish seekers of protection (and those who acquired and wished to preserve it) were sometimes adept at shaping supplications to their advantage, invoking histories and origin stories that, even if fictitious, could be taken by state representatives as fact—and could, in turn, influence the fate of individual protected subjects, create legal precedent for his or her descendants, and shape prospects for protégés elsewhere.

These creative histories sometimes even had wider consequences. Ottoman-born Jewish seekers of French protection included some who claimed to descend from Bayonne, thereby invoking a legal relationship that linked the early modern French state to the prosperous "New Christians" who settled in southern France after fleeing the Iberian Peninsula in the late fifteenth and early sixteenth centuries.[7] Despite the fact that these "Bayonnese Jews" had no verifiable link to Bayonne, their claims were validated by French representatives and came, at a sensitive moment in the First World War, to influence French policy regarding Mediterranean, Southeastern European, and Middle Eastern Jewish protégés—such that an origin story shaped within the Ottoman Empire, by ordinary women and men, swayed who was considered to belong to and in the French Republic. This array of permutations arose because state representatives and their supplicants interpreted the protégé relationship variously. Less a stable legal category, protection was a matter of perspective.

Making this picture all the more complex is the fact that regardless of which European state one speaks of, or whether one is concerned with Ottoman authority, the state was not a single, discrete actor in this drama. Each of the states of Europe, like the Ottoman Empire, followed its own path in shaping citizenship laws, of course; the "European citizenship" referred to in the title of this book bespeaks cacophony rather than harmony, in addition to hinting at the contemporary relevance of this story. That said, when it came to state oversight of Ottoman Jewish protégés navigating migration, war, and the dismantling of the Ottoman Empire, the states of Europe and the Ottoman authorities had one important quality in common: the absence of clear rules and regulations. Whether a given protégé was in dialogue with British, French, Spanish, Portuguese, Italian, American, Austrian, or Ottoman authorities, her ability to obtain or renew protection—and even the precise legalese that appeared on her paperwork—hinged on the mood, knowledge, and ambitions of the bureaucrats and offices with whom she dealt.[8] Indeed, local consular officials, police representatives, and government bureaucrats did not always understand or choose to follow foreign ministry directives pertaining to the protection of protégés, in some cases because they were themselves Mediterranean or Middle Eastern Jews with strong (if various) views on the matter at hand. For that matter, foreign ministry directives were themselves not stable, but open to constant reassessment, review, and audit. No rigid doctrine, protection emerged from negotiation and experimentation, and ultimately proved to be a measure of the diffuse and unruly nature of state power.

Consider this surprisingly honest 1881 account of what it meant for a representative of a foreign state (in this case, the United States) stationed in the Ottoman Empire to encounter the nuances of the capitulatory regime:

> It happens quite often that a newly-appointed consul arrives at his post in a Turkish city without a knowledge of the principles that govern the relations of his fellow-citizens residing in the consular district to which he has been sent with the authorities and natives of the land, between whom he is the only proper medium of official communication . . . Casting about to find some guide, some authority, from which he can obtain light upon the origin of the international principle that forms the basis of the multitudinous and multifarious duties and functions that have been conferred upon him by the statutes, he meets at the very outset with two difficulties. First, he knows not the native language, and has scarcely any, or in most cases, no acquaintance at all with the commercial and diplomatic languages of the Levant, which are the French and Italian. Second, he can find no one book that contains the information he so much requires before he can see through the maze of the rights, privileges, and immunities of foreigners, ecclesiastics, and protégés in Turkey, all of which prerogatives the small colony of his fellow citizens lay claim to under the elastic treaty stipulation commonly called the most favored nation clause. What he desires to find exists but is scattered throughout a large number of books, most of which are either in Italian or in French and, moreover, are not on the shelves of the consulate library. Besides, he cannot always afford the time to wade through so many works . . .[9]

Consular ignorance, combined with hubris and a genuinely confusing legal landscape, rendered protection as much a product of local practice as a matter of national or international law. State representatives often fudged (or even directly disobeyed) official directives, or simply realized them in an inventive fashion.

For much of the time, the protégé relationship cost the states of Europe little while affording concrete benefit. Protector nations collected modest taxes from living protégés and potentially enormous levies from dead ones. Individual consular representative accepted fees (and, in cases, bribes) in return for paperwork, despite vigorous Ottoman efforts to arrest such abuses.[10] Finally, rather more amorphously, protégés were viewed as valuable vehicles for the expression—and, at times, the expansion—of European interest.

These benefits persisted into the twentieth century, but over time came to be shadowed by novel risks. War, in particular, made protégés expensive and risky propositions. In wartime, an extraterritorial subject could require protection of person or property beyond what the state was able to provide. If a protégé became a refugee, he might demand repatriation or reparations, and migration only added to the complexity. The legal consequences of protection became similarly thorny with time. As the Ottoman Empire and the states of Europe sought to solidify the boundary between citizen and protégé (a process that began in the nineteenth century but that gained steam in the early twentieth), the adjudication of legal matters pertaining to protégés threatened to set precedents that neither the Ottoman authorities nor the states of Europe were willing or able to honor. This was particularly true during and in the wake of the First World War. For the leadership of the Committee of Union and Progress (or CUP, popularly known as the Young Turks) brought to power by a 1913 military coup, the war provided a pretext for a ruthless assault on non-Muslims—especially Armenians, but including other Christians and Jews—as well as some Muslim foreign nationals (including protégés) living in Syria and Palestine. The resulting refugee crisis tested the magnanimity of protector nations. It also hinted at far greater unclarities to come. After the war, the creation of protectorate and mandate regimes in the Middle East transformed millions of women and men into colonial subjects of the Western powers with ambiguous rights and responsibilities.[11] How risky it now was, from the perspective of the Great Britain and France, to treat Ottoman Jewish protégés generously while so many more potential protégés looked on.

Jewish holders of protection, for their part, recognized that protégé status had grown malleable by the turn of the twentieth century. Protection could be revoked, but it could also be leveraged and in certain cases even transformed into citizenship, notwithstanding laws to the contrary. At times (if, for example, it might insulate one from state conscription efforts) individual protégés saw it in their interest to interpret "protection" in the broadest possible fashion; at other times (if, in another configuration, it might insulate one from state conscription efforts), a more constrained interpretation proved desirable. In the absence of strict and coherent rules, clear directives, or fixed ambitions on the part of the states involved—and in light of so many border changes and migrations—protection was a plastic entity shaped by the competing dreams and nightmares of the parties involved.

TOWARD A HISTORY OF LEGAL MISFITS

In the course of the late nineteenth and early twentieth centuries, as Ottoman Jewish protégés migrated and experienced wars, border changes, and the radical reconfiguring of political geography, they struggled to comprehend—and, in many cases, stretch—legal categories that owed a historical debt to the capitulatory regime but that reflected only vaguely the norms of early modern protection. As they did so, they carried on extended conversations with officials at all levels of state bureaucracy, and these representatives puzzled over the elusive boundary between practice, policy, and law governing extraterritoriality. The aspiration of this book is to parse the resulting multi-partied and multi-sited dialogue—at times carried on over decades, or even generations—using it to rethink the relationship between the states of Europe and subjects (and descendants) of the Ottoman Empire, as well as the nature of European citizenship in and of itself.

Since at least the late nineteenth century, Ottomans, Europeans, and Americans condemned the capitulatory regime and the legally pluralistic environment it produced within the Ottoman Empire, calling it corrupt—particularly in comparison to the theoretically rational, mono-legal, and ostensibly superior European and American legal environments. Departing from this polarized and fundamentally skeptical view, my emphasis here is on the variety of debates and experiences that accompanied the gradual and uneven devolution of the protégé system. This approach seeks inspiration from the growing body of scholarship on legal pluralism (that is, environments of overlapping legal orders and competing jurisdictions) in the Mediterranean and Middle East that understands legally pluralistic environments as fonts of choice and strategy.[12] In keeping with this rich literature, my emphasis is not on an arc of decline nor on a linear movement from extraterritorial dreams to extraterritorial nightmares, but on the meandering paths of the actors involved. More specifically, this book offers a series of nested arguments about the nature of citizenship; the spectrum of legal identities inhabited by modern Jews; and the complex entanglement of European, Ottoman, Mediterranean, Middle Eastern, and diasporic histories.

This history of extraterritoriality contributes, first, to an ongoing conversation on the exceptionally messy nature of modern European citizenship. Extraterritoriality undermined regnant citizenship norms in Europe because the rights and limits associated with this legal identity were ill-defined; because even if being a protected subject was never the same as being a citizen, many Jewish protégés and state representatives perceived the two as equal or chose, for a variety of reasons, to treat them as one; because so many extraterritorial subjects never lived (nor ever intended to live) in the nation from which they held protection, causing particular trouble for the state at times of war; and because migration, regional violence, and the creation of new nations (and nationalizing projects) in Southeastern Europe and the Middle East created novel political demands to which Jewish protégés and their protector states were compelled to respond. To attend to extraterritoriality is thus to attend (borrowing loosely from Laura Tabili) to the "discrepancy between nationality [as it was] defined by states and citizenship [as it took shape] through local relations and daily life": and to look beyond binary understandings of citizenship or nationality, towards the subtle degrees of political belonging an individual could occupy in Europe and the Middle East in the late nineteenth century and the first half of the twentieth.[13] For this, the case of the Jewish protégé provides a most excellent optic. One could argue, indeed, that European state attitudes towards the legal institution of extraterritoriality ebbed and flowed in relationship to Mediterranean and Middle Eastern Jewish history—as it did in relation to the histories of other mercantile diasporas, including the Armenian, Greek, Syrian, and Maltese.

The second, related ambition of this book is to intervene into the historiography of the field of Jewish history. Too often, scholars within the field have viewed citizenship flatly, as something Jews either possessed or lacked. Similarly, it has long been assumed that Jews' possession or lack of citizenship is a metric by which to measure a range of cultural, economic, political, and gendered practices.[14] The story of Jewish protégés and their descendants pushes us to consider citizenship as a spectrum: a range of conditions or positions that Jews could access rather than a singular possession they could or could not claim. For the Ottoman Jews who aspired to protégé status, as for the states that extended it, extraterritoriality was not simply a legal niche but a potent concept, a framework into which one could invest one's fears, ambitions, and dreams. In this, Jewish tangles with legal belonging resonate not only with the history of Ottoman Christian protégés, but with the history of myriad other groups that defied easy categorization by the state because they muddied the legal boundaries meant to divide citizen from foreigner, colonial subject, and protégé.[15]

A correlated aspiration of this study is to introduce the agency of individuals to the story of Jewish emancipation. Citizenship has typically been understood by Jewish historians as something the state either offered or denied Jews, notwithstanding the recognition that Jews often agitated for it. Under certain circumstances, however, Jewish women and men could strategically navigate—or even manipulate—the existing legal options, exploiting loopholes and exploring opportunities to transform their official status to their advantage. This access to juridical fungibility hinged on ambiguities inherent to extraterritoriality as it was shaped in the Ottoman (and extra- and post-Ottoman) context. These opportunities for self-determination were not broadly available to all Jews, including (or perhaps especially) those with ambiguous legal standing such as the stateless, expelled, exchanged, or transferred. Yet, despite the particularity of this story, Ottoman Jewish experiences of the gradual, slumping collapse of the capitulatory regime upend enduring scholarly typologies and chronologies of emancipation. The point is not that empires granted their Jewish male subjects rights, including citizenship, as did the states of Europe—nor that the states of Europe were also empires that denied most of their Muslim and a portion of their Jewish and Christian subjects citizenship. These arguments have been ably made.[16] The principal insight, instead, is that some Ottoman Jews wiggled their way towards the possession of European citizenship; not as a result of migration, which we might expect, but through persistence, ingenuity, and luck. Though that which could be acquired could also be snatched away.

Third and finally, this project demonstrates the importance of considering the history of European citizenship in dialogue with Ottoman, Mediterranean, and Middle Eastern history. While recent scholarship on the early modern capitulatory system has downplayed (if not altogether dismissed) the role of imperial ambition in stoking the desires of capitulatory nations, the pursuit and rejection of Jewish subjects in the late nineteenth and early- to mid-twentieth century were motivated by imperial aspirations in many if not all instances: be it Portuguese desires to expand influence in southern Africa; British desires to exert authority in South Asia, East Asia, or the eastern Mediterranean; French desires to consolidate a hold in North Africa or the eastern Mediterranean; Austro-Hungarian desires to procure a direct trading route to the Aegean Sea and thence to the wider Middle East; or Nazi aspirations to create a globally dominant Third Reich. Each of these motivations directly or indirectly fueled a relationship between the states of Europe and Ottoman Jewish subjects, generating competing fantasies (at times philo-Semitic, at times anti-Semitic, and at times allosemitic—that is, regarding Jews as an ambivalent other) about the benefits and hazards that attended Jewish protected people.

This is not to suggest that Jewish protégés were pawns of European power. Jews brought their own sets of desires and demands to their negotiations with the European powers and, if they acquired protection, sought to use it to their own advantage, sometimes parleying one form of legal identity (that of protégé, say), into another (that of citizen). What's more, the paperwork that could result from the negotiation between Mediterranean and Middle Eastern Jews and state officials often proved of uncertain value to both parties. Sometimes the granting of protection weakened rather than strengthened the state's hand—in other instances, the acquisition of foreign protection backfired for the individual concerned. Finally, there were many instances in which a given state set out to recruit Jewish subjects for a clear set of reasons, only to have state officials frustrated—if not deeply troubled—when they did not achieve the results desired.

How are we to understand the protégé, if neither as a pawn nor as a victor? Becoming a protégé, and obtaining the papers to prove it, was an exercise of will and a political gamble. For some, protected status was a loophole to exploit in the pursuit of European citizenship. For others, it offered a modicum of shelter from the nationalizing policies of young states. The protection of a European power could provide individuals and families a means of confronting, resisting, or strategically manipulating the colonial order, or smooth the rocky transition from empire to informal colonial (including treaty port and mandate) regimes. For émigrés who carried their protégé status through the British or French Empires (or beyond), claiming protected status allowed one to situate oneself outside the dyads of colonial subject or naturalized citizen, colonizer or colonized, Eastern or Western, European or Occidental, even Sephardi or Ashkenazi, rendering protected Jews intermediary figures of imperialism.[17] All told, Jewish protégés of the European powers used their elusive status through a variety of means and to a variety of ends. The richness of their stories cannot be conveyed by resort to platitudes, nor by any quantity of legal doctrine or demographic statistics. Protégé encounters with protector nations and their multitudinous representatives—like protégés' relationships to the papers they sought, carried, and lost, folded and unfolded, treasured, and at times took for granted—were deeply personal: deserving of the vocabulary of intimacy employed throughout this book.

In the chapters that follow, I examine the dissolution and reconfiguration of the institution of protection through the prism of historical episodes selected because of their geographic, conceptual, and temporal range, and because they shed light on relationships between states and subjects that are less well known than others. I make no claims to offer a comprehensive history of the topic at hand, which could be told quite differently from myriad vantages.

We begin, in chapter 1, with the Balkan Wars (1912–13) and the competitive pursuit by various states of Europe of Sephardi subjects in Salonica. This contest, and the actions of Jews with which it was engaged, took shape at the uncertain moment at which Salonica was transitioning from Ottoman to Greek rule, and as Jewish emigration fissured the Judeo-Spanish cultural epicenter—factors that ensured that the worth of Jews' newly earned protection would shift uncertainly, over time and space. Chapter 2 reconstructs the abrogation of the capitulatory regime by the Ottoman authorities and the expulsion of Allied nationals from Ottoman Syria and Palestine by wartime governor Cemal Paşa in the course of the First World War. Here we consider how expulsion was experienced by protégés and the (erstwhile) capitulatory nations of Europe, triangulating with the Armenian genocide and forever shifting the symbolic and legal value of protection. Chapter 3, also rooted in the era of the First World War, takes us to Western Europe to investigate the creation, in France and Great Britain, of a novel wartime legal appellation for thousands of resident Jewish, Ottoman-born, would-be "enemy aliens." While unpacking this nomenclature as a vehicle of European neocolonial ambition, we also evaluate the creative means Jews employed to manipulate state law to their advantage. Leaving Europe once again, chapter 4 takes us to Ottoman Mesopotamia, East Asia, South Asia, and the young state of Iraq. Beginning with a sensational court case conducted in His Britannic Majesty's Supreme Court in Shanghai in the 1930s, it traces the complex legal history of Iraqi-born Jews who acquired (or lost) British protection in the course of multigenerational migration from the Ottoman Empire to and through the British Empire, all the while reflecting on the place of Middle Eastern Jewish protégés in the imperial order. Finally, the conclusion asks how legacies of protection influenced Jewish experiences of the Holocaust and Second World War in Europe and meditates on the enduring legacy of the capitulatory regime in postwar Egypt and across the twentieth-century Ottoman Jewish diaspora.

These chapters build chronologically, but each also looks backward in time to historical precedents and returns to shared turning points of the early twentieth century, especially the First World War, the dismemberment of the Ottoman Empire, and the extension of European imperial influence. While each of these chapters has a geographic center, these sites are not examined myopically, but treated as prisms that refract local, regional, imperial, transimperial, transnational, and diasporic histories, while at the same time offering different snapshots of the same general phenomenon.

Throughout, I am drawn to extraterritoriality partly because of its bedeviling amorphousness. Where does one look for the history of legal misfits? Seeking answers, my research has taken me to the archives of various national and imperial polities, nongovernmental organizations, global Jewish advocacy groups, as well as to families with papers they were kind enough to share. This very diffusion of material tells a story of its own. To think about extraterritoriality is to think in new ways about peoples, states, regions, and the lines that ostensibly demarcate them: it is also to unthink the organizational schema one tends to find in state archives. Finally, to think about extraterritoriality is to conflate the distinction between histories macro and micro, geopolitical and familial. In the pages that follow, our attention is drawn back and forth across these scales, mingling the voices of individual Jewish women and men with the representatives of state who dwelled, often with great puzzlement and consternation, on their legal states. Harboring innumerable shifting agendas and desires, these parties endlessly revisited the same set of complex and restless extraterritorial dreams.

OTTOMAN (JEWISH) EXTRATERRITORIALITY: A BRIEF HISTORY

The various legal categories that animate this study owe homage to precedents established in the early modern period, namely, the *ahdnameler* [pledges, or letters of promise], known by Europeans and Americans as the "capitulations" due to the *capitula* [chapters] they were typically divided into. The first of the bilateral treaties that made up the capitulations were signed between the Ottoman leadership and the European powers in the sixteenth century and conferred rights upon Europeans and their non-Muslim Ottoman representatives (including consular agents, dragomans, and their families) who lived or conducted commerce within Ottoman territories.[18] In return, the Ottomans required of the capitulatory nations reciprocal rights that allowed for the settlement and protection of Ottoman merchants abroad.[19] Within Ottoman territory, the rights guaranteed by the capitulations included the protection of persons, commerce, and property and a degree of legal independence, including the right to be judged in consular courts in many matters. Reviewed and renewed by successive sultans, the capitulations allowed European and Ottoman authorities to reevaluate continually their commercial and political relationship. Crucially every *berat* [deed of appointment, or grant of privilege: plural, *beratlar*] that was issued to a *beratlı* [beneficiary of a *berat*] required the authorization of the Sublime Porte, which reserved the legal right to monitor and rescind rights, and to place strict limits on the numbers of grants of privilege that capitulatory nations granted.[20]

Among the first Jews to pursue foreign protection were Tuscan merchants of Livornese and Iberian origin who came to Ottoman lands in the eighteenth century as French protégés, thereby earning themselves the Ladino moniker *Franko* [a term meaning, loosely speaking, "European"] and the appellation *Grana* in North Africa.[21] The resulting "collaboration between a stateless diaspora and state commercial power" was mutually beneficial, allowing France to become the ascendant European economic force in the Mediterranean in the eighteenth century and arguably to maintain semicolonial influence in the region thereafter.[22] First French, occasionally Dutch, often Tuscan, and—in the nineteenth century, after Italy became a nation—Italian, this population underwent a dizzying series of dramatic legal transformations, in most cases without ever leaving Ottoman lands.[23] All the while, the Frankos and Grana came to serve as an elite subset of the larger Jewish community, distinguished not only by legal status but by class and social status. In Salonica and Istanbul, Frankos such as the Allatini, Fernandez, and Modiano families emerged as visible beneficiaries of an Ottoman economy in flux, and as some of the most influential reformers of their day; in Tunis, the Grana families Borges, Ferreira, Mendez, and Silvera, among others, were considered, as one contemporary observer put it, "to be fierce defenders of their privileges."[24]

Throughout the early modern period and into the twentieth century, Jews were also exceptionally prominent among consular agents and dragomans of the capitulatory nations—and they and their families often received protected status as a result of these professional relationships.[25] In certain Ottoman cities (as elsewhere in the Mediterranean and Middle East, including Morocco, where treaty agreements inspired by the capitulatory regime granted foreign subjects extraterritorial status under the protection of local consulates), Jewish consular dynasties passed their protégé status through multiple generations. In extraordinary contexts—for example, eighteenth-century Aleppo or eighteenth-, nineteenth-, and early twentieth-century Salonica—Jews dominated the consular corps and dragoman population.[26] As a consequence of the protégé status, no matter what its genesis, generations of Mediterranean and Middle Eastern Christians and Jews and their descendants obtained privileges from foreign states despite, in most instances, never having lived in the polity in question. Their protectors, in turn, accrued financial advantage and the benefits of a relationship with a local mercantile class.[27] So, for centuries, functional—if always rocky—relationships existed both between the European states and their protégés and between the Ottoman leadership and its native-born "European" subjects, notwithstanding ongoing supervision and pushback by the Ottoman authorities.

Others have scrutinized Ottoman perceptions of the capitulatory regime in the early modern and modern periods, and I do not wish to reiterate what is already known. But it is important to emphasize that the Ottoman authorities made repeated efforts to end extraterritoriality and came to mistrust local non-Muslims who obtained foreign protection.[28] This determination extended to the policing of protégé dress, in order to prevent protected subjects from flaunting their status.[29] The Ottoman authorities' distrust of protégés grew with the Tanzimat ["Reordering"], a period of reforms that began in 1839 when sultan Abdülmecid I promulgated the Hatt-ı Şerif of Gülhane, or the Noble Rescript of the Rose Chamber, guaranteeing all Ottoman subjects equality and security of life and property without distinction of race or religion. In 1856, Grand Vizier Ali Pasha sought to abolish the capitulations as part of the negotiations that led to the Paris Peace Treaty, which concluded the Crimean War, only to be thwarted by his European counterparts.[30] Significantly, the signing of the Paris Peace Treaty marked the Ottomans' entry into a system of European public law, at least nominally, and led to the granting of the Islahat Fermanı [Reform Edict, also known as the Hatt-ı Humayün] of 1856. This edict, initially shaped by European statesmen invested in the granting of new rights to Ottoman Christians, was signed by sultan Abdülmecid and promised equal treatment of all the empire's subjects, regardless of religion; it also augured the erosion of the legal autonomy of the Jewish community by rendering all questions of commercial, civil, and criminal law subject to French commercial and penal codes.[31] Celebrated in the Ottoman Jewish press, the Islahat Fermanı emerged in tandem with a series of economic reforms that made it far easier for the European powers to guard their own interests in the empire.

In subsequent decades, as the Ottoman debt to the European capitulatory states rose dramatically, as the foreign-run Public Debt Administration (founded in 1881) assumed control of a third of the empire's revenues, and as growing numbers of Ottoman subjects proved immune to local justice, critics of the capitulations framed the institution as an impediment to Ottoman independence and, after the passage of the short-lived 1876 Ottoman constitution, the solidity of a young constitutional regime.[32] In the Ottoman popular press, the capitulations were equated with the very rape of empire.[33] With time, the capitulations had come to be perceived as acts of submission—the original meaning of the *capitula* notwithstanding. Jewish observers were among those who judged the capitulations severely. In 1909, Shlomo Yellin, a Jerusalem-born Ottoman Jewish patriot, graduate of Istanbul's prestigious Galatasary Imperial Lycée and Ottoman Imperial Law Academy, and author of the 1919 pamphlet *Les Capitulations et la juridiction consulaire*, condemned the capitulations as "the greatest obstacle" to development in the empire."[34]

The story of the capitulations is clearly a complex one, linking the Ottoman authorities, the states of Europe, Ottoman citizens, and Ottoman-born Christians, Jews, and (in some cases) Muslims who acquired foreign protection. Where do Jewish protégés fit into this story? To answer this question, we may well turn to an exchange between Ottoman and British representatives that unfolded in 1840, in the wake of two blood libel accusations in Damascus and Rhodes.[35] Lord Henry John Temple Palmerston, secretary of state for foreign affairs (and future prime minister) of Great Britain, seized on these events to call for the mass settlement of European Jews in Ottoman Palestine under British protection—an impractical proposal that had (from Palmerston's perspective) the double benefit of currying the favor of British millenarians and advancing British imperialist interests abroad. Palmerston's suggestion failed spectacularly. In a response issued through the British dragoman in Istanbul, the Ottoman grand vizier explained sniffily that the Ottoman authorities already had effective mechanisms for the protection of their subjects in place; and were the Ottomans to authorize Britain's right of rule over Ottoman Jewish subjects, "His Imperial Majesty's exalted administration will be divided into two parts," setting a precedent immensely dangerous to the Ottoman state. In the grand vizier's words:

> As is well known, they [the Russians, French, and Austrians] have obtained certain privileges from earlier capitulations. Claiming that [the Orthodox Christians and Roman Catholics] are their coreligionists, they would make the protection [of said Christians] the central issue of their foreign policies. In particular they would use the matter [of British mediation] as a precedent and the Russians would take the Greeks under their official protection, while the French and Austrians would do the same with regard to the Catholics. This would mean the complete ruin of the Great State's sovereignty.[36]

As the vizier's reply suggests, Jewish protégés did not exist in a vacuum. Instead, they were pieces of a puzzle that linked the states of Europe, the Ottoman authorities, and other protected (or would-be protected) non-Muslim subjects in the empire. This was as true for the states of Europe as it was for the Ottoman authorities. The capitulatory nations' treatment of protected Jews always reverberated with other relationships of protection, actual and imagined, existing and projected, including those concerning Ottoman subjects who were Greek Orthodox, Armenian, Melkite, Maronite, and Catholic, and extending to colonial subjects of the European powers who were Muslim, Hindu, Buddhist, or Sikh. Thus Jews who sought, held, or lost the protection of a European state stood (in the eyes of the states involved) for other relationships—and for both potentiality and risk.

While scholars have a fairly rich picture of the capitulations as they were shaped in the sixteenth, seventeenth, and eighteenth centuries, we have fewer tools (if ample sources) to allow us to understand the muddle that became of the capitulatory regime in the late nineteenth and early twentieth centuries. During this period, an endless series of wars led to massive intraregional migration and the birth of new countries in Europe and the Middle East, beginning with the establishment of the independent state of Serbia in 1830 and, in 1832, the Kingdom of Greece. After Greek independence, tens of thousands of Hellenic Greek Christians immigrated into Ottoman domains, settling in large numbers in Izmir and along the western Anatolian Aegean coast. Many of these migrants carried their newly acquired Greek citizenship with them, greatly bolstering the numbers of foreign citizens in Izmir and the surrounding region.[37] The Russo-Ottoman War (1877–78, also known as the Russo-Turkish War) precipitated further Ottoman territorial loss and the creation of an autonomous Bulgaria under Russian protection. After this war, thousands of Jews along with hundreds of thousands of Muslims retreated to within the empire's shrinking borders, in rare cases preserving their status as Russian protégés.[38] Three decades later, the Italo-Ottoman War (1911–12, also known as the Italo-Turkish War) resulted in the expulsion of Italian citizens from the provinces of Beirut, Syria, Aleppo, and Jerusalem and the fearful flight of others from Anatolia and Macedonia—though many who left subsequently returned.[39] That war, and the Balkan Wars (1912–13) that would follow, generated further losses for the Ottomans, including Libya and the bulk of the empire's territory in Southeastern Europe. The First World War (1914–18) pitted the leadership of the Committee of Union and Progress against the Entente Powers and provided the excuse for the temporary abolition of the capitulatory regime, as well as a selective assault on non-Muslims within the empire. After the First World War, the Ottoman Empire lost all of its Middle Eastern holdings, leading to the creation of British and French mandates and protectorate regimes in Palestine, Lebanon, Syria, and Mesopotamia. All told, these events legally fractured Ottoman Jewry, which now inhabited many regimes rather than a single imperial entity.

Jewish responses to these developments were manifold. As Julia Phillips Cohen and Michelle Campos have demonstrated with great eloquence, many Sephardim expressed a newfound affinity for Ottomanism (imperial state patriotism) in the face of these developments.[40] Tens of thousands of Ottoman Jews voted with their feet, leaving the empire or region for Western Europe, Great Britain, the Americas, and southern Africa (among other locations).[41] Others remained in their place of birth and gravitated to new forms of political expression, including socialism, Zionism, or other forms of nationalism (Serbian, Greek, Bulgarian, Turkish, and Iraqi, among others).[42]

The quest for foreign protection, yet another expression of the times, is arguably the Jewish response least understood by scholars. Far more Jews retained their Ottoman-era subject-hood or took on the citizenship of a successor state or adopted country than became protégés. The choice to become extra-territorial would always prove the exception rather than the norm. Still, the numbers of those who did acquire foreign protection or who were forced to contend with the uncertain meaning of extraterritoriality rose tangibly in the decades that straddled the turn of the twentieth century, provoking intense (and revealing) responses. So palpable, and so threatening, was this trend as to elicit the disapproval of Jewish and non-Jewish observers who perceived the rush on foreign papers as a form of betrayal—whether of international law, Ottomanist ideals, the nation-state, a nationalist cause, the working class, the Jewish community, or a particular urban culture. Some of these reactions were narrowly partisan; but perhaps the protégé status provoked such an intense range of reactions because it cast light on the fundamental instability of citizenship itself, which protégés seemed all too easily to cast off or acquire anew.

In the face of such criticism, Mediterranean and Middle Eastern Jewish women and men sought the protection of European states for a variety of reasons: for commercial advantage, social clout, political security, to avoid conscription or taxation, or to travel or migrate with greater ease. In some instances, an individual could seek protection from more than one nation. This was true of Abraham ben Israel Rosanes, who has recalled in an unpublished Ladino-language memoir how a family dispute in his hometown of Rusçuk prompted him to play the Prussian, Russian, and Ottoman consuls off one another, seeking the form of legal protection that appeared to gain him maximal advantage.[43] The legal immunity that attended protection could also be a draw, and not only for a would-be consular official or dragoman: brothels in fin-de-siècle Alexandria were flush with protégé prostitutes whose legal status insulated them from state oversight.[44] Others, fearful of the shifting political tides, sought protection at the instant at which their citizenship was poised to shift from Ottoman to that of a successor nation—this was true of thousands of Salonican Jews, as it was of Samuel Behar-Menahem, who appealed for Spanish protection in the course of the Siege of Edirne [Adrianople] during the First Balkan War (1912–13), as his city was falling to Bulgarian hands.[45] Whatever an individual's reasons for pursuing protection, one always *chose* to become and remain a protégé—even if one could not prevent the state (or the Ottoman authorities) from revoking this status. Paperwork had to be renewed and, conversely, a protégé could choose to allow his or her protection to lapse. Some also lost protection after failing to meet renewal deadlines.[46] In this important sense, for Ottoman Jews and their descendants extraterritoriality (like emigration or the embrace of Ottoman patriotism) was a choice, even if it could also feel like a strategic necessity.[47]

Protégé status was available to so many Jews because over the course of the nineteenth century the capitulatory states of Europe had grown laxer—if not downright profligate—in their granting of protection. Protégé Jews were among a rising tide of foreign citizens (a term whose slipperiness provided the lubricant for much of this action) who lived within the boundaries of the empire—a population estimated at roughly 200,000 in 1907.[48] In larger cities such as Izmir, Istanbul, and Salonica, holders of European papers could constitute as much 15% of the urban population; Izmir alone claimed more than 50,000 of the 55,467 foreigners who dwelt in western Anatolia in 1889.[49] Nor were smaller cities immune. When Alexandria transitioned from Ottoman to British protectorate control, somewhere between 50,000 and 60,000 foreigners could be counted among its residents, totaling 34% of the overall urban population.[50] In the first years of the twentieth century, the (admittedly extraordinary) administrative district of Palestine counted 30,000 foreign Jews out of a total population between 700,00 and 750,000.[51] The number of consular courts swelled to accommodate the growing number of protégés and foreign citizens in the empire—in 1895, no fewer than thirty-two British courts operated in the Ottoman Empire.[52] These numbers suggest that with the exception of Palestine, Jews constituted a relatively small percentage of the protégé population relative to their percentage of the Ottoman population writ large.

Who was counted among the "foreign citizens" (or so-called "Franks") of the late nineteenth- or early twentieth-century Ottoman Empire? The answer is not a simple one, for the boundaries between "Ottoman subjects" and "foreigners" and "protégés," never rigid, were growing more blurry with time. Ottoman censuses at times counted foreigners and at times did not. When there were centralized attempts to measure this population, various definitions were employed.[53] The class of protégés, though initially reserved for non-Muslims, proved rather more fluid than anyone might have anticipated. A protégé could convert to Islam, confounding socioreligious distinctions.[54] By the late nineteenth century, meanwhile, an unknown number of Algerian Muslims lived within the boundaries of the Ottoman Empire, maintaining the French protection they acquired as colonial subjects.[55]

Jewish and Christian protégés, too, were not always where the authorities wanted them to be, or easy to track. Attempts by European authorities to count and control their protégés were usually thwarted, producing confused conversations that extended over decades and multiple governmental offices but that frequently came to naught. Consider the case of Michael Houri, an Ottoman Christian born in Istanbul who acquired British protection in Aleppo in the late nineteenth century. By the 1890s, Houri had earned the enmity of British representatives due to an unspecified malfeasance. Memos circulating within the Foreign Office in the last years of the nineteenth century stated baldly that "we do not like Houri. . . . we should, indeed, be pleased to get rid of him."[56] Legally speaking, British authorities had every right to strip Houri of his protégé status—not only because the state reserved the right to withdraw protection from any subject at any time, but because of circumstances particular to Houri's case. (Houri had inherited his protection from his great-grandfather, thereby straining the legal limit of three generations beyond which British protection was meant to pass.)[57] Still, Foreign Office representatives resisted taking action against the protégé, acknowledging that there was a "large number of other people at Constantinople and elsewhere in Turkey who are registered as British subjects, although they can only claim that status on the ground of descent from British ancestors more remote than the second generation, and who consequently, are not British subjects at all according to English law."[58] In violation of British—let alone Ottoman—law, the practice of protection had run rampant. When Houri's case came to light, the British Foreign Office viewed the reversal of Houri's protection as risky because it "raise[d] the question of [the] competency" of certain British consuls—and thereby threatened the integrity of the state as a whole.[59] One subject's extraterritorial dream, it would seem, could prove a state's extraterritorial nightmare.

A lack of clear doctrine bore some of the blame for confusion in this and many other cases; additionally, across the protector states of Europe, record keeping pertaining to protected subjects was decentralized and unsystematic. Protégés too played a role in producing a degree of disorder. As we shall see again and again, Jewish holders and seekers of protection participated in the elision of easy categorization, strategically drawing upon inventive self-descriptors in hopes of achieving legal advantage. During his travels through Egypt, France, and Britain in the late nineteenth century, the Aleppan-born A. Hamwee carried an Ottoman-issued *laissez-passer* [certificate of safe conduct] in a leather carrying case imprinted in gold with his name and the (counterfactual) word "PASSPORT" (figure I.1). Was the dressing a costume meant to disguise a legal truth; or, for Hamwee, did the *laissez-passer* function as a passport—and hence was perceived and presented as such? The answer indeterminate, we are left to marvel at the confounding of official doctrine and documents effected by ordinary people in everyday situations.[60]

Ottomans, like Europe's protector nations, bristled in the face of this chaos. As already mentioned, in the course of the peace negotiations that led to the Paris Peace Treaty of 1856 that concluded the Crimean War, Grand Vizier Ali Pasha tried unsuccessfully to negotiate the eradication of the capitulations—the

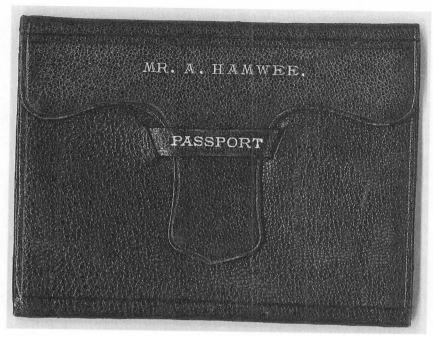

FIGURE 1.1 Passport case of A. Hamwee, c. 1882. Courtesy Manchester Jewish Museum Archive, 2010, 45, 3.

first of many such thwarted attempts. Just over a decade later, the Ottoman Law of Nationality of 1869 sought to formalize the boundary between Ottoman subjects and foreign citizens to prevent further "losses" of native-born subjects to European protégé status.[61] However, though the Law of Nationality was intended to clarify the legal difference between Ottoman citizens, Ottoman subjects, and foreign citizens, there was little effective mechanism to stop non-Muslims from seeking protection. When it came to supervision of the empire's protected subjects, the muscle of the Ottoman authorities had atrophied.[62]

The whittling away of the capitulatory regime, begun in the nineteenth century, was accelerated as the Ottoman Empire was dismembered by regional irredentism and by losses at war. The peace treaties that followed the Balkan Wars dictated that the capitulations were to be abolished in territories and among populations annexed from the Ottoman Empire. Just prior to their entry into the First World War, the Ottomans annulled the capitulations. Soon, various Ottoman successor states, including Greece, Bulgaria, and Yugoslavia (and eventually the Turkish Republic and Italy), would seek to override the foreign protection of their subjects, pressuring them to conform to evolving nationalist norms.[63] The capitulatory system was temporarily reintroduced in Turkey in 1918 in the wake of the Allied victory at war, but the death knell was nigh. In 1923, the Treaty of Lausanne formally abolished the institution of protection.[64] Still, the resentment of protégés lingered on, taking anti-Semitic form in the Turkish Republic in the 1920s, when Jews were accused of harboring greater loyalty to Spain than to Turkey.[65]

Jewish holders of foreign papers were not subjected to the aggressive "unmixing of peoples" that shadowed the signing of the Treaty of Lausanne, as most of the formerly Ottoman Jews who did not emigrate from Southeastern Europe chose to accept citizenship from whatever successor state engulfed them.[66] For a similar reason, Southeastern European Jews were not, as a group, perceived as *heimatlosen* [or *staatenlosen*, stateless] and therefore not as potential recipients of the Nansen passports granted by the League of Nations beginning in 1922.[67] This was so because in every instance, Jews had the option of accepting citizenship from an Ottoman successor state, as was their right by the terms of the Treaty of Berlin (1878) and various national constitutions.[68]

This general trend did not prevent individual Jews from acquiring Nansen passports, or from perceiving themselves—or being perceived by state representatives in their adopted homes—as stateless. Raphael Isaac [Joseph] Souhami, a British-dwelling Izmirli Jewish protégé of France, acquired (through successive offices in London) French registration, a Nansen passport, and, eventually, British naturalization.[69] When Vidal Coenca appealed to the British authorities for naturalization, on the other hand, he "described himself as of no nationality." Coenca had migrated to England from his native Salonica before that city became Greek. Fifteen years later, neither the Greek nor the Turkish consulates in London would affirm his nationality.[70] According to the Ottoman Jewish émigré José Vidal Sassoon, many Salonican-born young Jewish men living abroad were in comparable straits, having failed to exercise the option to become either a Greek or an Ottoman citizen in the wake of the Balkan Wars.[71] Then again, there were times at which the acquisition of citizenship by an émigré was simply overridden by a host nation. Sassoon himself emigrated to Great Britain with Greek papers, but when he applied for a marriage certificate in December 1916, officials in London's Somerset House disregarded his claims to Greek citizenship. Pursuant to the fantastical logic that "as his father was of Ottoman nationality his nationality must be the same," they described Sassoon as "Ottoman" on his marriage certificate. Now neither the Greek nor the Ottoman consulate in London would accept Sassoon as their own. Though not technically stateless, Sassoon had become as much through clerical error.[72]

Despite its eradication in Europe and the Ottoman Empire, the legacy of foreign protection continued to carry import into the mid twentieth century. It influenced the legal sensibilities of Jews in Iraq into the 1930s, continued to structure a system of legal pluralism in Egypt until 1949, and would influence the legal—and perhaps rather more metaphysical—mentality of Middle Eastern Jewish émigrés thereafter. Within Europe, the aftereffects of the capitulatory regime persisted in unexpected form well past its formal expiration date of 1923, influencing policies relative to the Ottoman-born across Europe and mottling the fate of Sephardi foreign nationals who fell within the Nazi dragnet.

All the while, with the emergence of a passport regime, with (voluntary and forced) migrations, and with the endless shifting of political boundaries in Southeastern Europe and the Middle East, many Ottoman-born extraterritorial subjects and their descendants ceased to be *beratlı* in the early modern sense—that is, European subjects whose status was monitored and authorized by the Ottoman authorities. They became, instead, legally liminal subjects with ill-defined rights and responsibilities. This proved threatening to many Ottoman successor states intent on nationalizing their populations, and these polities in turn pressured their extraterritorial subjects to adopt the citizenship of the country in which they lived. There were some erstwhile Jewish protégés who took on new citizenship at this time (whether out of desire, due to a sense of defeat, or in deference to pressure), but the nation-states involved did not always succeed at converting extraterritorial subjects into citizens. At times, this effort provoked more trouble than it solved. This was true in Greece, where in the 1920s the state attempted to obligate all members of the Jewish community to hold citizenship but abandoned its efforts after extensive pushback by the community. The effects of this communal victory are felt in the present; to this day, members of Thessaloniki's small Jewish community, as well as members of the Salonican Jewish diaspora, continue to hold foreign papers inherited from protégé ancestors.[73] This point allows us to end much as we began, in the present moment, which the ghost of the capitulatory regime continues to haunt.

CHAPTER 1

Seductive Subjects

The passports were magnificent in comparison with those one could obtain from other consulates in Salonica. The presses on which they were printed had been obtained, with some difficulty, by Portugal's consul in Salonica, Solomon/Salomão Arditti, himself a Jewish native of the city, in the summer of 1913. Arditti was anticipating a surge in need, for Portugal's Foreign Minister—at Arditti's urging—had only just approved the granting of provisional protection to Jews in Salonica. The Foreign Minister's directive, issued in the course of the Balkan Wars (1912–13) and during a time when the political future of the city itself was indeterminate, was in Arditti's view sure to result in a flood of paper seekers. Whether by accident or by the consul's design, the new presses were equipped to do more than generate a great deal of handsome paperwork quickly. They were also capable of printing passports whose impressive aesthetic qualities visually overrode the theoretically "provisional" nature of the papers themselves.[1] Some of the Salonican Jews who obtained Portuguese protection from Arditti's hands found that elegant provisional papers proved astonishingly durable. Carried outside of Salonica to cities elsewhere in Europe or any number of émigré settings, Arditti's grand passports were accepted as proof of citizenship itself. With ink, paper, and a state-of-the-art printing press, Arditti was providing Portugal's new protégés with the tools to contravene Portuguese law.

At the turn of the twentieth century, Salonica was among the most important ports of the Ottoman Empire and one of very few cities in the world in which Jews constituted a plurality of the population.[2] Salonica's Jewish community (like the Jewish population in surrounding regions) was overwhelmingly

Sephardi—consisting primarily of Ladino (Judeo-Spanish) speaking Jews descended from Iberian exiles who settled in the Ottoman Empire in the late fifteenth century. Over five centuries, Sephardi Jews became an integral element of Ottoman society, particularly in cities where the community was most densely concentrated: Istanbul, Izmir, Edirne, Sarajevo, Sofia, and especially Salonica, where Jews formed the backbone of the mercantile and industrial workforce. The city had an almost fabled place in the Jewish world, in which it came to be known as "the Jerusalem of the Balkans."[3]

The loss of Salonica to Greece in the course of the Balkan Wars heralded the end of an era for the city's Jews, as for Ottoman Jewry as a whole. In the course of the conflict, Salonica's Jews witnessed a rash of anti-Muslim and anti-Jewish violence and anticipated (rightly, as it turns out) a decline in their city's economic vitality. The war also sparked great fear within the Jewish community that a further rise in anti-Semitism would accompany Hellenic rule.[4] In response to what many perceived as an increasingly traumatic situation, Salonican Jews pursued security along a number of divergent paths. Many found themselves seduced by novel political affiliations taking shape in their city, evincing sympathy for socialism, Zionism, or the notion that *if* Salonica was not to be Ottoman, it should be the international capital of a politically neutral buffer state.[5] Others chose to emigrate: between 1911 and 1912 alone, the number of Salonican Jews passing through Ellis Island doubled.[6] With the annexation of the economically vital Salonican hinterland by Macedonia (in 1912) and the growing vibrancy of Christian-owned firms, local Jewish merchants scrambled to respond dexterously to a shifting commercial terrain.[7] Finally, several thousand Salonican Jewish women, men, and families rushed to acquire protégé status, hopeful that the resulting papers would provide a measure of political security in a world turned upside down.[8]

Salonican Jews' pursuit of protection was enabled by a highly particular set of circumstances generated by the Balkan Wars. During the uncertain months between the Greek occupation of Ottoman Salonica in October 1912 and the formal designation of the city as Greek (with the Treaty of Bucharest, in August 1913), Portugal, Spain, and Austro-Hungary set out to entice the single largest Jewish mercantile population in Southeastern Europe, the Sephardi community of Salonica, as protégés. These polities had their own complex reasons for pursuing Salonican Jewish subjects: what they shared was the realization that in this moment of political uncertainty it was possible to recast a faded legal category to their advantage. Within Salonica, the official Jewish Community was continuing to register certificates of identity to members of the community that could be used as proof of identity both domestically and internationally.[9]

Simultaneously, during the few months in which Salonica's political future was indeterminate, the Spanish, Portuguese, and Austro-Hungarian consulates in Salonica—in the face of British and French restraint—began registering the city's Jews (as well as lesser numbers of Jews in Istanbul, Edirne, and Izmir) as protégés. Roughly 2,500 Salonican Jewish women, men, and children took advantage of the opportunity—roughly 5 percent of the urban Jewish population.[10]

This chapter untangles the intersecting desires and dynamics that fueled the competitive scramble for Salonican Jewish protégés during the course of the Balkan Wars. It explores how these wars provided the occasion for certain European states to reimagine the protégé status: and how individual Ottoman Jews sought to navigate the rapidly shifting political environment of Southeastern Europe to their advantage. In the pages that follow, I hone in on the evolution of Portugal's unusual (and unusually tentative) legal relationship to Ottoman Jews—and those from Salonica, in particular—from the late-nineteenth century to the eve of the Second World War. I consider in what ways the extension of consular protection served Portugal and local consular representatives in the course of the Balkan Wars, and why Ottoman Jews came to appear less "seductive" to Portuguese officials in years to come. In this chapter we ask; What legal rights, and what limits, were placed upon those who inscribed themselves on the ledgers of foreign consulates? How did individual Jews and Jewish families come by their protection, and in what ways did this status serve—or work against—them over time? To address these questions, we visit the same history from various perspectives: that of Portuguese officials in Lisbon; Portuguese consuls in Europe, North Africa, and the Middle East; non-Jewish Greek observers and the Greek authorities; and, finally, individual Jewish seekers and holders of Portuguese papers—women and men who acquired Portuguese papers and subsequently sought to leverage this protection to their advantage over the course of the First World War, with the rise of Prime Minister António de Oliveira Salazar's authoritarian and corporatist regime in Portugal, and during the frantic lead-up to the Second World War.

IMPERIAL AMBITIONS AND THE PATH TO PROTECTION

The relationship between the Portuguese state and Jews athwart the Sephardi diaspora did not begin with the Balkan Wars but had roots deep in the early modern period. For much of this era, in all the centers of the western Sephardi diaspora (that is, in the European centers of Sephardi culture that existed outside the Ottoman lands and northern Morocco), the descendants of Jews expelled from Spain in 1492 and of those forced to convert to Catholicism in Portugal in 1497 were known and referred to themselves as *nação*, members of "the Portuguese nation." The *nação*, a community bound by commercial as much as ethnic ties, was granted a unique—and uniquely advantaged— collective legal status by various states of Europe. This nomenclature also served to provide "members of the nation" with a means of demarcating their community from that of other Jews and non-Jews.[11] Crucially, "Portuguese" was, for the western Sephardim, an affirmative diasporic identification formed in the absence of a legal relationship to Portugal. Indeed, Portugal was annexed to Spain for nearly a century of the early modern period (from 1580 to 1640), and thus lacked the wherewithal to extend subject-hood of any form. With the Inquisition active until the eighteenth century, most of the early modern Jewish merchants who conducted commerce in Portuguese territories did so as Italian protected subjects.[12]

In the Ottoman context too, an indirect connection was drawn between the empire's protégé Jews and Portugal. As early as the eighteenth century, Ottoman sources referred to the empire's Frankos as *portakal taifesinden* [Portuguese], likely because they were assumed to descend from converso émigrés from Portugal who settled in the port of Livorno, whereupon they returned to Judaism.[13] Still, it appears to have taken until the late nineteenth century for the label "Portuguese" to gain a measure of legal standing for Southeastern European Jews.

Some among the first Ottoman Jews to appear on Portugal's citizenship rolls were registered in the North African commercial hub of Tunis in the late nineteenth century. The catalyst to these registrations lay in the realm of colonial geopolitics. According to the terms of the capitulations, France had granted protection to a great number of Jews, Muslims, and Christians in Tunisia in the nineteenth century in hopes of strengthening French influence over the Regency. After Tunisia became a French protectorate in 1881, however, France withdrew its protection from these extraterritorial subjects, leaving them under the jurisdiction of Tunisia's civil code.[14] Under pressure from the French, Italy and Britain soon closed their consular courts in Tunis, agreeing to suspend the capitulations within the realm of French protectorate Tunisia. These developments provoked great consternation among Tunisian Jewish families who had come to take for granted the rights, security, and privileges that foreign protection afforded. And these families in turn sought legal alternatives: engaging, in Mary Dewhurst Lewis' evocative term, in "jurisdiction jumping."[15]

The pursuit of Portuguese papers proved a readily available option. Beginning in 1894, Portugal's consulate in Tunis opened its citizenship rolls to four extended families of Portuguese origin—those of Borges, Ferreira, Mendez, and Silvera. These families, residents of Tripoli, Constantina, Sousse, Tunis, and Sfax, were among the Livornese mercantile families who had begun settling and/or creating commercial bases in the North African entrepôt in the sixteenth century.[16] By the late nineteenth century, Livornese Jewish families (or Grana, as they were known locally) had established deep roots in the North African landscape, but they nonetheless continued to think of themselves as a discrete cultural and communal population. These sentiments were compounded by community member's possession of foreign protection, which set Livornese Jews apart from the native-born Arabophone (so-called Twansa) Jewish community. These dynamics explain why, when French, British, and Italian protection was denied the Livornese Jews of Tunisia, they turned to the Portuguese consul in Tunis for succor. Between 1894 and 1923, the Portuguese consul in Tunis registered over one hundred thirty members of these families. (In 1923, when the Morinaud Law allowed for the naturalization as French citizens of wealthy, highly educated Tunisian Jews, it is likely that many of these same Jewish families transferred their allegiances back to France.)[17]

In extending papers to Livornese Jews in Tunisia in the late nineteenth century, Portugal was to a certain extent pursuing the selfsame goals that would be pursued by the consul in Salonica decades later: embracing as protégés a wealthy mercantile population while vying with other European powers to deepen its commercial and cultural toehold in the Mediterranean. But one crucial element differentiates these stories. In late-nineteenth century Tunis, a small number of Jewish families came to the Portuguese consulate seeking protection. In early twentieth-century Salonica, a zealot consulate seeking Jews actively recruited large numbers of would-be Portuguese citizens. During the Balkan Wars, the pursuit of Salonica's Jews was the concerted (if short-lived) policy of a young constitutional monarchy seeking economic opportunity, international visibility, and a revitalization of Portugal's imperial past.

The momentum came from Spain. Its heralded mastermind was Ángel Pulido Fernández, a physician, anthropologist, and Spanish senator who zealously advocated for Spain's embrace of the Ladino-speaking diaspora. Senator Pulido's campaign, launched with his 1905 study *Españoles sin patria y la raza sefardí*, centered upon the idea that Spain ought to welcome into the nation's fold Spanish Jews living in lands from Morocco to the Balkans, in part by offering these "Spaniards without a country" the opportunity to acquire citizenship. Pulido's ambitions were as practical as patriotic. His *Españoles sin patria y la raza sefardí* noted that the Ottoman Empire's economy hinged upon the contributions of its Jews, and furthermore that 70 percent of the commerce between northern Morocco and Spain was in Jewish hands. On this evidence, he argued that Spain's reintegration of its "hemorrhaged" Jews might prove a catalyst to the restoration of the commercial and cultural might lost by Spain when the country relinquished the remains of its overseas empire in 1898.[18] In defense of this position, Pulido formulated a claim that would inform not only Spain's policies towards Ottoman- and Moroccan-born Jews, but those of various other countries in years to come: that Sephardi Jews were a commercial tool for an aspirational nation, and the extension of citizenship the key to unlocking their fiscal utility.

Pulido's gestures towards Sephardim sparked a range of reactions in the Judeo-Spanish heartland, as in Spain. In Southeastern Europe, Pulido was mocked by some Jewish observers and embraced by others, catalyzing a surge of academic interest in Castilian and medieval history, and animating a sense of Sephardi identification with Spain that was perhaps Pulido's lasting achievement.[19] In Spain, the senator's efforts found favor among a liberal circle of Jewish and non-Jewish intellectuals—Spanish Judeophiles who attempted to pressure their government (as well as a number of foreign regimes) to protect Sephardi Jews displaced or legally marginalized by global events.[20] Most importantly for the purposes of our story, Pulido's efforts sparked a copycat reaction that reached Lisbon, Vienna, Athens, and beyond.

With this context in mind, we return to Salonica and the frame of the Balkan War. In November 1912, a month after Greek forces occupied the city, the Spanish consul in Salonica, parroting Pulido, extended protection to all Jews in that city who "spoke Spanish and were of Spanish origin, whom modern Spain recognized as her sons."[21] Some weeks later, the consul engaged in ambitious outreach. He met with representatives of all the Jewish organizations of Salonica and delivered a series talks in which he called Sephardim the "beloved children of modern Spain" and emphasized that Spanish representatives in Salonica were prepared to do everything possible to accommodate those who desired Spanish nationality.[22] The Spanish consul to Istanbul now made his own visit to Salonica, welcoming the Ottoman Chief Rabbi Haim Nahum aboard the *Rena Regente* and noting that "the occasion was doubtless the first for almost five centuries that the head of the Jews in the East had set foot upon a Spanish warship."[23] Quipped the Salonican Jewish intellectual Joseph Nehama in a letter to Paris: "If, after all this, the Catholic King does not mobilize his army and fleets to defend the interests of the Jews of Salonica, it is not for want of eloquence."[24] By the end of 1913, the Spanish consul in Salonica had registered as Spanish subjects 175 Salonican Jewish men on behalf of their families, representing roughly 850 souls.[25] Half of these registrations were conducted between February and May, after the Bulgarian army entered Salonica and initiated a wave of violence against the city's Muslim and Jewish civilians.[26]

The Portuguese authorities were not alone in watching these events unfold. To the political cauldron in Salonica, the Austro-Hungarian monarchy added its own motives and actions. In 1883, the Habsburg monarchy had secured the right to connect Vienna to Salonica by railroad, affording the empire a coveted outlet to the Aegean Sea and the promise of greater economic influence in the Balkans. Since these ambitions would be thwarted were Salonica to fall into Greek or Bulgarian hands, during the Balkan Wars Austro-Hungarian diplomats agitated for the transformation of Salonica into a free and neutral city headed by a Jewish mayor; simultaneously, as if to hedge their bets, the Habsburg consular representatives sought their own Salonican Sephardi subjects. These efforts began in the late nineteenth century, but accelerated in the course of the Balkan Wars, when the Austro-Hungarian consulate registered 450 Sephardi men and their families as protected subjects. Among them were seven patriarchs of the Amar family and their wives and children, who supplied the requisite paperwork and paid a fee of 7.50 kronen (each) before taking oaths of allegiance to Austria. The Ottoman passports submitted by the Amars to Austro-Hungarian bureaucrats reveal an uncommon Sephardi affection for the name Felix; historically Germanic nomenclature was rare among Jews in the Sephardi heartland of Southeastern Europe, but it appears to have been strategically embraced by those in pursuit of Austro-Hungarian protection. Hence the name was added, ex post facto, to Haim Jacob Amar's *laissez-passer*, which was granted by the Ottoman consulate in Budapest in 1908. A Salonican-born Jew, Amar was granted Austro-Hungarian citizenship in April 1913 along with his wife Ida and newborn son Jakob [Jossué Salvator]; [see caption 1.1] his "Certificate of Good Character" emphasized that Amar had a preexisting commercial relationship with various Austrian factories, and his naturalization was sure to promote Austrian exports. How ironic that this documentation was coupled, seemingly without guile, with a copy of Amar's 1913 Ladino- and French-language registration by the Jewish Community of Salonica—a document that legally bound Amar to neither nation nor state, but to a Jewish community and city (figure 1.1).[27]

As the Spanish and Portuguese authorities busied themselves in Salonica, in Lisbon the Portuguese parliament was vetting a proposal to allow for the massive settlement of European Jews in Angola. This plan, which was widely covered in the Ladino- and French-language press of Southeastern Europe, was motivated by the assumption that an influx of Eastern European Jewish

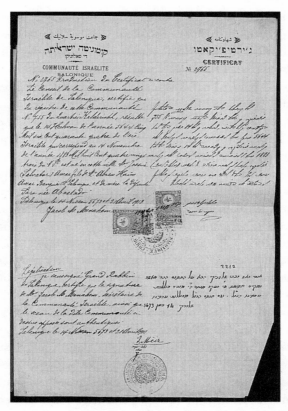

FIGURE 1.1 Registration of Jossué (Salvator) Amar (b. 1883) by the Jewish Community of Salonica, 1913. Courtesy Austrian State Archives, dept. Haus-, Hof-, und Staatsarchiv.

immigrants to the colony would provide Portugal with a middle-class, white, settler population that would further its imperial ambitions.[28] The proposal was met with widespread favor in Portugal's parliament, where it was ratified in June 1913. Even before the bill was passed, the Zionist press in Southeastern Europe responded with enthusiasm, lending support to the idea that Russian and Ottoman Jews could serve Portugal capably and loyally, bringing a dose of "colonial heroism and civilization to the entire Jewish nation."[29] Almost as an aside, these articles noted that Jews who settled in Angola would be asked to adopt Portuguese citizenship and educate their children in Jewish schools in which Portuguese would be the primary language of instruction.

The Portuguese consul in Istanbul, Alfredo Mesquita, registered this coverage with satisfaction.[30] Mesquita, a (non-Jewish) Portuguese journalist and career diplomat, had his own entrepreneurial vision of how the young Portuguese Republic could benefit from a relationship with Ottoman Sephardim. Some weeks earlier, the consul had commissioned Albert Algrante, a Sephardi middleman from Istanbul who had spent time in Portugal, to prepare a report on Portugal's commercial potential in the Ottoman Empire. The results emphasized that Portugal could expand its investments and influence in Southeastern Europe, picking up the slack in commercial relations between Italy and the Ottoman Empire produced by the Italo-Ottoman War (1911–12).[31] Buoyed by the Portuguese parliament's ratification of the Angola plan, Mesquita registered two Ottoman Jewish subjects as Portuguese: Elie Condoi, the Portuguese vice-consul in Damascus (who, at sixty-two years of age, had served the government for twenty-two years) and his son, Joseph Elie Condoi.[32] At roughly the same time, Jacques Missir, Portugal's honorary consul in Salonica, began inscribing select Salonican Jews as Portuguese subjects. Among the first was Isaac Yacoel, who had served as dragoman for the Portuguese consulate in Salonica from 1907 to 1927. From Missir's hand, Yacoel obtained what he called "*la nationalité Portugaise*" for himself and his children.[33]

It is unclear whether the Portuguese Foreign Minister authorized Mesquita's or Missir's actions—in these instances, as in others to come, local consular representatives of the Portuguese state juggled national interests with their own (rather more locally moored) set of priorities, with the latter sometimes taking precedence over the former. To Great Britain's representative in Salonica, Consul Wratislav, Missir would later claim that he had received written authorization from the Portuguese government before embarking on this course of action. But Wratislav himself was skeptical. "I doubt if he [Missir] was very critical in examining [applicants'] proofs," the consul confided to a colleague in Athens.[34] Perhaps; and yet, at the time, the granting of protection to select Jews of perceived or actual value was a time-honored consular tradition—for Portugal as for many other European nations. Even the skeptical Wratislav had to concede that many consuls "have on their books local Jews who would find it hard to justify their original acquisition of foreign nationality or protection if the matter were strictly enquired into. The Turks [e.g., Ottomans] were extremely easy-going in such matter[s] and would often, for a consideration, wink at such transactions."[35]

Wratislav's suspicions were not entirely unfounded. Something new was taking shape in Salonica. Early 1913 found Mesquita strenuously advocating for the systematic addition of Salonican Jews to Portugal's registration rolls—not simply as protégés in the early modern sense, but as citizens.[36] Echoing Pulido, Mesquita's appeals to the Foreign Minister emphasized that just as the

Spanish Jews of Salonica were a discrete community with their own synagogue (the Aragon Synagogue), the Portuguese Jews of that city also maintained a private synagogue (the Lisbon Synagogue), were of honest reputation, primarily mercantile in class status, and financially secure. (The latter point apparently aroused the interest of the Foreign Minister, who marked the relevant passage of Mesquita's letter with a bold red "X." Mesquita's reportage from Salonica, it seems, was most tantalizing to the Foreign Ministry when it hinted at commercial possibility.) Consul Mesquita went on to acknowledge that granting Portuguese citizenship to Jews in Salonica could not fulfill Article 19 of the 1911 Portuguese Civil Code, which mandated that a foreign national live on Portuguese soil for at least three years before acquiring Portuguese nationality. And yet, the consul reasoned:

> If the Republican government recognizes the applicants as descendants of ex-pelled Portuguese; if it recognizes, moreover, that they have no ties binding them to their adopted country [e.g., Greece], [then] they remain intimately and effectively a part of this country [e.g., Portugal] . . . [Therefore] I believe it possible for the [Foreign Minister] to grant me the necessary authorization to accept via the respective consulate [in Salonica] the declarations of those who. . . . want to preserve their first nationality.[37]

Consul Mesquita concluded his missive by reminding the Foreign Minister that Spain, seeking to augment its prestige and develop its commercial interests, had already begun extending Spanish nationality to the Jews of Salonica—and that the Jews of that city were responding with enthusiasm. "Now is the time for Portugal to reassert its old prestige in this part of the Orient," Mesquita insisted; and if Portugal were to provide Salonica's Jews with protection, "we will assure ourselves of their gratitude."[38] In addition to reflecting the dominant position Sephardim occupied within Salonica's economy, these statements hint at more general, allosemitic assumptions about Jewish influence and power: Mesquita, like Albert Algrante before him, made no reference to the corresponding advantage that Salonica's Christian mercantile population might broker for the Portuguese state.[39]

Pressured by Mesquita, stoked by a sense of competition with Spain and Austro-Hungary, the Foreign Minister relented. In March 1913, the minister granted the consuls of Istanbul and Salonica the unique authority to approve "provisional registrations" to Jews, urging them to exercise the greatest caution as they did so.[40] A few weeks later, the Foreign Minister clarified why he was authorizing "provisional" rather than "definitive" registration as was being extended by the Spanish and Austro-Hungarians at the same time. "Provisional registration will allow us the freedom to implement [the policy] if we wish, or reject if it could cause us harm," he explained; "It will allow us to attend to the issue either way, with ease."[41] Provisional registration was thus a fruitfully vague strategy, designed to reap benefit without incurring obligation. Over the ensuing four months, the Portuguese consul in Salonica, Solomon/ Salomão Arditti, registered five hundred Jewish families as Portuguese subjects.[42] So vigorous were Arditti's efforts that he was obliged to acquire for Portugal's consulate the new printing presses with which this chapter began.

THE LIMITS OF "PROVISIONAL REGISTRATION"

Even as Arditti's printing presses rolled out passport after elegant passport, motley questions loomed. What did "provisional registration" entail? By adding one's name to the registration books of the Portuguese consulate in Salonica, was one acquiring citizenship? Was one becoming a protégé in the same sense as had the Livornese Jewish subjects of Tunis decades earlier? Could a provisional status become permanent and, if so, how? How far could protection be passed; beyond the traditional vectors of husband to wife or father to child, could it travel from a deceased husband to a widow, from brother to sister, between brothers, or from son to mother? In the near-end and immediate wake of the First Balkan War, the involved parties—Jewish holders or seekers of papers, Portuguese consuls, the Foreign Ministry—answered these questions variously. Even Portuguese Foreign Ministry's views of these matters shifted with time, in part because of the constant and rapid turnover in this office over the first sixteen years of the First Republic (1910–26), and in part in dialogue with the unfolding of dramatic events in Portugal, Greece, and Europe more generally.

Certain Jewish families registered in 1913, unsure of the legal value of the papers they held—or possibly intent on maximizing their worth—found themselves commencing a decades-long bureaucratic dance with Portuguese officials. The de Botton family offers one example. During the Greek occupation of Salonica, Mair de Botton and at least eleven of his children registered in Salonica as Portuguese subjects.[43] Over subsequent years and migrations, the family leveraged their registrations to claim other forms of official paperwork. Mair de Botton's children (and at least four of their spouses) were granted Portuguese passports from the consuls of Istanbul, Milan, Barcelona, and Rio de Janeiro; another brother obtained Portuguese citizenship from the Portuguese consul in Rome for his new wife, a French citizen who had become denaturalized upon her marriage to a foreign man.[44] All told, the de Bottons appealed to no fewer than seven Portuguese consuls over a period of two decades.[45] Yet other members of the family make appearances in the Austro-Hungarian Foreign Ministry, British Home Office, and Spanish consular archives, suggesting that the extended de Bottons (carrying on a time-honored Mediterranean tradition) may have hedged their bets by diversifying their political fealties.[46]

Nor does the story end here. In 1924 José de Botton undertook the extraordinary measure of traveling to Lisbon to obtain documentation from the Foreign Ministry that would testify to the Portuguese status of all members of the extended family. De Botton's unprecedented voyage prompted the Foreign Minister to review the records of the family and the Salonican consulate whence their Portuguese papers came. Labeling the de Botton history "fussy," the Foreign Ministry noted that though the Salonican embassy had granted the de Bottons' provisional registration in keeping with the Foreign Minister's mandate of 1913, the family's reinscriptions in Rome and Barcelona did not state whether they were provisional or definitive. Despite the evident displeasure of the Foreign Minister, José de Botton left Lisbon with the certificates he demanded. Arditti's short-term passports had morphed into definitive ones by dint of bureaucratic convolution. The Foreign Ministry might have protested, but apparently did not perceive the metamorphosis as threatening. In time the office would prove less generous.

In Istanbul, too, the legal waters were muddy. After being informed by Portugal's Foreign Minister in 1913 that the state sanctioned the provisional registration of Jews in Southeastern Europe and Ottoman Anatolia, Consul Mesquita assured his superior that he would be "meticulous" in carrying out his demands.[47] And yet Mesquita was well aware that the Spanish and Austro-Hungarian consuls in Istanbul (as in Salonica) were extending definitive rather than provisional passports to Jewish applicants, and over the months to come he urged the Foreign Minister to follow suit.[48] Mesquita's principal concern was that provisional registration would produce provisional loyalty. He noted with anxiety that hundreds of Jewish families who had registered with the Portuguese consulate in Salonica were procuring the flags of other nations to display outside their homes.[49] These Jewish supplicants to the Portuguese state, it would seem, were strategic with their patriotism. For them, the pursuit of Portuguese papers did not necessarily entail the attenuation of loyalty in other directions.

Confronted by these happenstances, Mesquita was soon tempting Jewish would-be applicants with the promise of citizenship itself. Early 1914 found the consul delivering a talk to the B'nai B'rith Society of Istanbul on the subject of Portugal's newfound affection for its diasporic Jews. Before an audience that included the Sephardi scholar Rabbi Abraham Danon, Mesquita cited Portugal's 1913 law (designed to encourage the migration of European Jews to Angola) as providing legal precedent for the *naturalization* (rather than the provisional protection) of would-be Portuguese Jews.[50] This event was heralded in the local Ladino- and French- language Jewish press, and this coverage prompted a swell of Jewish applicants to approach the Portuguese consul in Salonica, where they in turn were granted Arditti's magnificent passports.[51] If the registration of these individuals was provisional, its finite nature was counterbalanced by perception. For Mesquita and the Jewish families to whom he granted papers, citizenship, it seems, was as much a matter of discernment as of law.

Questions of gender further complicated the meaning of "provisional registration," reiterating that the value of this status was not fixed but rather shifted jerkily. Portugal's consulates employed a spectrum of strategies for registering women, children, and families. Some consular representatives chose to list only men in their registration ledgers, presumably assuming that the man's unidentified dependents would automatically inherit their husbands' or fathers' legal status. In other instances, women and children were listed as dependents of husbands and fathers (or, in the case of widows, sons), sharing their registration number and documentation.[52] Still other consular representatives registered women and children as discrete subjects, granting them each their own entry and registration number in the relevant ledger (figure 1.2).

Nor were women treated in a static fashion throughout their lives. In 1929 the Portuguese consulate in Athens issued Rebecca Benveniste, a native of Salonica, her own travel papers. These documents, which were heavily used, featured a photograph of the young woman with her son Jacques and bore no mention of Benveniste's husband, Vital (Haim). Ten years later, the family was issued a group passport—again from Athens—under Vital's name: here, Rebecca and her children were featured as dependents.[53] Esther Algrante traveled in the other direction, legally speaking. When she divorced her husband, Elia, who had served as Portuguese consul in Istanbul, she was reregistered independently of her husband, gaining rather than losing legal autonomy.[54] For women, documentary independence could be reevaluated and even constricted over time, according to the whim of an individual bureaucrat. These cases suggest that Jewish women and children faced their own layers of uncertainty as they sought, carried, or renewed Portuguese protection. To be

FIGURE 1.2A Portuguese registrations of Isaac and Julie Beja, c. 1913, 1925, and 1931. Isaac Beja was among roughly 2,500 Salonican Jews who acquired foreign papers during the Balkan Wars (1912–13), after which Salonica transitioned from Ottoman to Greek rule. In subsequent years Beja renewed his "provisional" Portuguese protection in Salonica and Paris; after his marriage, his papers listed his wife Julie and children Esther and Albert as dependents. To be a dependent of a provisionally protected person was to skate at the outer limits of citizenship. Portuguese protection was stripped from many Mediterranean Jews after a consular audit in the mid-1930s. Courtesy Divisão de Arquivo e Biblioteca, Instituto Diplomático, Lisbon, 3PA12M312.

a dependent of a provisionally protected person was to skate at the outer limits of citizenship.

From a certain perspective the whole Jewish community of Salonica was vulnerable to the ambiguities of extraterritoriality, even if only a small minority of the city's Jews sought foreign protection. The most poignant evaluation of the ramifications of extraterritoriality may have come from local Salonican

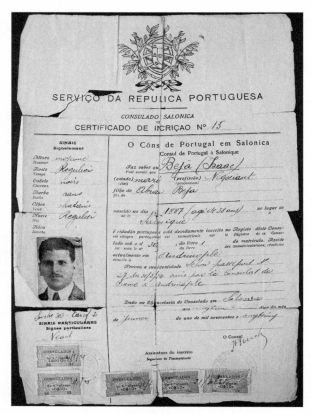

FIGURE 1.2B *continued*

Jewish historian Joseph Nehama. Writing from his native city in the spring of 1913, Nehama described the onslaught of foreign registrations by Jews in his city as a threat to the health of the Jewish community and the city as a whole. "All who think, who have thought, who have agitated, who have argued in Salonica are now foreigners," Nehama wrote. "It remains for the government to come to the aid of the little people . . . and the riff-raff. It poses a very grave danger to the community because all these foreigners are without political rights, and a municipal and communal [voice], too. Who will represent the great community of Salonica? She is being decapitated. It is truly a bad thing, with terrible economic consequences."[55] In Nehama's eyes, the acquisition of foreign protection (like emigration) was a luxury of the elite, and a dangerous manifestation of their effective disengagement from communal and local politics, as evidenced by their forfeiting the right to vote in local elections.

FIGURE 1.2C *continued*

This was an ironic position given that Nehama belonged to the elite and would himself take on Spanish citizenship some three decades later.[56] Still, Nehama's point remains: from an economic perspective, Salonica's middle class, already shrunk by a wave of emigration, was being cherry-picked, leaving the community less and less able to function collectively.

Criticism of the class-based nature of foreign registration in Salonica came from non-Jewish observers as well. Among the earliest public efforts to parse the legal contours of Portugal's policy was an article published simultaneously in at least four regional newspapers in the spring of 1913: the Greek-language Trieste-based *Nea Imera*, the French-language *Liberté* of Salonica, the Greek-language *Embros* of Athens, and the Greek-language *Macedonia* of Athens.[57] The article, ostensibly written by a "correspondent" in Salonica, ruthlessly criticized foreign consuls for registering Salonica's Jews.[58] Calling the officials

FIGURE 1.2D *continued*

in question "cunning agents," the author accused them of "exploiting the fears" of city dwellers anxious that Greece would impose conscription on the city's residents. To draw attention to the ostensibly crass nature of this process, the article emphasized that Jewish applicants paid 2,500 Ottoman lira for their registrations—and that Portugal's representative in Salonica, Consul Missir (among others), was all too happy to accept the remuneration.

This article also waded into the choppy legal waters surrounding the institution of consular protection. Its author labeled the actions of the consulates "pointless and invalid," arguing that since the individuals being registered were already Ottoman subjects, their legal fate would necessarily mirror that of all other "Ottoman residents of Thessaloniki [*sic*]," regardless of their registration. This argument hinged upon careful phrasing and a twist of legal logic. By calling Salonica by a Greek name, "Thessaloniki," the author evinced a nationalist view of the city's destiny.[59] At the time of the article's publication, after all, Salonica was occupied but not annexed by Greece, its "Greekness" a matter of historical and future projection rather than state law. How ironic, then, that the letter rested on a legal valorization of Ottoman history. According to the author, Salonica's Jews could not be Portuguese, Austrian, or Spanish because they were Ottoman; therefore they, like Salonica itself, were destined to become Greek.

Portuguese representatives responded to this criticism with outrage, but there was an element of prescience in the reportage. Immediately after the Greek annexation of Salonica, Greek officials commenced a Hellenizing effort in the city: street names were changed to reflect a Hellenic past, a population of Greek bureaucrats was imported, and many Muslims who refused Greek citizenship were fired from their jobs.[60] At the height of these efforts, the Portuguese consul in Istanbul complained that Greek authorities were objecting to the legality of Portugal's registrations as well as those of Spain and Austro-Hungary—an eventuality Joseph Nehama had predicted. In response, the Spanish consul in Istanbul traveled to Athens to defend the claims of Jewish holders of Spanish papers, while the Austro-Hungarian representative issued formal complaint. Consul Mesquita sought to maintain "an entirely dignified attitude" in public while seething in his exchanges with Lisbon.[61] Individual Jewish holders of Portuguese papers also jockeyed to obtain assurances. Haim Perez and his son Levy Perez, both of whom had been "provisionally registered" as Portuguese months earlier, appealed directly to the Foreign Minister for any form of paperwork that might testify to the family's foreign status and placate Greek officials.[62] Other Jewish families who were granted Portuguese papers in 1913 took on Greek citizenship at this time. Whether this was done out of desire, under pressure, or by resignation cannot be ascertained.

Within the year, Europe was at war. In Salonica and Greece more generally, there was a fierce divide over whether the country should enter the conflict and, if so, on whose side. The nation was literally divided, with the liberal-democrat Eleftherios Venizelos, a supporter of the Allies, forming a provisional government in Salonica and King Constantine, who wished to see Greece support the Entente, ruling in Athens. Once Venizelos proved victorious in the contretemps—due, in no small part, to the landing of sympathetic Allied troops in Salonica—he declared his support of the Allies. Six months later, King Constantine retreated into exile, the halves of Greece were united, and the country officially entered the war on the Allied side. Venizelos now mobilized the Greek army, imposing conscription upon Greek men of fighting age, including holders of foreign protection.[63] In Greece, as elsewhere, the war provided an excuse for the authorities to accelerate the nationalizing process by reigning in protégé freedoms. Incensed, the Austro-Hungarian, Spanish, and Portuguese consulates in Salonica began inquiries into the legality of this development.[64]

The families of Portuguese protected Jews conscripted by Greece were also struggling to determine their sons' legal rights. Frustrated by the seeming impotence of their protector, a subset of this population formed a delegation that intended to travel to Lisbon to advocate on behalf of "the Portuguese colony of Salonica."[65] Though the trip was postponed due to the hazards of maritime travel during a time of war, the delegation appealed to the Portuguese Foreign Ministry in print, arguing that the conscription of their sons was sure to have a deleterious effect on the moral and commercial relationship between Portugal and her subjects in Salonica. This ad hoc group also weighed in on the legal meaning of protection by arguing that Greek conscription of protected Jews violated their sons' "civil status."[66] The accusation bore the implication that provisional protection was equated with citizenship in these supplicants' eyes—or, at least, suggested that they saw opportunity in such a legal loophole. This interpretation apparently satisfied Consul Arditti, who referred to the conscripted young men as "those under our jurisdiction" [*nos ressortissants*].

Across the Sephardi diaspora, other Portuguese consuls were grappling to reach their own conclusions. The Portuguese consul in Barcelona, having been approached by Jewish holders of Portuguese papers seeking exemption from Greek military service, was told by his superiors in Lisbon to authorize renewal of the applicants' "provisional papers" without conceding their right to a military exemption.[67] Similar instructions were delivered to Portugal's representative in Berne.[68] In Rio de Janeiro, Consul d'Oliveira, blindsided by the number of like appeals directed to his office, offered his own (astute) rumination on the legal status of the applicants, writing, "I believe this is a question of protection [*proteção*] and not of naturalization [*naturalização*] or Portuguese nationality [*nacionalidade*]."[69] Representatives of other governments were splitting the same hairs. Writing in 1918, Great Britain's consul in Salonica concluded that the actions of the Portuguese consul in that city were "based on no recognized principle of international practice," reflecting further that: "it is hard to believe that the Greek government will recognize [the Portuguese consul's] right to confer Portuguese nationality on inhabitants of Turkish territory annexed to Greece."[70] This terse reading did not misrepresent facts on the ground, but it did ignore the complexities of the past. The vagaries surrounding Portugal's protection of Salonican Jewry far exceeded the question of whether "provisional protection" offered fewer assurances than more permanent forms of protection—or (Spanish or Austro-Hungarian) citizenship itself. These nuances were of interest to so many state representatives, including the British, precisely because indeterminate forms of legal protection had been extended by so many European states, for so long.

IN WAR AND IN FIRE: PROTECTION AT TIMES OF CRISES

Whether the representatives of foreign regimes, Portugal's consuls or Foreign Minister, or Jewish protected subjects themselves were aware of the fact, the legal implication of "provisional registration" would soon become not simply a local, consular, or regional concern, but of the utmost international import. With the advance of the First World War, states and extraterritorial populations across Europe were increasingly attentive to the importance of passports, residency permits, and official papers. For the Portuguese Foreign Ministry, the war supplied myriad cautionary tales, for Portugal—even more, it seems, than other European countries—lacked the experience and ability to monitor its protected subjects abroad, let alone to carry through on promises of protection, however provisional.

The wartime travails of Alfredo/Aron Nahum are illustrative in this regard. Nahum, a Salonican-born Jewish merchant, was added to the registration books of the Portuguese consulate in Salonica in the summer of 1913. Some time thereafter, Nahum used his Portuguese papers to leverage the permits required for travel to Berlin, whence he successfully applied for a provisional Portuguese passport from the Portuguese representative in Vienna. Passport in hand, Nahum traveled to Paris and was there when the war broke out.[71] In accordance with French wartime legislation mandating the registration of "friendly aliens" (the topic of chapter 3), Nahum registered with the Parisian police.[72] Recognizing Nahum's passport as provisional and cognizant that he had reached France from Germany, officials in Paris suspected him of espionage. Portugal's representative in Paris was contacted and he in turn appealed to the Foreign Minister for assistance. The Foreign Minister's response was unequivocal: Nahum's status was not "clear enough" to justify intervention.[73]

This ostensible lack of clarity was endemic to Portuguese policy rather than Nahum's portfolio. Jewish holders of Portuguese provisional protection confounded the authorities because they were in a sense doubly extraterritorial. By acquiring Portuguese protection, over a thousand Salonican Jews had become extraterritorial without ever leaving their homes. If they subsequently traveled with Portuguese documentation in hand—as did many, including Nahum—they were still subjects living outside their chosen country, but they were also removed from the local territory and consulate that had provided the social and legal framework for (and, in a sense, lent logic to) their foreign protection. This unpredictable set of events strained the limits of Portuguese officials' imagination and, no less, their sense of legal responsibility. Small wonder that as the war unfolded, the Foreign Minister advised the consul in Lausanne to be "meticulous" in extending new visas or passports to Jewish holders of papers from Portugal's consul in Salonica, and, "above all," not to grant them the papers required to travel to the Allied countries.[74] The Foreign Minister reminded another consul to grant Salonican Jewish applicants "very limited protection," reminding him that they were "very recently Ottoman subjects"— that is, would be enemy aliens of the Allied countries.[75] Taking this one step further, the ministry announced that Portugal's legal obligation to Jewish paper holders from Salonica should be comparable to that granted by the Allied countries to their own protected subjects.[76] And yet Portugal's protection of Salonican Jews—by dint of its provisionality—was not, in fact, akin to that which Great Britain or France had extended to resident Mediterranean and Middle Eastern Jews. As if to intensify the contrast, the Portuguese Foreign Ministry tightened its policies yet further in late 1917, advising its representatives to grant "no more protection or renewal of registration or passports or new documents [of any kind]. . . . in favor of people who do not possess Portuguese nationality by birth without consulting first with the representatives of Allied nations in Salonica to certify that these individuals were not suspect from their point of view."[77]

While global politics were altering the implications of provisional protection, an event in Salonica provided the Portuguese government with the ultimate opportunity to harden its policies towards its Jewish protégés. In August 1917, a massive fire swept through Salonica, wreaking particular damage upon its historic center, a commercial district overwhelmingly populated by Jewish families and Jewish cultural and religious institutions.[78] The devastation was catastrophic. Some 52,000 Jews were left homeless, along with 10,000 Muslim and 10,000–15,000 Christian residents of the city. Thirty-two synagogues and nine rabbinical libraries burned, along with countless private libraries, archives, and schools.

Like so much else, the Portuguese consulate in Salonica was destroyed. With it burned all documentation associated with the registration as Portuguese subjects of Southeastern European Jews that had begun in the city in 1913. As news of the devastation in Salonica rippled across the Sephardi diaspora, Salonican-born Jews across Europe and as far away as Rio de Janeiro awoke to the realization that crucial documentation pertaining to their legal status was likely lost in the conflagration. As the Jewish community initiated an ambitious census, émigré Jews from the city began flocking to consulates (of Portugal and other nations) across the globe, seeking to renew their papers or confirm their status as citizens.[79] Among them was Moises Benveniste, a young man of twenty-three years of age. Just two days after the fire in Salonica, Benveniste, an advanced engineering student, approached the Portuguese Consul in Lausanne requesting a passport. Benveniste carried a certificate from October 1913 showing proof of his registration by the Portuguese Consulate in Salonica, and explained that he required the passport to travel to France, where a job awaited him.[80]

Benveniste's request was one among scores. The Portuguese consul in Rio de Janeiro complained to the Foreign Minister with evident exasperation that in the months after the fire of 1917, "Jews from Salonica holding Portuguese passports and visas from Portuguese consulates in Europe, [that have been] verified by the Foreign Minister, continue to present themselves at this consulate and others in Brazil."[81] Witnessing the proliferation of Jewish requests for papers and paper renewals, and the concomitant mounting of consular inquiries, the Foreign Minister commenced an inquiry into the history of Portugal's legal relationship with Jews of Iberian origin. The investigation that followed concluded that the practices implemented by the Salonican consulate beginning in 1913 were of an irregular nature—not only because of their provisionality, but because they violated Portugal's civil code. The Foreign Minister's office now declared that all future registrations were to adhere strictly to Portuguese nationality laws, granting papers only to individuals born in Portugal who could demonstrate "moral and material assurances" of allegiance to the country. All other protections were to be annulled, and, in the future, Portugal's legions and consulates were to reduce dramatically the number of protections extended.[82]

These were, on the face of it, bold words, but they did little to settle the legal ambiguities that swirled around Portugal's Jewish subjects in and from Salonica. With the registration rolls of the Portuguese consul in Salonica destroyed, all parties involved—the Foreign Ministry, local consuls, and Jewish paper holders and would-be paper holders—found themselves in newly ambiguous waters. Notwithstanding the Foreign Minister's novel legal benchmarks, the state lacked definitive documentation testifying to who had been granted protection in violation of state law and who might rightfully be called a Portuguese subject. The Foreign Minister's intervention in 1917 did little to redress the legal fallout of Portugal's "provisional registrations": if anything, Portugal's Jewish subjects from Salonica were now harder than ever to identify, monitor, and control.

The last, dramatic interwar chapters of Portugal's relationship with the Jews of Salonica took shape against the backdrop of the 1926 military coup in Portugal, António de Oliveira Salazar's rise to power, and the consolidation, under his rule, of a corporatist, nationalist, stubbornly imperial, and conservative "New State" of Portugal.[83] Writing but weeks before the coup that dismantled Portugal's First Republic, Foreign Minister Brederode ordered his consul in Salonica—J. D. Missir, son of the honorary Consul Missir who granted the first papers to Salonican Jews—to consider any passport held by "an individual who is not Portuguese in origin and did not conduct military service for Portugal" to be worthless.[84] Missir responded in a desperate tone. He rehearsed to his superior the many cultural and historical ties that sutured Salonica's Jews to Portugal, reminding the Foreign Minister of the 1913 order issued to the elder Consul Mesquita, and emphasizing that both Portugal and Spain had exempted its diasporic Jews from the burden of military service. "Under these conditions, after thirteen years, after the government of Greece has recognized a great number of these families as Portuguese, can we refuse them protection?. . . . I shall find myself in a very delicate situation vis-à-vis the Greek authorities if I am obliged to change my attitude and not recognize as citizens of my consulate those people that I have protected until now."[85] Missir was not greeted with a sympathetic audience. "There are no rights without responsibilities," responded the Foreign Minister. "We can not allow for a privileged status among citizens of the state." The dismissive retort went on to upset the historical fantasy that had underpinned the Republican promise to Salonica's Jews. Sephardi Jews of "the Orient," the Foreign Minister expanded, were not speakers of Portuguese but of Spanish, "which they have guarded carefully and which is the language of their true origins." This statement shifted attention from the problematics of provisional protection to the problematics of the claim that Sephardi were Portugal's diasporic children. Reminding Missir that his job was to represent Portugal, not Spain, the Foreign Minister repeated his orders, demanding that Missir follow them strictly.[86]

The Foreign Minister's words of 1926—like the military coup of that year—were but a harbinger of things to come. Under Salazar's watch, Portugal's Foreign Ministry retreated from the opportunistic, self-serving, and colonial fantasies that had driven Portugal's policy of registering in Salonica, only to invest tremendous efforts in other opportunistic, self-serving, colonial fantasies (particularly as concerned Angola, which Salazar would fight to maintain as a Portuguese province in the course of the Angolan War of Independence of 1961–74). By the late 1930s, the Foreign Ministry had become deeply suspicious not only of Jews like the de Botton family (who, over some two decades, had leveraged Portuguese protection to the greatest extent possible), but of the Portuguese consuls who permitted such practices. As Avraham Milgram has aptly put it, this hostile attitude "can be traced back to the opportunistic way the liberal Republic treated the Jews in 1910–26—seeking to exploit their economic capabilities, but never expressing genuine willingness to integrate and embrace them as liberal members." In Milgram's opinion, Salazar's hostile views on Ottoman Jews were "based, among other things, on his tendency to link the problem of Jews of Levantine origin with the liberal Republican regime, which had created it in the first place."[87]

The state's crackdown on Jewish holders of Portuguese papers took form with an elaborate investigation by Jorge Roza de Oliveira, the Foreign Ministry's consular auditor. De Oliveira's inquiries, conducted over 1936–37, were not instigated with the explicit goal of ferreting out Jewish holders of Portuguese papers, but they nonetheless focused on the records of Portuguese consuls that had, since the late nineteenth century, granted papers to Jews in disproportionate numbers (including those in Vienna, Istanbul, Salonica, Athens, Naples, Cairo, Alexandria, Tunis, and Casablanca).[88] The auditor paid particular attention to Jews who had been registered in Salonica beginning in 1913 and the smaller number of Jews who were concurrently registered in Istanbul. (De Oliveira also chose to sanction roughly a dozen registrations that had taken place in Port Said in 1915, when, it seems, a dozen or so distinguished Jewish and non-Jewish mercantile families from Goa jumped on the bandwagon led by Salonica's Jews.)[89] These registrations, de Oliveira concluded, were "certainly illegal in the juridical sense, as these naturalized persons claim a vague and very doubtful Portuguese genealogy." Shedding doubt on the strategic value of this population—a perceived value that had convinced the Portuguese Foreign Minister to grant Salonican Jews protection in the first place—de Oliveira noted that "all of the persons registered in the Istanbul consulate are of modest means. They do not speak Portuguese, with exception of the consul, they do not maintain ties with Portugal, and I do not think they have ever visited [the country]."[90] Finally, he concluded that Jewish applicants were insincere in attesting to their Portuguese heritage or evincing loyalty to Portugal. They were motivated, de Oliveira asserted, simply by the desire not to be "subjected to the sovereignty of the winner [e.g., Greece]." Having completed his inquiries, the consular auditor proposed that the Foreign Minister consider all suspect registrations null and void.[91]

Jewish holders of Portuguese protection were not the only subjects of de
Oliveira's disdain. The auditor also railed against Portuguese consuls "of the
fourth rank" who were unfamiliar with Foreign Ministry circulars and issued
passports with undue lenience. He directed particular animus at those Portuguese consuls who were themselves Sephardi Jews, namely, Solomon/Salomão
Arditti (whom he considered "not the best individual to serve" Portugal) and
Jacques Abravanel, the then-serving consul in Istanbul. Abravanel was, in fact,
an exceptional servant of Portugal, who had not only lived in Lisbon for a time,
but also served in the Portuguese military. No matter: de Oliveira called Abravanel "not the best person to occupy the position" of consul, noting that he
was "of humble means and a Jew."[92] (The auditor also ruthlessly condemned
Portugal's non-Jewish consul in Athens, B. Lencastre e Menezes, who was dismissed as a result.)[93] Extending his reach yet further, de Oliveira argued that
Portugal's consulates in Istanbul and Salonica should be closed not only to
circumvent the employ of Arditti and Abravanel, but to "thwart the possible
pretentions of the old illegally-registered individuals that want to be considered Portuguese again," due to "the notorious lack of honesty that is almost
ubiquitous to the Middle East and, especially, Greece."[94]

Beyond its evident Orientalist bias, de Oliveira's writing reveals a revisionist sense of Salonica's strategic value. In the auditor's view, Portugal would do
well to shift its attention south and east of Salonica and Athens to the eastern
Mediterranean, the Mashriq, and North Africa. "The Oriental Mediterranean
does not, in my opinion, have satisfactory consular representation," de Olivera
explained to the Foreign Minister. "The region from Turkey to North Africa
(Asia Minor, Palestine, the new states of the Levant, Iraq, and [Saudi] Arabia)
is of interest due to the emergence of new countries. The transference of a consular post from Athens to that region would be convenient. I think that Egypt,
where there are Mixed Tribunal Courts, would be the best country for this new
consulate. . . ." Here, de Olivera was astonishingly canny. Salonica's economy
was unraveling, and if Portugal were to seduce a Jewish protégé population
suited to the mid-twentieth century, it would be in Cairo, Beirut, or Baghdad
rather than Greece. In North Africa, the Mashriq, and the eastern Mediterranean, after all, the Ottoman capitulatory system—like European imperialism
more generally—was experiencing an after-life, assuming various convoluted
forms including the Mixed Tribunals of Egypt.[95] The auditor's plea was well
crafted to appeal to President Salazar's own evolving agenda of reinvigorating
the Portuguese empire.

De Oliveira's audit of Portugal's consuls resulted, in the short term, in
the annulling of protection for many Jewish subjects, the demotion of select

consuls accused of malfeasance, and the diminishment in responsibilities of consular representatives of anything but the first rank. These outcomes laid a foundation for an inflexible policy towards Sephardi refugees (including some who held papers acquired in Salonica in or after 1913) who sought Portuguese protection in the course of the Second World War—a subject we shall return to in the conclusion.

In the midst of the Balkan Wars, middle- and upper-class Jews in Salonica (and, in lesser numbers, Istanbul) were sought as protégés by a number of countries, including Portugal, that wished to bolster economic growth by enlisting a successful and rooted mercantile population with desirable footholds in new countries and markets. Portuguese state representatives imagined Salonica's Jews as would-be settlers who would further nationalist colonialist projects, including the settlement of Angola, and as agents who would, in theory, abet European influence into formerly Ottoman territories (such as Salonica) or yet intact Ottoman territories (in the Middle East) over which the Western powers were beginning to angle for control.

In the case of Portugal, the protection offered Jews was ambiguously phrased: provisional in nature but devoid of a definitive expiration date. This ambiguity resulted in anxious exchanges among state representatives and between Portuguese bureaucrats and Jewish supplicants seeking to define the legal limits of and opportunities afforded by "provisional registration." These very ambiguities produced a decades' long crossing of perspectives—conflicting interpretations of law and policy that were all the more confounded in times of war, threat, and hopeful expansion. In the preceding pages, I have been particularly invested in these confused responses, for they illuminate the competing nationalist, local, and transnationalist interests of myriad involved parties, including protector nations, individual consular representatives, invested observers with competing interests and investments, and the Jewish men and women who sought to make use of the protégé status. For Salonica's Jews, anxieties associated with the end of Ottoman rule and the meandering course of Hellenization came to include the ambiguous nature of extraterritoriality. Jewish protected subjects of Portugal were both privileged and endangered by their status, even more so because of the provisional nature of their protection, the value of which was revisited with every change of the political wind.

CHAPTER 2

Protégé Refugees

In Jaffa, a stone building containing a soap factory and store; in Jerusalem, four houses, one with a kitchen and cistern, another with a library and kitchen; a collection of ancient and modern religious books; a dresser and mirror; a buffet; silverware; glassware; a clock; a rug; a full set of utensils for Passover; an estate, all told, worth 88,000 francs—this is what the brothers Askenazi (Salomon, Abraham Haim, and Israel), French citizens of Algerian Jewish origin, left behind when they were expelled from Palestine in the early years of the First World War.[1]

The Askenazis were among some 11,000 holders of papers of an Allied or neutral country, the vast majority of them Eastern European Jewish immigrants who were subjects of the Russian Empire, to be labeled enemy aliens and expelled by the Ottoman authorities from Palestine and the Syrian provinces of the Ottoman Empire in the course of the First World War.[2] The wartime governor of Syria and commander of the Ottoman Fourth Army, Cemal Paşa, one of three leaders of the Committee of Union and Progress (or CUP, popularly if less accurately known as the Young Turks) brought to power by a 1913 military coup, oversaw these deportations as part of a reign of terror marked by mass conscription, harassment, detention, and expulsion—especially of local Muslim leaders and former opponents, and including prominent Zionists. Cemal Paşa's martial rule was designed to reassert Ottoman state control over the peoples of Syria and Palestine.[3] However, Cemal Paşa's reign coincided with a catastrophic famine which resulted in the death of half a million people in Syria and Lebanon, and which was used by the British and French as a weapon of war; these dynamics, coupled with Cemal Paşa's own extreme tactics, meant that the war was marked by profound suffering and subsequently remembered as "the war of famine."[4]

The expulsion of enemy aliens from Syria and Palestine unfolded in sixteen rounds beginning in December 1914, three months after the Ottoman Empire entered the war on the side of the Central Powers and sultan Mehmed V abrogated the capitulatory regime, and but a month prior to the Ottoman declaration of jihad [*cihad*].[5] Those expelled came from a variety of backgrounds. They were subjects of Russia, France, Great Britain, Italy, Spain, Portugal, and the United States. Some, like the Askenazis, were wealthy at the time of their forced departure; others came from humble backgrounds. Some were locals; others were passing through for work, to visit family, or on religious pilgrimage. Some were foreign citizens, others protégés, others colonial subjects, still others held Ottoman citizenship and were mistakenly caught up in the sweep for foreign nationals. For their differences, one striking fact remains. Many of those forced to leave their homes by dint of their foreign status were Jews—not because Cemal Paşa's policies targeted Jews per se, but because so many Jews in the region held foreign papers.

This story unfolds against the backdrop of mass displacement in Europe and the Middle East, lending a Mediterranean corollary to the European refugee crises associated with the First World War that have already commanded scholars' attention.[6] (Precedent was provided in the course of the Italo-Ottoman War [also known as the Italo-Turkish War, 1911–12], during which Italian nationals—including many Frankos—were expelled or fled from Ottoman territories.) More specifically, it developed alongside the forced expulsion of some 200,000 Greek citizens from Izmir and the Aegean Islands in 1914, and the genocide and displacement of Armenians that was begun in the spring of 1915 by various CUP authorities. That genocide and displacement entailed the mass arrests and executions of Armenian intellectuals and political figures, the widespread confiscation of Armenian-owned property, the abduction and forced conversion of Armenian women and children, and massive, and forced marches of men, women, and children to the deserts of Syria and Iraq, during which as many as a million died of exposure, starvation, and massacre.[7] (Most of those forced to leave Izmir and the Aegean Islands in 1914, by comparison, returned during the Greek occupation, only to be compelled to leave again in 1923 as part of the population exchanges of that year.)[8] These were not only human catastrophes: they were also breaches of the Ottoman Empire's various treaty-based obligations towards its non-Muslim minorities.

The events that transpired in Syria and Palestine under Cemal Paşa's watch, like the CUP's assault on Armenians, was part of a broader Ottoman wartime strategy to use jihad flexibly, to various ends: to signal hostility to non-Muslims within the empire, to draw the sympathy of Muslims across the globe to the Ottoman version of pan-Islamism, and, simultaneously, to welcome strategically certain non-Muslims into the Ottoman fold.[9] The multidimensionality of this strategy was not evident to the (erstwhile) capitulatory nations whose subject populations were under threat in Syria and Palestine. The principal fear of the British, French, and American authorities was that the CUP assaults on enemy aliens would proliferate, intensify, and bring yet more violence to the already blood-soaked soil of Asia Minor and Anatolia, and they made determinations of policy and strategy based on this fear. Most influential among these parties was American ambassador to Istanbul Henry Morgenthau, one of few foreign consuls to remain in the Ottoman capital during the First World War and among the most vocal international critics of the Armenian genocide. Cognizant that the CUP oversaw both disasters, Morgenthau (like other Allied representatives) filtered his perception of the refugee crises in Syria and Palestine through the Armenian genocide. This connection fanned fears that the Ottoman leadership might reproduce its genocidal actions in Palestine or Syria, or extend its assault on enemy aliens to the Ottoman interior, putting a broad range of protected subjects at risk.

The expulsions of Muslims and Jews from Syria and Palestine, and the violence associated with Cemal Paşa's rule, have loomed large in historical scholarship as the crucial triggers to three discordant forms of political awakening: the shaping of Arab nationalism in Syria and Lebanon, the beginnings of Turkish nationalism, and the move towards militancy by Zionists in Palestine.[10] My interest is in thinking about the refugee crisis less as a catalytic political force than as a legal problem—one that plagued not only the Ottoman authorities and the refugees themselves, but protector states. The expulsion of foreign subjects from Syria and Palestine was a turning point of sorts for the erstwhile capitulatory regimes of Europe, for it forced them to contend with the tremendous financial and logistical risks associated with protection at a time of war. The "protégé refugee" was, after all, a novel category—one filament of the international refugee crisis generated by the Great War.

Here, then, we situate the expulsion of foreign subjects from Syria and Palestine within a transimperial context and as a set of juridical challenges. Among the questions I shall ask are: How, amidst the chaos of expulsion, did the Ottoman authorities and supervising states of Europe (especially Great Britain and France, the protector nations of the vast majority of Ottoman-born refugees whose stories I attend to here) identify or misidentify their refugees and would-be refugees? How, if at all, did they differentiate between citizens and protégés, or between wealthy and poor refugees? Who became a refugee upon deportation; who had the right to be repatriated? Finally, how and when did the people involved cease to be refugees?[11]

THE CAPITULATIONS, ABROGATED

By the late summer of 1914, with an Ottoman alliance with the Central Powers ever more likely, European consuls across the Ottoman Empire noted a growing disregard for the terms of the capitulations and a concomitant flaring up in hostility towards their citizens and protected subjects. In August 1914, American vice-consul Leland Morris reported that in Izmir "the officials. . . . are showing a desire to disregard the privileges enjoyed by the franks. Since last Sunday, there have been several breaches of capitulatory rights, which surely would not have occurred before the out-break of this awful conflagration. Even though the intervention of the consulates concerned was effective it is clear that the prestige of Europe has been sadly diminished in the eyes of the Ottomans. . . . There have been many cases of the authorities entering upon foreign property and seizing horses, carriages, and automobiles by force and giving no receipt for them . . . In general the officials show a scant lack of consideration towards foreigners."[12] Morris' superior, American Ambassador Morgenthau, confided to the American Secretary of State: "It is feared that Turkey, taking advantage of general conditions, may abrogate capitulations."[13] The ambassador's fears were well founded. The capitulations were in their death throes. On 30 October 1914, the Ottoman Empire officially entered the war on the side of Germany and Austro-Hungary, formally realizing an alliance with the Central Powers secretly brokered in early August.[14] A week after entering the conflict (on 8 September 1914) sultan Mehmed V signed an *irade* [official declaration] abolishing the capitulatory regime. The following day, the authorities notified all ambassadors in the imperial capital of the ruling, sharing with them an identical circular explaining the policy and its motives.[15]

The contents of the 1914 *irade* were not terribly original. On the contrary, the declaration recycled objections to the capitulatory regime that had been aired in Ottoman circles for nearly a century, and which were directed with particular force at places like Palestine, where the population was extraordinarily legally pluralistic.[16] The circular criticized the way in which the capitulatory regime limited Ottoman judicial power by exempting holders of foreign papers from Ottoman law—and addressed the way in which the institution of protection economically crippled the state by exempting protected subjects from local taxes. Calling the capitulations a "hindrance to all progress in the Empire," the 1914 pronouncement concluded by emphasizing that an abrogation of the capitulations neither reflected "unfriendly thought[s] on the part of any Power," nor did it intend to contravene future commercial treaties "on the basis of the general principles of public international law."

The overturning of the capitulatory regime elicited a range of reactions across the empire, the Jewish protégé diaspora, and the states of Europe that claimed citizens and protégés in Ottoman lands. Critical coverage of the *irade* was muted in the Jewish press of Southeastern Europe, where the hand of Ottoman censors was felt keenly: in Palestine, however, discussion was more robust. Spanish Consul Antonio de la Cierva, Conde de Ballobar, stationed in Jerusalem, noted in his diary that "the effect of such a notice can scarcely be described: Christians fell victim to a tremendous panic, given that the demonstrations immediately began against the Europeans."[17] Jews living in the same city were divided in their reception of the sultan's pronouncement. According to Sephardi journalist Abraham Elmaleh, non-Ottoman immigrant members of Jerusalem's Jewish community who held foreign citizenship received the sultan's announcement with enthusiasm, for it appeared to pave the way to their legal integration into the state. Palestinian-born Jews, on the other hand, were more skeptical. They—like Ottoman Jews throughout the empire—were (according to Elmaleh) accustomed to leaning on foreign consuls for assistance of various kinds, and therefore perceived that the potential power vacuum left in the wake of the capitulatory regime could bode ill.[18] Practical concerns preoccupied other observers. A journalist for the Hebrew-language, socialist newspaper *Ha-Po'el ha-Tsa'ir* noted that the majority of Jewish holders of foreign papers would be unlikely to afford the fee (or roughly 40 francs) associated with obtaining Ottoman papers.[19] Many, however, accepted the fundamental premise of the 1914 *irade*: that an abrogation of the capitulations would fruitfully unify and strengthen the Ottoman state. These same observers—many Zionist leaders among them—tended to criticize those who clung to their foreign status in the face of the extension of Ottoman citizenship.[20]

For at least some who held the protection of a foreign power, the *irade* was experienced as a near existential insult insofar as it equated holders of foreign papers with foreigners—an equation some did not recognize in themselves. Writing in Jerusalem's Hebrew-language press, A. Kretschmer described the most painful consequence of the Ottoman entry into the war was "the sense of feeling foreign in this land. . . . 'Foreigners!' they yelled at us from every direction, 'foreigners,' whispered every gaze of a neighbor or passerby, 'foreigners,' murmured every stone in our house, every tree we had planted." Noting that there was great irony in the Ottomans "seeking to revenge Russia by attacking the Jews who had escaped from it," Kretschmer nonetheless agreed with most Zionists of the day that a demonstration of loyalty to the Ottoman regime was the best means to advancing the cause of Jewish national autonomy.[21] Those who did not reach the same conclusion were widely criticized as disloyal in the Hebrew press—dismissed by one account as "unsettled and unfixed elements who were about to leave anyway."[22] Such polemics did not pay heed to the broad range of legal niches occupied by those who lived in Syria and Palestine and held the protection of a foreign power. Some, as we shall see, were indeed foreign citizens: but others were protégés, or locals who worked in foreign consulates (or both), or colonial subjects, and they often lacked the range of rights the states of Europe granted their citizens.

For the erstwhile capitulatory states of Europe (including, at least initially, the Central Powers) the abrogation of the capitulations was not an event to be celebrated. The sultan's *irade* stripped legal immunity from protected subjects, thereby depriving the protector nation of a tax base and leaving the subject prone to arrest, denaturalization, or expulsion. The response of the European powers therefore, was predictable and instantaneous. In Istanbul, the Italian ambassador, acting as intermediary, submitted identical protests to the authorities on behalf of the six foreign powers represented in the empire—France, Great Britain, Russia, Austro-Hungary, Germany, and Russia—objecting that the capitulations, as a series of bilateral agreements, could not be unilaterally abrogated by a single contracting party. In the eyes of the Americans, the protest brokered by the Italians was "weak," but (as American representatives in Istanbul admitted) it mattered little, for nothing could be done to persuade the Ottoman authorities to reconsider their decision.[23] Other parties proved more flexible. Germany and Austria would later consent to the abrogation of the capitulations as the price of an alliance with Turkey—Germany in January 1917, Austria in March 1918.[24]

At the time at which sultan Mehmed's 1914 *irade* was promulgated, the Ottoman authorities gave no indication of their intention to expel holders of foreign papers from the empire. On the contrary, certain Ottoman representatives encouraged those protected by a foreign power to remain in their homes, emphasizing that the empire intended to serve as protector of its noncitizen subjects by guarding their security and treating them judiciously.[25] Still, the Allied states responded to the Ottoman entry into the war (and concomitant abrogation of the capitulations) by calling back their representatives from Ottoman territories, cognizant that they could no longer promise them legal immunity. As mentioned, American Ambassador Morgenthau was one of the few foreign envoys to remain in Istanbul, where he represented the interests of multiple Allied powers in the course of the war; in Jerusalem, only the Spanish and American consuls persisted at their posts.[26]

The Ottoman authorities now occupied various consulates of the Allied states, including the French consulates in Beirut and Damascus, using their confiscated papers to identify opponents of the regime.[27] This left local servants of the European powers—including Jewish dragomans and consular representatives—immensely vulnerable.[28] Such was the case with Alesander Akras, a Jewish translator and clerk of the British consul in Aleppo who was left in charge of the British consulate in that city after other British employees had been recalled from their post. With a wartime assault on Allied subjects underway, police in Aleppo arrested Akras and sent him to Adana, where he was obliged to resign his position. The archival trail on Akras might here have grown cold were it not for the fact that when he was forced to abandon his post in Aleppo, the dragoman entrusted the British consular archive to representatives of the American government. After those representatives fled, the British papers fell into the hands of the Ottoman police. Within the pages of this archive, the police discovered that Akras had been lauded by the British authorities for his "most valuable service in obtaining the mandatory information so continually recognized by the military attaché at Constantinople." Like that of many dragomans, Akras' service to the British was expansive, and could, under the circumstances, easily be perceived as espionage. A warrant for Akras' arrest was issued, and his trial and imprisonment thought likely to follow. Akras, however, was by now in hiding and appears to have remained so for the duration of the war.[29]

Akras' story was not exceptional: in Istanbul, Noureddin Ferouf [Nur al-Din Faruq], dragoman and (likely Muslim) secretary to the British in Istanbul, was said to be spending the war years smoking in the vacated British embassy, doing little aside from calling his superiors in London "to ask what is going to happen to him."[30] The question was more complex than Ferouf himself might have realized. He and Akras were neither citizens nor diplomats, but protégés and consular employees. The very amorphousness of these legal statuses posed little challenge to the state in a time of peace, but in a time of war matters were more complex. To Akras the authorities extended no assistance whatsoever—to Ferouf they offered the promise of diplomatic immunity in The Hague, should he be able to find his own way to the Netherlands. The

protégés of the Allied powers, it seems, were vulnerable not only to the Ottoman authorities, but to the whim of foreign ministries in Europe.

(MIS)IDENTIFICATION, ARREST, DENATURALIZATION, EXPULSION

How much more vulnerable were those outside of consular circles. Beginning
in December 1914, Cemal Paşa's administration ordered the first of a wave of
expulsions of Allied subjects who remained in Palestine and Syria and resisted the extension of Ottoman citizenship. These actions were not without
precedent. The regime could lean, for legal model, on the 1897 expulsion of
Greek nationals who refused Ottoman citizenship—a policy that took shape in
the course of a war waged between the Ottoman Empire and the Kingdom of
Greece over the status of Crete. That expulsion resulted in the displacement
of some 25,000 Greek citizens from the city of Izmir, leading to the acquisition of Ottoman citizenship by a large number of Greek citizens who chose to
remain in the city.[31] Ottoman animosity towards this population was renewed
in the course of the First World War—as mentioned earlier, between January
and June 1914, the state forced the emigration of 200,000 Greeks from Asia
Minor.[32] (Though a portion of these individuals returned, many would be
forced to join the 192,000 Greeks compelled to leave their homes pursuant
to the population exchange brokered between Greece and Turkey in 1923).

In December 1914 and over the subsequent three years, local police working under the direction of Cemal Paşa haphazardly identified and rounded up
the so-called enemy aliens of Syria and Palestine, ushering them to the ports of
Jaffa, Haifa, Jerusalem, and Beirut—in some cases weeks before any ship that
could carry them to refuge was allowed to dock. Some were prone to arrest
and stints of imprisonment even before they reached points of egress. Salomon
Padova, Abraham Amado, and David Arditti recalled being taken from their
homes with chains on their wrists and ankles after refusing to renounce their
French nationality. The men were incarcerated and told they would not be
released without significant payment.[33] In Tiberias, the temporary imprisonment of Jewish foreign nationals was also common.[34]

The expulsion decrees crossed class lines, leading poor as well as wealthy
families into destitution. Many of loftier means—like the Askenazi brothers,
with whom this chapter began—watched their homes looted as they prepared
to flee or were murdered as they tried to escape.[35] According to one particularly vivid account (which may merit the designation "atrocity propaganda"),
"The roads to the Jewish colonies north of Jaffa are lined with thousands of

starving Jewish refugees. The most appalling scenes of cruelty and robbery are reported by absolutely reliable eye-witnesses."[36] Rabbi Jacob Moses Toledano, a scholar raised and educated in Tiberias who was expelled from his hometown along with a large community of Jewish foreign subjects, described how multitiered this dramatic process was. According to Toledano, the refugees were not only uprooted from families, homes, and belongings, but forced to walk miles from their homes to the requisite port of exit; found themselves trapped at ports awaiting safe passage; and were confined to ships for weeks while their destinations were sorted out, sometimes moving back and forth between ports while other refugees were being boarded.[37] (After being settled in a refugee camp in Corsica, Toledano would come to serve as the exiled community's spiritual leader and to represent his refugee community to the AIU and French authorities, to whom he wrote in elegant, calligraphic Hebrew. He would subsequently serve as a member of the Tangier rabbinate, deputy chief rabbi of Cairo, and Sephardi chief rabbi of Tel Aviv, among various other distinguished functions.)

Those targeted for expulsion were usually granted forty-eight hours or ten days to renounce their foreign citizenship and (for a fee of approximately 40 francs) accept Ottoman citizenship rather than face deportation.[38] As many as 15,000 complied with this ruling, the bulk Russian Jews.[39] However, a portion of those who sought or acquiesced to Ottoman citizenship faced obstacles. In Jerusalem, Ottoman clerks (a class that had been criticized for its loyalty to the old regime since the rise of the CUP) were said to be "reluctant to assist in the Ottomanization process."[40] Elsewhere, those who took on Ottoman citizenship felt coerced into doing so, or were labeled Ottoman citizens against their will. In Beirut, 175 Jewish subjects of France and Great Britain were denied the right to leave Ottoman territory because local officials claimed they had taken an oath of loyalty to the Ottoman Empire—a claim denied by the women and men in question.[41] In Istanbul, Jean Hasson (who faced an imagined rather than imminent deportation threat) renounced his French citizenship in favor of Ottoman nationality only to rush to the American embassy to plead that its representatives contact the French authorities and assure them that his choice to denaturalize was born of desperation rather than desire.[42] Other protégés or colonial subjects found that the option of renouncing "foreign citizenship" placed them in a quandary, for they were not fully citizens of Europe in the first place.

Others recalled being rushed to a port without the time to gather clothing, supplies, money, or legal papers. After he was labeled an enemy alien, Isaac d'Avilla, a Jewish protected subject of Portugal living in Jerusalem, was sent by foot from Jerusalem to Jericho with a group of sixty Italians and Americans and "nothing but my skin and the clothes on my back." This happened so fast, in d'Avilla's telling that "it was possible neither to see my parents at this last, rude moment of separation nor to take money, bedding, or bedclothes." D'Avilla was shuttled from Jerusalem to Jericho and thence to Aleppo, where the Spanish consul advanced him money enough to buy shoes, clothing, and writing materials.[43]

Between December 1914 and May 1915, approximately 12,000 foreign subjects from Syria and Palestine found asylum in Egypt. Far smaller numbers were deported to Anatolia.[44] In Alexandria, where the bulk of the refugees were taken to two camps, those of Wardian and Gabbari (likely the first refugee camps created in Egypt), as well as settled through the city, the situation was said to be "pitiable." According to one witness, the refugees

> were completely destitute, without shoes, clothing, or linen. Some had been rudely arrested in the street and forced to embark without being able to carry anything with them; others had been withdrawn from prisons in which they had been confined for several weeks as suspects of an enemy, and conducted directly on board ship; others, finally tired of struggling against misery and frightened by the prospect of greater sufferings to come, left the country of their own free will. It was heartbreaking to see this dejected crowd come from the steamers and land on the docks. Husbands looked for wives, parents for their children, a large number of whom were seeking their mothers. The exile had separated members of the same family.[45]

Relief aid came from various directions, including the Egyptian, British, and French governments, the Red Cross, the Alexandrian Jewish community, various Jewish philanthropies (including the Alliance israélite universelle), and an emergency relief organization, the Committee for the Assistance to Refugees in Syria and Palestine, that was founded upon the arrival of the first group of refugees in December 1914.[46] But Alexandria was already economically strapped by the war, housing large numbers of soldiers as well as refugees, and roughly 3,000 of these early exiles (some of whom were housed in camps) slid quickly into poverty.[47] Those who could sought "repatriation"—a slippery word for reasons we shall explore momentarily. This option proved most accessible to Russians and Americans, of whom as many as 8,000 may have left Egypt during the war, and to small numbers of Tunisians, Moroccans, and Algerians (about whom we will learn more in time).[48] For the Ottoman-born Jewish refugee, however, options for exit were all but nonexistent.

Despite the vast amounts of aid funneled into Alexandria in particular and Egypt more generally, the wartime economy made the city inhospitable for the poor arrivals, who were said to be "in absolute misery."[49] By the late summer of 1915 Alexandria was saturated with refugees; strained, in the words of British High Commissioner in Egypt Henry McMahon, "to the outmost limit" (figure 2.1).[50] Now British and French officials sought frantically for alternative sites of refuge. The British considered Malta and Cyprus: the French Algiers. Even as their deliberations continued, hundreds of citizens of Great Britain, France, Russia, Greece, the United States, and Italy were being loaded onto American warships in Haifa and Beirut after Ambassador Morgenthau successfully negotiated for their safe passage with the Ottoman Foreign Minister. Some of these ships docked briefly in Egypt, allowing those with family in that country or the proven means to support themselves to disembark. The remainder of the refugees was ferried to Cyprus, in the case of most British subjects, and Corsica (by way of Canea, Crete), in the case of most French subjects.[51]

Finding a place to house the refugees and the means to feed, clothe, and otherwise assist them was, predictably, an immense challenge for the states and institutional bodies involved—but it is not the story upon which I am focusing here.[52] More relevant for our purposes are the varied challenges that surrounded the refugees' legal status. Precisely because so many refugees arrived in such desperate straits, it was often not easy to determine their legal identity—let alone a given state's or institutional body's legal obligation to them. Documenting the paperless proved a constant vexation. Among the refugees were Muslim pilgrims caught en route to Mecca who weren't registered with the local French consulate, or whose papers were damaged or lost in the course of expulsion.[53] Many Jewish "enemy aliens," meanwhile, had labyrinthine legal histories such as those this book unpacks, and these histories were unintelligible to the authorities involved. When Isaac d'Avilla arrived in Alexandria, the Portuguese consul in that city prepared him a temporary passport, valid for one year, that retraced the means by which d'Avilla had acquired Portuguese protection in the first place (through his father Massoud, who acquired it in Jerusalem in 1831).[54] But consular generosity could sometimes be challenged by the legal complexities associated with the refugee population. None other than Henry Morgenthau, among the bureaucrats most sympathetic to the plight of the refugee, noted with exasperation that of the fifty British and French citizens living in Istanbul in 1915 who were potentially prone to expulsion by the Ottoman authorities, "only two were born in England and two in France. All the rest are born in Turkey and few, if any, have ever visited either France or Great Britain."[55]

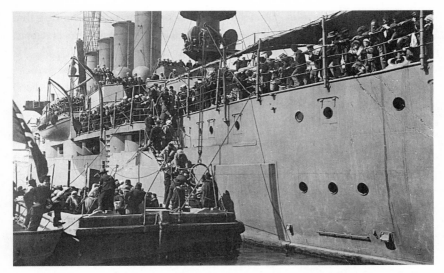

FIGURE 2.1 Disembarking refugees from the *U.S.S. Tennessee*, Alexandria, c. 1915. During the First World War, Ottoman authorities abrogated the capitulatory regime and began an uneven assault on non-Muslim minorities, as well as on dissident Muslims. In Palestine and the Syrian provinces of the empire, wartime governor Cemal Paşa used the conflict as an excuse to initiate martial law and conscription, harassment, and expulsion of Muslim leaders and opponents, prominent Zionists, and "enemy aliens." Jews, Christians, and Muslims—protégés, colonial subjects, and foreign nationals—were caught up in the expulsions. Many of the refugees were ferried by American warship to camps in Egypt, as pictured here. The unfolding crisis was legal as well as humanitarian in nature, raising questions about the obligations of protector nations at a time of war. Courtesy Ministère des Affaires étrangères et du Développement international, Direction Les Archives, La Courneuve. Correspondauce politique et commerciale, A. Guerre 1914–1918, Carton 947, f° 73v and f° 75r.

As Morgenthau and various European representatives were fretting over how British or French the refugees were (and therefore just how expansive the states' obligation to them as individuals or a group was), others were dwelling on their Jewishness—and thus just how indebted were Jewish institutions to them as a group. Edgar Suarez, a banker, outspoken critic of Zionism, and wartime head of Alexandria's Jewish community, was adamant in insisting that his community should not be expected to support the refugees, as "it was not Jews who were expelled from Jaffa but Russians, French, Belgians, etc." In Suarez's view, the protector nations should be held accountable for the refugees' care, and the government of Egypt should be responsible for appealing to the relevant consuls for that support. Suarez himself participated in petitioning Hussein Kamal, sultan of British Protectorate Egypt from 1914–17, for the requisite funds. This money Kamal promised, with the understanding that the British authorities in Egypt would subsequently demand reimbursement from the relevant protector nations.[56]

Locally and internationally, Suarez had his critics. David Yudelowits, Alexandrian manager for the Palestine-based company Carmel, devoted himself to working on behalf of the refugees in Egypt once the war broke out; after the war, he recounted his wartime experiences (often in self-aggrandizing fashion) in the Hebrew-language *Mi-yamim rishonim*. In the pages of this journal, Yudelowits emphasized that not all shared Suarez's legalistic approach, but were, rather "committed to Jews on all fronts, regardless of which side they fought on."[57] The major international Jewish philanthropies of the day (the American Jewish Joint Distribution Committee, the World Zionist Organization, the Alliance israélite universelle, the Board of Deputies of British Jews) were similarly attuned to the crisis as a Jewish one, offering philanthropy of one sort or another. To these institutional bodies, as to Yudelowits, the refugee crisis was not simply a problem of and for states, but of and for Jews.

In whatever conceptual manner the refugees were named, they had to be accounted for. The task of registering refugees in the course of their journey or at intake sites such as Alexandria and Canea was rendered complicated by the fact that one Allied state was often charged with registering the citizens of another, and the authorities realized that "it would be impolitic in the circumstances to differentiate between Jewish subjects of this country and her allies."[58] So the British in Egypt registered most incoming refugees on behalf of the states in question.[59] This system, in turn, raised the possibility of fraud. British representatives in Egypt and Crete were instructed to approve the papers of other Allied nations only with the greatest care, as "many passports granted to Allied and British subjects have passed into enemy hands and are a source of danger to this country."[60] Whether this instruction was paranoid or reflective of genuine threat is unclear—but it does reveal that representatives of the erstwhile capitulatory nations looked upon the refugees (and, just as importantly, the papers they carried) with a degree of suspicion. War, combined with forced migration, diluted the perceived integrity of state-issued documentation, blurring the boundary between ally and enemy.

For similar reasons, Zionist activists driven out of Palestine by Cemal Paşa's forces alarmed Allied authorities. A portion of these refugees—who constituted a minority of the overall refugee population—was Ottoman by birth and held paperwork demonstrating this fact. To the Allied authorities supervising the arrival of the displaced in Egypt, this population was confounding. Were the enemies of one's enemy to be trusted as friends? Or were they to be judged solely by the paperwork they carried—that is, as Ottomans, and hence enemy aliens of the Allies? To these questions the supervising authorities had no easy answers. Some of the Zionist activists pushed out of Syria and Palestine by the Ottoman authorities arrived in Egypt as refugees, only to find themselves identified as Ottoman subjects and thus arrested as enemy aliens by Allied authorities.[61]

Errors of categorization were arguably inevitable under the circumstances. When I. Barouch was elected president of the Franco-Syrian Jewish refugees in Corsica, he wrote the Alliance israélite universelle to inquire whether he was qualified to hold this position despite being of Ottoman nationality—that is, despite his having been expelled from Syria by accident.[62] Barouch's experiences with misidentification were not anomalous. When Amélie Nahon was expelled from Syria with her family in 1915, she carried papers that labeled her an Ottoman citizen. The daughter of AIU teacher and school director Isaac Ben Abraham Nahon, the Haifa-born Amélie had been registered as a French citizen of Algerian background by the French consulate in Alexandria in 1907. Resettled in Alexandria in the wake of expulsion, Nahon obtained permission from AIU secretary Jacques Bigart to relocate to Morocco to teach in an AIU school. But her resettlement in North Africa required new documentation that contravened that which she carried. Only with the intervention of Bigart and the Paris Prefecture of Police (who issued Nahon the necessary French travel papers) did the young woman clarify her legal quagmire, obtaining the French papers that allowed her to leave Alexandria for Morocco.[63] On the Ottoman side, as on the side of the Allies, identifying enemy aliens was hardly foolproof—in part because the refugees had legal histories and papers that bore evidence to the shortcuts and inventive strategies on which European consulates had depended for so long.

Nahon's story suggests that class and connections could work to the advantage of a refugee. All who were expelled from Palestine and Syria, regardless of class, were compelled to abandon their property, sell their possessions at reduced value, or watch their belongings seized by looters. In the words of David Yudelowits, the volunteer in Alexandria whom we encountered earlier, "The refugees included property owners, merchants, craftsmen, rabbis, teachers and students, school principals, lawyers and doctors—all had to leave with nothing."[64] Still, refugees carried class differences with them, and European representatives charged with overseeing the destitute population perceived these differences readily (figure 2.2). Correspondence between local

FIGURE 2.2 "Extra feeding of young children at Wardian" [refugee camp, Alexandria], c. 1915. Refugees expelled from Ottoman Syria and Palestine by wartime governor Cemal Paşa in the course of the First World War carried class differences with them, and European representatives charged with overseeing the destitute population perceived these differences readily. Muslim, Jewish, and Christian refugees who could document their ability to support themselves were allowed to stay in Egypt when other refugees were sent to camps in Cyprus and Corsica, or were "repatriated" to legal "homes" such as Morocco, Algeria, Tunisia, and India, even if they had never lived there before. Courtesy Ministère des Affaires étrangères et du Développement international, Direction Les Archives, La Courneuve. Correspondauce politique et commerciale, A. Guerre 1914–1918, Carton 947, f° 73v and f° 75r.

representatives of the European powers and their superiors in the metropole frequently subdivided the refugees by class—pointing out that those from Aleppo were wealthier than those "of indigent and parasite class" from Tiberias and Safed, for example, or that a group of women and children from Alexandretta were "of a better class"—and (or, one assumes, *hence*) "real British subjects—Englishwomen."[65] The British consul in Athens went so far as to query his superiors whether those of privileged background might merit preferential treatment, including the payment of higher relief, as "it is certainly very hard for people who have evidently seen better days, fairly well dressed women and men, to have to sleep on the ground amongst the very poorest class of Syrian Jews."[66] To this particular inquiry the British Foreign Office replied unequivocally, "There should be no discrimination between classes in the amount of relief afforded."[67] But in fact the supervising parties did not apply an even hand across class lines. Individual refugees who could document an ability to support themselves or be supported by others were repatriated to Morocco, Algeria, Tunisia, and India, or taken to Egypt at a time when most refugees were being taken elsewhere. When it came to class, policy norms towards refugees proved fungible, with state representatives revealing themselves to be more or less willing to exercise creativity in the face of chaos.

"REPATRIATION," WOULD-BE REFUGEES, AND THE LIMITS OF PROTECTION

In 1915, the secretary at Downing Street appealed to the British Foreign Office, asking whether the refugees in the Mediterranean couldn't simply be "sent to the part of the Empire to which they belong."[68] Alas, due to the diversity of the refugee population and the complex legal histories so many carried with them, "repatriation" proved a frustratingly slippery notion, both to the supervising states of Europe and the refugees themselves. Indeed, the question of repatriation proved not to be a single question (to repatriate or not to repatriate?) but a tangled knot of questions: Who had the legal right to transition from refugee to repatriate? Where was "home" to the extraterritorial subject at a time of war? Who might become a refugee in the future? What was the state's duty to its protected subjects in a time of war—and the refugee's duty to the state? These questions, as we shall see, only became more acute as the war approached its end.

In early 1915, the French Foreign Minister was informed that three categories of people under French protection had been affected by the expulsions of the preceding months: "Indigenous [Muslim] subjects of Algeria and our colonies," "indigenous [Muslim and Jewish] subjects from Tunisia and Morocco," and "Ottomans and those without well-defined nationality, in general Jews, who have always been under the protection of our consulates.[69] Handling the first two categories of refugees, the Foreign Ministry mused, would be relatively easy. The 400 Algerian and 2 Tunisian refugees were roughly on a par in the eyes of French law—they were *indigènes* without citizenship, colonial subjects of France. This group, the Foreign Minister mused, could be immediately repatriated to their place of origin. Muslim and Jewish refugees who were subjects of colonial Morocco—a population thought to number roughly 330—could be repatriated under the same logic. Most troublesome to the French was the third category of protégés: individuals the Ottoman authorities determined to be foreign, but who in many cases were neither French citizens nor colonial subjects.[70]

Consider the astonishing case of Moïse/Maurice Sidi. A Jew born in Bulgaria who held French papers, Sidi was directing the Alliance israélite universelle school in Beirut when the war broke out. Sidi left Syria for France, where he attempted to enlist with the French army in Marseilles. When army recruiters found him medically unfit to serve, he returned to Damascus, was interned as by the Ottomans an enemy alien, and (extraordinarily enough) obtained permission to return to Beirut from Cemal Paşa, whom he knew personally from his days as a school director in Baghdad. The authorities in Beirut informed Sidi that he could remain in the province if he acquired Ottoman citizenship: if, on the other hand, he was unwilling to renounce his affiliation with France, he was compelled to leave Ottoman territory. Choosing flight, Sidi managed to board an Italian boat destined for Alexandria with his wife and children.[71] If the Allied authorities supervising the refugee population in Egypt were to seek to repatriate Sidi, where would he be sent? Bulgaria, his native home, was enemy territory; France, a country in which he had never lived. How, in this case and so many others, was the ambiguous nature of extraterritoriality to be squared with wartime exigency?

Even those who wished to be repatriated to North Africa, whom the French considered "easy" repatriates, raised questions. Writing from the French refugee camp in Ajaccio, Salomon Lévy (who was expelled from Syria in 1915) repeatedly appealed to French officials to be sent to Casablanca, where his three brothers resided. The Foreign Ministry directed the French embassy in Morocco to locate Lévy's brothers, but none could be found. Despite the fact that Lévy and the Foreign Ministry shared the ambition of reuniting Lévy with his family, the refugee's request was denied.[72] Home, in Lévy's instance, was an elusive entity. Something similar could be said of the Askenazis, with whom this chapter began. French citizens of Algerian origin, the Askenazis appear to have lived in Palestine for some time—it is possible, indeed, that they never dwelled in North Africa, but inherited their French legal status from a family patriarch. Within the logic of war, to which place did they belong? A similarly confounding question arose in the case of Amélie Nahon, the AIU teacher we met moments ago. Born in Haifa, a resident of Syria, registered as French by dint of Algerian ancestry though a holder of Ottoman legal papers, a refugee in Egypt, an employee of the AIU—Nahon was as elusive a subject as one could fathom. For the refugees themselves, as for the supervising authorities, determining where "repatriation" might take an individual was no small matter, nor, in the end, an exclusively legalistic concern.

As the French Foreign Ministry struggled to resolve cases like Sidi's and Lévy's, the realm of law and the realm of myth began (neither for the first nor last time) to bleed into one another. The Foreign Ministry, though invested in assisting refugees claiming French protection, was nonetheless nervous creating a legal precedent that the French would have to honor in the event that the Ottoman expulsion of enemy aliens spread beyond the province of Syria and Palestine. Fretted the French Foreign Minister: if the French protégé refugee population in Alexandria (a mostly Jewish population estimated at 1,300 in 1915) were to be "repatriated" to France, would the far larger population of French protégés living in the Ottoman interior (estimated at 7,000) demand to follow suit? In Izmir alone, the Foreign Minister was informed, there were some 900 French Jewish protégés out of a suspected total of 3,000 French subjects claiming to hail from Bayonne who were threatened with expulsion; in Athens, 400 Jewish families from Algeria, Tunisia, and Bayonne were demanding repatriation; in Istanbul, 2,500 others were thought ready to lodge similar claims. All told, the potential cost of a strategy of repatriation was prohibitive, ranging from 80,000 to 100,000 francs.[73] Faced with mounting numbers of refugees fleeing Syria and Palestine, the over-saturation of refugees in Egypt, and the threat of a legal precedent that might snowball, the French Foreign Minister resisted repatriating the bulk of its refugee subjects to continental France. Instead, once the refugee camps at Alexandria filled, the administration created two new sites of temporary internment in French Corsica—one in Ajaccio, the other in Bastia.

What is so interesting about this determination is that it relied on faulty data—or rather, recycled as fact a mythic vocabulary that appears to have been crafted by Ottoman Jews themselves. For years, Ottoman Jewish supplicants appealing to the French for protégé status had claimed ancestry in Bayonne. This fictive designation invoked a connection, on the one hand, to a notable commercial center of the early modern western Sephardi diaspora and, on the other, to the very particular legal relationship that linked the French state and the prosperous community of "New Christians" (also called members of the "Portuguese nation") that had settled in southern France after fleeing the Iberian Peninsula in the late fifteenth and early sixteenth centuries.[74] That the Bayonnese ancestry of these Jews was, in the vast majority of instances, neither documentable nor credible seems not to have prevented Jews from employing this rhetorical subterfuge; but neither did it prevent the French authorities from accepting the applicants at their word. For example, when the Izmir-born David Levy and Isaac Chicourel (business partners and Ottoman-born Jewish protégés of France living in Rio de Janeiro) sought to travel to Paris in the course of the war, they applied for and were granted travel papers that identified each as "a beneficiary of French protection as a Jew originally from Bayonne."[75] Fearful of the existence of thousands of Jews like Chicourel, French Foreign Minister saw mass repatriation as a credible threat. Thereby, a fantastical Jewish origin story subtly influenced French policy towards its refugees.[76]

Like the French, the British were vexed by the thought of the unspecified number of Jewish holders of British papers who might seek repatriation to the metropole should the Ottoman expulsion orders spread. This in turn raised two practical questions. Did would-be refugees have a legal right to seek repatriation? And did Britain have the resources to aid them?[77] In answering these questions, British suspicions (like those of the French) circled back to Izmir, where as early as 1902 British officials suspected there to be "in large numbers of cases a practice of irregular registration" of protégés past the third generation, which exceeded the bounds of British law.[78] There was no evidence that the protégés in Izmir would be expelled, nor, upon that eventuality, that they would seek repatriation to Britain. But the fear of such potentialities proved trigger enough. In early 1915, the Foreign Office cast about for resolution to these hypotheticals, approaching Leopold Jacob Greenberg, editor of the influential journal *The Jewish Chronicle*. Greenberg's reply was remarkably disengaged. "There is so much in the way of relief to be accomplished just now for Jews affected by the War that funds should not be diverted for British subjects who are Jews in Constantinople," the editor replied, lamenting that there was "no body at present constituted that can deal with them."[79] For this war-weary public intellectual, it would seem, the state's obligation to its Jewish protégés abroad was less a question of law than of resources. Subsequent Foreign Office correspondence with the Board of Deputies of British Jews resulted in more ambitious assurances: that the board would represent the Central Charities Committee in obtaining and distributing aid should a refugee crisis along these lines emerge.[80]

In the vast majority of instances, holders of foreign papers expelled from Ottoman Palestine and the provinces of Syria in the course of the war were not repatriated to Great Britain or France, even if some were returned to British or French colonies. Extraordinarily enough, one of the very few exceptions to this rule was a young Jewish woman (and French protégé) in the Alexandrian refugee camp who was accused of "causing a scandal by her conduct." With great speed, French administrators arranged to transport the woman and her family to Marseilles.[81] Perceived female misbehavior was the rare factor that abutted the general trend—perhaps because it threatened to provoke disturbances among the refugee population in Alexandria. Logistical reasons (including associated costs) stood in the way of the mass repatriation of Syrian and Lebanese refugees to France and Britain.

As the French and British struggled to determine who among the refugee population deserved—or might in the future deserve—to be sent "home," the Ottomans were "repatriating" a different extraterritorial population: an unidentified number of Muslim protégés of French Algeria and Tunisia whom Cemal Paşa's forces found to be living in Syria and Palestine. As already mentioned, some of these North African Muslims were expelled to Egypt, where they awaited repatriation to Morocco, Tunisia, and Algeria. But others were placed under the protection of the caliphate, sent to the Ottoman interior, and enlisted into the Ottoman army as so-called *muhacır* [Muslim refugees who migrated to the Ottoman lands].[82] These actions infuriated the Allied authorities, who insisted that according to international law any individual had the right to preserve their subject-hood. Representing France to the Sublime Porte, American Ambassador Morgenthau argued that "this action of the provisional authorities is not only incompatible with all rules of international law, but is in perfect contradiction with the repeated statements of the Sublime Porte that it will give reciprocal treatment to the subjects of the belligerent countries."[83] There was some truth to this claim; and yet the Ottomans' treatment of the *muhacır* was delicate in ways that Morgenthau did not concede. The Sublime Porte's actions could be read, first, as a denunciation of Britain's and France's right to rule over Muslim subjects abroad and, second, as a component of the Ottoman use of jihad as tool of wartime international and domestic policy.[84] Seen in this light, the Ottoman provocation had far-reaching implications. Such was the impression of Britain's Governor General of India, Charles Hardinge. In Hardinge's view, it might be "advisable not to denounce publicly the action of Turkey . . . as Mohammedans not at present affected will regard such action as a powerful expression of the unity of Islam."[85] What Hardinge appreciated was that the CUP's treatment of Muslim protégés in Palestine and Syria (which carried forward sultan Abdülhamid II's reliance on the vocabulary and symbols of pan-Islamicism) was at least partly motivated by the desire to gain support of Muslims abroad.[86] Were Britain publically to denounce the enlistment of the *muhacır*, might Muslims around the globe—in the subcontinent, among other places—respond with outrage? Cognizant of the symbolic potency of the *muhacır,* the British Foreign Office and French Foreign Ministry pressed the Sublime Porte to desist in its actions. The Allied demands were ostensibly heeded in January 1916. Nevertheless, enlistments continued—according to Ottoman authorities, not due to outright defiance by the central authorities but because "the rescinding order has not reached all the recruiting places."[87]

When it came to weighing the state's responsibility to its refugees deported from Ottoman Syria and Palestine, it was not only bureaucrats who had matters of strategy in mind. Refugees were also seeking to comprehend the extent of the state's duty to them, and, in some cases, to nudge circumstances to their advantage. In 1915, for example, four young refugees from Haifa and Tiberias who were lodged at the British camp at Canea expressed a desire to enter the British army. After the group was questioned by the British Vice Consul stationed on the island, it was determined that the young men "do not appear to want to go and fight, which is what one might naturally expect from a person desiring military service." Additionally, none of the four young men proved able to speak English.[88] Whether the petitioners genuinely wished to render themselves useful or whether they felt they had something to gain through service to the state, it seems they determined that enlistment, for them, came at too high a cost.[89]

At the French refugee camp in Ajaccio, similar negotiations were underway. As the war drew to a close, the French Foreign Ministry mused whether its refugees ought to be asked to serve their state militarily. The suggestion provoked alarm within the camp, and a group calling itself the Franco-Syrian Jewish Committee issued a number of demands to the Alliance israélite universelle in response. These petitioners acknowledged that they did not want to bring shame upon their families by a failure of patriotism. Yet they insisted that as French *protégés* native to Syria, Palestine, and Morocco, they could not be expected to serve the state in the same manner as French *citizens*.[90] The group's logic flew in the face of French wartime policy. In the course of the war, France used conscription to muddle the difference between citizen and subject, deploying roughly half a million colonial subjects in "indigenous troops" that were sent to the battlefields of Europe.[91] In Ajaccio, the refugees were either unaware of this fact or felt themselves to be exceptions to the trend. The four not only demurred on conscription but demanded their own immediate repatriation to Morocco or Tunisia. Before the contretemps could be resolved, the Ottoman Empire signed an armistice signaling the near end of war.

PROTECTED IN WAR, REFUGEES IN PEACE

The refugee crisis we have been exploring, like all that were linked to the First World War, did not end with the conclusion of combat. Despite earlier appeals for repatriation by refugees in Ajaccio, many dwelling there resisted repatriation after the war's end. The political climate in Palestine, controlled by the

Occupied Enemy Territory Administration, remained turbulent; it was an un-stable home to which to return. The refugee camp on Corsica would remain intact until August of 1920, when the last remaining refugees boarded the ship that would carry them to Palestine.[92] Among the last requests for repatriation to be fielded by the Alliance israélite universelle and the French government concerned the bodies of those who had died on Crete but who had wished to be buried in Palestine.[93] Aïcha Coublu, mother of eight young children, saw her husband and brother-in-law die in the course of their internment. Having obtained authorization from the French and British authorities to ferry their bodies to Palestine in the summer of 1920, she beseeched the AIU to contrib-ute the requisite sum, as she was destitute.[94] The war was over, but the trauma of expulsion lived on.

By early 1918 many of the 11,000 who had been brought to Egypt on their flight from Palestine and Syria had been repatriated, reunited with family, or managed to find employment and housing in Alexandria. Approximately 1,500 remained in refugee camps by the war's end; these were said to be "old people, widows and their families, and the mentally and physically unfit."[95] Those in charge of supporting the camp financially hoped that they would still be able to marshal the funds to repatriate the poorest among this group when the war concluded.[96] The first families to return to Palestine left Egypt in October 1918.[97] Some refugees of Great Britain, France, and Italy would receive modest indemnities after the war, including the Askenazis, with whom this chapter began. Others, like the Portuguese subject Isaac d'Avilla, received nothing and petitioned the authorities in vain for years to come.[98]

In a time of war (as in its wake), it proved inconvenient for the erstwhile capitulatory regimes to treat their Ottoman protégés as citizens, or in the same manner as they treated consular representatives called back to the continent in the early years of the war. To do otherwise was financially costly and poten-tially dangerous: because the refugees were poor and needy, because it was difficult to police rigorously the line between real protégés and false ones, and because the Allied powers couldn't be sure which (and how many) of their protected subjects would find themselves in comparable straits in the future. While philanthropic dollars were funneled toward the refugees by the pro-tector states involved (as well as by a large number of other parties), the war provoked the authorities to dial back their sense of debt to their subjects with-out ever clearly formulating or reformulating the state's legal obligation to its extraterritorial subjects.

What is striking, nonetheless, is that so many holders of foreign papers de-termined to retain their legal status rather than accept Ottoman citizenship.

For those in Syria and Palestine, protection came with an enormous cost: loss of property, impoverishment, displacement, incarceration, the separation of families. In the face of so much loss, the protection of a European power still commanded a certain value. The capitulatory regime was dead, at least temporarily, but for many, the cachet of being a protégé lived on—whether out of credulity or cognitive dissonance one can but speculate.

CHAPTER 3

Citizens of a Fictional Nation

Before he was a stowaway, Jacques Azose was an Ottoman subject. Upon his arrival in France he was undocumented and a suspected spy, until, with the assistance of Paris' Prefecture of Police, he became "a foreigner of Jewish nationality from the Levant" [*un étranger de nationalité Israélite du Levant*] in the eyes of the law. It was the Great War. On his arrival in France, Jack was fifteen, claiming to be eighteen.[1] The legal nomenclature granted him did not exist prior to the First World War and would disappear soon after the war's end.

The fact of being Jewish was not yet a guarantor of citizenship to any national or international body: the Levant an amorphous geographic entity. And yet in the course of the First World War and its immediate aftermath, thousands of Jews who were Ottoman by birth but extraterritorial by circumstance came to be codified in new and inventive fashion in France and its colonies. Immediately after the Ottoman Empire's entry into the First World War, the Third Republic determined that most of the 7,000 "Ottoman subjects" living in France, the majority of whom were Jewish and a significant minority of whom Armenian Christian, would be deemed "*protégés spéciaux*" [special protégés]. The formulation and application of this nomenclature was the result of careful orchestration by the police prefect [head of police], local police prefectures, the Foreign Ministry, the Ministry of the Interior, and (when it came to cases including Jews) two Franco-Jewish philanthropic organizations—the Alliance israélite universelle and Association cultuelle orientale—which aided the administration in identifying and allocating papers to Mediterranean and Middle Eastern Jews. The papers issued as a result of these collaborations allowed thousands of Ottoman Jewish (as well as

Armenian Christian and some Muslim) women, men, and children émigrés to avoid surveillance, deportation, or (with tens of thousands of Germans, Austrians, and Ottomans) internment as enemy aliens; to travel within their country of residence and abroad; and to acquire the passports, residency permits, and official papers that were ever more indispensable to the modern world.[2]

The statist designation "Ottoman" was, as we shall see, a crude amalgamation of those who actually claimed Ottoman citizenship and those whose family history was impacted in the Ottoman Empire, but who carried the papers of successor states or protectorates such as Bulgaria, Greece, Italy, or Egypt. But when it came to official paperwork, the legal field was more complex even than this complex history allowed. Ottoman Jews who lived in France at the outbreak of the First World War reached the country in possession of myriad papers and legal identities. Some could claim French protection, or the protection of another Western European power. Others emigrated with little more than an Ottoman birth certificate. In the course of his migrations, Fritz Ephraim Reisner, editor of the Istanbul-based French-language newspaper *Le Journal d'Orient*, carried communal, rather than state, documentation: two birth certificates issued by the chief rabbi in 1911 and 1939 (and stamped by the German and French consulates in Istanbul, respectively) attesting that Reisner was an Istanbul-born subject of the Ottoman Empire.[3]

As the boundaries of the Ottoman Empire retracted, most Jews filed for citizenship in the country that now claimed territorial possession of their place of birth (e.g., Greece, Bulgaria, Italy, and Egypt), as was their right by the terms of the Treaty of Berlin (1878) and the various national constitutions formed by Ottoman successor states; if these Jews emigrated, they did so not as Ottomans but as citizens of other nations.[4] Other émigré Jews ignored associated deadlines, either intentionally or accidentally, thereby becoming stateless. Many of the "Ottoman" Jews who lived in France at the war's start possessed only the *laissez-passer, permis de séjour,* or *carnet de séjour*: temporary documents of the French state that attested to the holder's ability to reside in, enter, or travel in France, but which were not proof of citizenship. In peacetime, one could comfortably occupy legal gray zones such as this for years, or even generations.[5] In times of war, matters were otherwise. With the outbreak of the First World War, amidst a climate of heightened anxiety about loyalty, thousands of foreigners living in France were targeted for arrest and deportation, and surveillance became more sophisticated and the checking of papers more common.[6] Desperate to shoehorn legal categories born of the empire-state into the logic of a nation-state at war, the Third Republic and the many nonnaturalized

Mediterranean Jews living within its borders sought new legal fixity, reversing a trend that was generations old. This fixity found impermanent form in the label "a foreigner of Jewish nationality from the Levant."

When the Quai d'Orsay granted Ottoman Jews the status of special protégés in 1914, it did so to solve a pressing problem. France had a long history of protecting Ottoman-born Jewish merchants who provided financial benefit to the French state. By the outbreak of the First World War, Jewish merchants of this description were not only numerous, but had a powerful lobby behind them. With the Third Republic at war with the Ottoman Empire, the administration was obliged either to subject Ottoman Jews to arrest, internment, and expulsion (thereby ending an enduring relationship and putting the regime at risk of public critique) or to engage in deft legal maneuvering. For self-serving reasons, the administration chose the latter course. In this instance, as in so many others that took place across France's colonies and protectorates, the Third Republic distorted itself in the interest of creating legal categories that suited its own interests.[7]

To be specific, the Foreign Ministry and Ministry of the Interior cannily borrowed a category born of the early modern empire state (the protégé), legally codified an amorphous geocultural entity (the Levant), and strategically repackaged an element of Ottoman foreign policy (the capitulatory regime) to craft wartime policy at home. What makes this story all the more interesting is that these legal sleights of hand unfolded at the very instant that the Ottoman authorities suspended the capitulations (the subject of chapter 3) and indeed confronted the dramatic dismemberment of their empire amidst a climate of ascendant nationalism. A centuries-old Ottoman policy towards Levantine subjects—and with it an early modern extranational legal sensibility—was thus reincarnated in wartime France even as these phenomena were being denuded of meaning in Southeastern Europe and the Middle East, soon to be replaced by various forms of colonial rule.

Here I also engage in a comparison of French and British wartime policies towards Ottoman Jewish foreign nationals, reflecting on the contrasting ways in which "the Ottoman born" were defined, subdefined, and imagined differentially by these Allied states. As we shall see, the British, like the French, saw fit to create a wartime legal loophole that exempted most of this population from persecution as enemy aliens. However, the British Foreign Office understood "Ottoman subjects of Jewish nationality" to be an internally diverse class composed of subcommunities that deserved differential treatment by the state. The finely calibrated policy that emerged as a result of this perception reflected the unusual nature of the Ottoman Jewish émigré population in Britain (at least compared to that of France)—but also reflected ways in which British and French policy, though dialogically shaped, differed in important respects.

Returning to France, we trace a chain of implications that stemmed from France's protection of Ottoman Jews that stretched through the war and the interwar period, up to the cusp of the world war that followed. I propose that the Third Republic assigned new value to its determination to protect certain "Ottoman" subjects as the First World War progressed. Now, the Foreign Ministry marshaled its historic protection of Southeastern European, Mediterranean, and Middle Eastern Jews in the attempt to urge American Jewry to pressure the United States to enter the war on the side of the Allies, emphasizing that the granting of papers to Levantine Jews had been based on humanitarian motives. Simultaneously, the Quai d'Orsay came to see these policies as a tool of realpolitik. By 1916 and 1917, this office flaunted France's protection of Ottoman Jews as evidence of the Third Republic's claims on Syria and Lebanon—in this case, as in Tunisia, Morocco, and the Sahara, French claims of protection proved a precondition of formal control of one form or another. As the symbolic value of special protection shifted, what remained constant was the surprising fact that in an environment of heightened nationalism, and in tandem with France's zealous denaturalization of hundreds of foreign-born and/or recently naturalized Frenchmen and Frenchwomen, Jewish nationals from the Levant continued to be codified as citizens of their own fictional nation. This legal reality outlived the war, only to be definitively shattered (as we shall see in the conclusion) by the Vichy regime.

PROTÉGÉS AND PAPERS, A PREWAR HISTORY

Many of the Ottoman Jewish immigrants who came to France before the First World War lacked proof of protégé status (unless, of course, they arrived as French citizens), a birth certificate, or a passport. If they held any state-approved paperwork, it was likely to be the more temporary *carnet de séjour, permis de séjour,* or *laissez-passer* extended by French consuls in the applicant's place of origin. None of these permits was meant to grant or provide proof of French citizenship. But the authorities tended to reextend them blithely, and many Jews had come not only to see them as a right, but to invest the papers with an almost metaphysical meaning. When, in 1916, thirty-one-year-old Youda Leon Nissim requested permission from the Foreign Ministry to travel with his wife and French-born children to Vichy for medical care, he informed the ministry that he had arrived in France in 1903 as a medical student, on a *permis de séjour*; thirteen years later, he felt himself to be "Ottoman in name alone."[8]

These complex dynamics reverberated in wartime France. When the Allies declared war on the Ottoman Empire in the late winter of 1914, between six and seven thousand Ottoman Jews were thought to live in Paris, with additional smaller communities in Marseilles and Lyon.[9] This community represented somewhere between 50 and 58 percent of all Ottoman subjects living in France, and it included some 2,500 men who had enlisted in the French military.[10] (Armenians constituted the next largest population of Ottoman subjects in the country, numbering roughly 4,000 in the years preceding the outbreak of war.)[11] The Ottoman Jewish community in France was recent; a decade earlier, the number of Ottoman Jews living in Paris numbered less than one hundred.[12] But as we have seen, the Balkan Wars catalyzed a tremendous wave of Jewish emigration from Southeastern Europe, prompted both by the violence of war and by Jewish fears that regional irredentism would spark a rise in anti-Semitism.

With the onset of war, France could no longer serve as a casual, temporary dwelling place for Ottoman Jewish businessmen and their families, travelers, students, or teachers-in-training. Now, holders of foreign papers—and subjects of countries at war with France, especially—found themselves prone to heightened state surveillance and control. The number of French naturalizations plummeted in the course of the war (from 2,117 in 1914 to 282 in 1918), while tens of thousands of Germans, Austrians, and Ottomans were interned in camps for enemy aliens and hundreds of French citizens who were German, Austrian, or Ottoman by birth were stripped of their citizenship.[13] The first step, taken on 2 August 1914 (even before the Ottoman Empire entered the war) was to expel many so-called enemy aliens and to require all so-called friendly aliens living within France to register with the authorities.[14]

This ruling posed a problem for undocumented immigrants like Jacques Azose. Azose had sneaked into France by stowing away on a Turkish ship bound for Marseilles. Upon arrival, the young man evaded passport control by sliding down his boat's rigging. Penniless, he boarded a train to Paris, eluding the ticket agent at his arrival station by helping an unassuming porter unload an armful of suitcases. Luckily, Azose had met a schoolmate while still en route to France, "a young man from Istanbul, Turkey, who was going to France, just like me, with the exception that he had all his papers in order and plenty of money with a rich uncle in Paris who he was going to meet." The friend took Azose to his uncle's house, and the uncle helped Azose find a night's lodging above a nearby restaurant.[15] Thus far, Azose's illegal journey to France had been marked by good fortune. Now his troubles began. Recalls Azose:

> No one in Paris could rent a room in a hotel or rooming house without first obtaining a visa or a permit from the prefecture de police. The penalty was very severe if anyone would be caught on that offense so everyone was afraid to give me a place to sleep, knowing that I was a stowaway and that I did not have a permit.[16]

Fortunately, Azose's friend had an idea. He urged his undocumented companion to lie to the Parisian police, telling them that he had entered France legally but had his pocket picked in Marseilles, whereupon he lost money and passport. The plan worked. The police granted Azose his temporary permit, making him promise he would not stray from his stated address—that of a nearby hotel. Permit in hand, Azose returned to the restaurateur who had lodged him the night before. The owner offered Azose work and allowed him to sleep above his restaurant.

Three months after the Foreign Ministry reshaped its laws relative to enemy aliens, the Allied powers declared war on the Ottoman Empire. Now, the Quai d'Orsay was obliged to fine-tune its policies yet again, this time relative to the treatment of Ottoman subjects (and those whose family histories were impacted in the Ottoman Empire, but who themselves had held the papers of successor states) who lived in or who wished to gain entry to France. While the ministry was stringent in its treatment of German, Austro-Hungarian, Bulgarian, and some Ottoman citizens, it saw fit to grant an exemption to "honorable" Christians of Ottoman background who "professed Francophilic sentiment."[17] Those who qualified were entitled to live in and travel through France. However, these individuals were not to be considered citizens, nor could they receive French protection when in another country or in the event that they returned to Ottoman soil.[18]

Immediately, the Alliance israélite universelle lobbied the administration to extend protection to Ottoman Jews of good character. The organization had reason to believe its voice would be heard. Created in 1860 by members of the Franco-Jewish elite, the AIU aimed to provide education and social "uplift" to Jews across the Levant, and had, by the First World War, established hundreds of schools in the Ottoman Empire and North Africa, educating generations of Middle Eastern Jewish girls and boys in the French language, according to French bourgeois norms. The AIU's prominence and relationship to the leadership of the Third Republic predated the war—the organization gained prestige after successfully lobbying for Romanian Jews' acquisition of equal rights by the Treaty of Berlin (1878). In subsequent decades, the AIU had deepened its ties with the leadership of the Third Republic by successfully repackaging the regime's civilizing mission for Southeastern European, Middle Eastern, and Mediterranean Jewry, and because its own graduates, founders, and leaders were well represented in the upper echelons of French society and government.[19] In November 1914, the organization was, in short, well positioned to exert influence upon the Foreign Ministry. Its position on extraterritorial Ottoman Jews was embraced by the Quai d'Orsay only nine days after the Foreign Minister announced its policies towards Ottoman-born Christians, paving the way for a cooperative wartime relationship between that office and the AIU.[20]

When the Foreign Ministry allowed Jews to be recognized as "honorable Ottomans," it took but one step toward the fine-tuning of a policy that proved far less practicable than it might have first appeared. Many questions remained: How were "Ottomans" to be identified? How was honorability to be gauged? What papers would these extraterritorial subjects hold?

THE SHAPING OF A WARTIME FICTION

Immediately after the Foreign Ministry adopted its wartime policy towards Ottoman subjects living in France, it initiated an ambitious, thirty-two month-long effort to count and evaluate all the relevant parties who were living in France. Working closely with the Ministry of the Interior, Prefecture of Police, local police prefectures, and various organizations representing the communities in question, the Foreign Ministry assembled 7,000 dossiers.[21] Based upon this information, the Third Republic tried to draw distinctions between "Ottoman" subjects residing in France. On the one hand, the administration grouped those who were "Turkish," considering them "enemy aliens" who ought to be subject to expulsion or internment. On the other hand, it classed together groups who had fallen under "the Turkish yoke." These groups were to be considered *protégés spéciaux* [special protégés]. If a given individual from within this class was considered honorable, he or she was deemed to merit a so-called "Ottoman" identity card that stated their "nationality"—in the case of most Ottoman-born Jews, *"un étranger de nationalité Israélite du Levant"* (figure 3.1).

Building on Orientalist tropes from the nineteenth century, the Foreign Ministry's list of privileged Ottoman subjects combined and admixed racial, religious, subreligious, linguistic, and regional categories. This list included "Arabs from the Arabian Peninsula, Armenians, Levantine Greek Orthodox,

FIGURE 3.1 Travel papers issued by the Prefecture of Police, Paris to Jack Azouz [Azose], 1920. With the outbreak of the First World War, as thousands of foreign nationals living in France were targeted for arrest and deportation, surveillance became more sophisticated and the checking of papers more common. The French Foreign Ministry and Ministry of the Interior insulated thousands of Ottoman Jewish émigrés from this assault by labeling them "foreigners of Jewish nationality from the Levant." This curious designation, which had no legal precedent, was a tool of realpolitik, signaling the Third Republic's selective view of history and geopolitical ambitions for the future. Courtesy Isaac Azose and the Sephardic Studies Digital Collection, University of Washington, Seattle, ST00705.

Levantine Jews, Levantine Latins, Italian protégés from Rhodes, and Syrians." This last category ("Syrians") was further divided to include Chaldean Christians, Druze, Greek Melkites and Greek Catholics, Lebanese Christians, including Maronites, and Muslim Arabs.[22] The central unifying feature of this list is its crude characterization of the Ottoman *millet* system as a tool of repression wielded against Jews, Christians, and other religious minorities. The Jews of the Levant were seen as worthy of being saved, according to this vision, precisely because they were thought to be subjects of a despotic Turkish empire. The Third Republic's wartime policy towards "Ottoman" subjects living within French territories was in this sense born of an essentially sectarian view of Ottoman society combined with a republican commitment to *laïcité*.[23] According to this vision, persecuted religious minorities from the Ottoman Empire could find protection from the claims of Islam at the hands of a benevolent French state. At the same time, the Third Republic could overshadow (if not entirely explain away) its agile legal maneuverings by presenting itself as savior to the oppressed.

From the perspective of Jewish history, the Foreign Ministry's expressed preference for "Italian protégés from Rhodes" [*Rhodiciens protégés italiens*]—a group that was almost entirely Jewish in constitution—reflects the regime's strategic deployment of Mediterranean history. At the outbreak of the First World War, the vast majority of Rhodes' 4,500 Jews had been born when the island was Ottoman—which it had been since 1522. Many members of this community (along with many Rhodesli Jewish émigrés) received Italian protection after 1912, when Italy wrested the Dodecanese Islands from Ottoman control. By the start of the First World War, these Jews had been "protégé Italians" for but a few short years. Indeed, those who lived in émigré settings (including South Africa, Rhodesia, the Belgian Congo, Tunisia, and Egypt) received Italian protection through local consuls and representatives despite having never foot on the island in its Italian incarnation.[24] French authorities might well have chosen to fix the general label "Levantine" upon this community. By labeling them "Italian protégés from Rhodes," the regime honored recent history and politics over a more complex past, naturalizing Italy's sovereignty over this population.[25]

Even the Foreign Minister had to concede that given the ethno-religious diversity of Ottoman subjects, errors of categorization were inevitable. The ministry initially advised that police functionaries in charge of overseeing a given district might invite would-be Ottomans who lacked official documentation to volunteer their religion or race. This procedure was soon superseded by a rather more bureaucratic system by which sanctioned organizations were relied upon to testify to the honorability of a given individual; when it came to Jews, the Foreign Ministry relied on the Alliance israélite universelle and a smaller Franco-Sephardic philanthropy, the Association cultuelle orientale, to identify, vouch for, and deliver papers to worthy Jews living in France.[26] No matter the number of its institutional allies, the process of identifying and assigning appropriate paperwork to all Ottoman Jews living in France proved to be thorny for the Third Republic. Though it was evidently the intention of the Foreign Ministry and Ministry of the Interior to treat the majority of Ottoman subjects (and those of Ottoman descent) leniently, local police who were responsible for gathering data on these individuals viewed them with rather more suspicion. Indeed, though publically the Foreign Ministry spoke in the most glowing terms about its "precious" collaboration with the Ministry of the Interior, police prefect, and local prefectures in managing those perceived to be "Ottoman subjects" dwelling in France, there were many instances in which the offices of the Foreign Ministry and Ministry of the Interior were obliged to mop up after police error.

Lines of communication seemed particularly faulty between the Foreign Minister's office and French representatives outside of continental France, with Tunisia providing a particularly muddled context. France had granted protection to a great number of Jews (as well as Muslims and Christians) in Tunisia in the nineteenth century in hopes of strengthening French influence over the Regency. When the French Protectorate was formed, protection was retracted from Tunisian Jews and Muslims.[27] Subsequently, after France entered into a belligerent relationship with the Ottoman Empire, it was unclear whether these erstwhile French protégés should be treated as native subjects of Tunisia, Ottoman Jews, or former French protégés. The Foreign Ministry erred on the side of leniency, extending the reach of its policy towards Ottoman subjects to France's colonies and possessions, and offering specific assurance to Alliance israélite universelle representatives in Tunisia that Jews dwelling there "would be treated in the same fashion as Christians." Nevertheless, mere weeks after France announced its protection of honorable Ottomans, large numbers of Ottoman Jews living in Tunisia received notification of their imminent expulsion, despite their having obtained the appropriate *permis de séjour* required of foreigners at the outset of the war. (Whether this action was due to confusion about the novel policy, anti-Jewish sentiment, or obstinacy is not clear.) The AIU protested this action, arguing that most of the Jews living in Tunisia who held Ottoman papers were graduates of AIU schools, including some 2,500 who had served the French army. These Jews, the AIU maintained, deserved the government's protection.[28] The Foreign Ministry's commitments towards Jews in Tunisia were honored, but it was not the last time that this office's instructions would be misinterpreted or badly executed by French officials.[29]

French bureaucratic formality (as well as a concern for public opinion) kept the Foreign Minister's office from sparring publicly with the Prefect of Police or local police prefectures—but tensions between the units ripple through their correspondence.[30] Consider, for example, this exchange prompted by the Foreign Minister's dismissal of a writ of expulsion issued against ostensible Ottoman Jews living in the department of Alpes-Maritimes. In explaining its decision, the Foreign Ministry noted that the individuals in question, Isaac Matalon and "the wife of Albert Adoutte and their children" had lived in Alpes-Maritimes since 1903 and 1915 respectively, that none carried on trade in violation with wartime sanctions, and that each was able to support him- or herself economically. Rather more impressionistically, the ministry noted that in targeting Matalon, Adoutte, and other Jewish Ottoman subjects living in Alpes-Maritimes, officials in the district had fallen prey to "regrettable generalities that do not accord with the feelings of loyalism and devotion that have animated the great majority of *protégés spéciaux.*"[31]

Such recriminations belied the essential imprecision of French policy. Vagaries produced by labyrinthine paths of Jewish migration, by the shifting of political borders across Southeastern Europe and the Middle East, and by uncertainty—on the part of French officials and Jews themselves—about the legal and social categories imposed by the Quai d'Orsay ensured that confusion surrounding the Third Republic's course of action towards the Ottoman-born and Ottoman-descended would persist throughout wartime and indeed linger beyond its end. These intricate factors obfuscated policies in France that seemed more practicable in the abstract than they proved to be in reality. How else to explain the conundrum facing Lina Covo, Tamar Ovadia, Allegra Taboh, and Renée Benveniste in the summer of 1916. Each of these Jewish women was born in Ottoman Salonica, graduated from the local AIU school, attended the AIU's elite teaching college in Paris, and sought to visit their childhood home. The women's papers declared them Ottoman nationals, but the place of their birth was Ottoman no longer. France considered them Jewish nationals from the "Levantine nation", but with Salonica now a Greek city, they could no longer claim this title. As per the Treaty of Bucharest (1913), international law allowed the four to claim Greek citizenship, but none had filed the requisite paperwork. The AIU appealed to the Foreign Minister to give the Police Prefecture the instructions necessary to grant the four women appropriate passports; but what, under these circumstances, was appropriate? For French as well as British bureaucrats, the question was as philosophical as it was legal.[32] No wonder that local police representatives erred as they struggled to manage these and comparable cases.

Some Jewish applicants for paperwork objected to the rigidity and anachronism implicit in the classification "of Jewish nationality from the Levant."

Nahum Vidal, a native of Salonica, sought in December 1917 to register with the French authorities in Marseilles as a "Salonican" by nationality. This appeal may have reflected the applicant's support of the short-lived movement (shaped in the denouement of the First Balkan War, before Greek claims to Salonica were consolidated) to "internationalize" Salonica, in which Jews once existed as the plurality of the urban population.[33] It may have been born of Vidal's understanding that his first official registration likely came at the hands of the official Jewish Community of Salonica, which (as mentioned earlier) had the authority to grant Salonican-born Jews registration papers that carried a measure of legal weight domestically as well as internationally.[34] Or, finally, it may have reflected that the appellation "Levantine" had little resonance to a Jewish supplicant more tightly moored to his hometown than an impressionistic zone of the French and British imagination. No matter; the police accepted Vidal's application, but unceremoniously overruled his semantic quibble. The inspector on staff simply crossed out the word "Salonica" on Vidal's application, inscribing Vidal's completed identity card with the phrase "Levantine Jew."[35] For Vidal, this was but a temporary legal designation, to be supplanted first by Greek and subsequently French citizenship.

Perhaps the most poignant dossiers gathered by the Foreign Ministry concern French-born women married to Ottoman-born men. Since 1803, the French Civil Code mandated that any French woman who married a foreigner automatically forsook her nationality for her husband's. During the First World War, the Civil Code, combined with novel laws concerning the foreign-born, resulted in the denaturalization of thousands of French-born women. Patrick Weil has noted that "between 1914 and 1924, France 'lost' almost twice as many Frenchwomen (130,000) than it gained (53,000)."[36] Jewish women were among these ranks. Mathilde Levy [née Arditi], an erstwhile French citizen living in Izmir with her Ottoman-born husband, sought permission to travel to or through France not once but three times in the course of the war. Official correspondence pertaining to Lévy's first request, in July 1916, affirmed her as a French national by birth. Nonetheless, as per the terms of the Civil Code and wartime regulations, Lévy was labeled an *Israélite ottomane, d'origine française* [an Ottoman Jew of French origin] and granted the *laissez-passer* required of a foreign visitor. Lévy's subsequent requests were also positively received: in 1917 and again a year later, she sought permission to travel with her children to Saint-Honoré-les-Bains and Narbonne. In each case, the Foreign Ministry granted Lévy and her children travel visas, mandating that they register with the appropriate authorities in their new locations.[37]

Suzanne Nassi [née Gargallo] was in a similar position. In 1918, the twenty-year-old filed for a certificate of safe conduct with her husband, Albert Nassi, who wished to leave their home in Versailles to conduct a business transaction in Baule. Albert, a dealer in "Asian rugs," was born in Istanbul; together with his wife, who was born in Nogent-sur-Marne, he had lived in Versailles for a decade. The Nassis' application to the Foreign Ministry declared them Ottoman (in Albert's case) and "Ottoman by marrige" (in Suzanne's case). The authorities found both applicants' paperwork to be in order—both possessed the requisite foreign identity card as per wartime policy—and granted them certificates of safe conduct.[38] Suzanne Nassi's story, like that of Mathilde Lévy, has less to do with Jewish history per se than with the history of women and nationality in wartime Europe; as Laura Tabili has argued (regarding the British context), "the wartime context raised the stakes in . . . gendered ways." At times of war, a British or French woman's marriage to a foreigner—and, all the more, a subject of a warring nation—could transform her into threatening body. "Such a woman was not to be trusted," explains Tabili; in wartime, a woman's marriage to a foreigner rendered permanently suspect "her loyalty to the state as well as her respectability, bound up as the latter was with sexual probity."[39] For Nassi and Lévy, as for so many other women, gendered law and wartime circumstances conspired to exclude them from the notion of *jus soli* [the principle that one's place of birth determines one's nationality] that had ostensibly guided French nationality policies since the turn of the nineteenth century. These subjects (like most Algerian men and women) were French nationals without being citizens.[40]

If French policy and legal praxis sutured the label "Ottoman" upon certain native-born women—even if the Foreign Ministry reserved the right to subsequently expunge this label through the granting of 'special protégé' status—it actively erased the Ottomanness of select Ottoman men. Labeling Syrians, Armenians, and Italian protégés from Rhodes as "special protégés" had precisely this effect, as did the classification "a foreigner of Jewish nationality from the Levant." In all instances, French bureaucratic parlance eschewed the term "Ottoman" as a legal designation, even as it acknowledged its protected subjects as Ottoman-born. This impulse was made explicit, on occasion, as French officials approved a given set of papers. The Police Prefect labeled one Ottoman-born Jew *"en qualité Ottoman, Israélite non-suspect."*[41] Isaac Delbourge, an Egyptian Jew who inherited French protected status from his father, was granted a *permis de séjour* that "lacked indication of nationality," perhaps in deference to the fact that the place of his birth was Ottoman no longer.[42] Individuals in pursuit of permits cottoned on to the advantages of discursive slights of hand. In Youda Leon Nissim's appeal for paperwork, he called himself "Ottoman in name alone"; Moise Nichli described himself as being "born in Turkey of Jewish parents"; Elia Levy wrote that she "loved France more than her own country"; and Raphael Lévy carefully edited his handwritten appeal to the Foreign Ministry, such that it read: "I am an Ottoman subject ~~originally from Spain,~~ it is true, but a Jew originally from Spain."[43] These individuals appreciated that for select Ottoman Jewish men, an Ottoman (and even Spanish) past could be rhetorically manipulated to suit the exigencies of war.[44] French nationality could be taken from Frenchwomen married to Ottoman men, replaced with an illusory "Ottoman" status that the Ottoman authorities would surely not recognize. However, when it came to "honorable" Jewish and Christian men who sought to live in, travel to, or relocate within France, Ottoman subject-hood could be strategically ignored.

Class also mattered. Azose traveled to France because he "had a yearning for travel" and a brother who lived in France, and because he spoke French. He traveled as a stowaway because he lacked the funds to accord with the policies of the French Consulate in Istanbul. In Azose's words, "If I were to start taking steps towards securing the proper identification papers for my passport it would probably take me three months to get them at a cost of about 40 liras or twenty American dollars, something I did not have."[45] Azose's poverty conditioned his subsequent vulnerability as an undocumented immigrant to Paris. After he lied to the police about the theft of his would-be papers, the police (apparently suspicious of his claims) contacted the French consul in Istanbul. That office announced it had no record of an émigré by the name Azose, and feared he might be a spy. The Parisian police intensified their search but the young man eluded arrest, because—in violation of the law—he was not staying at the hotel listed on his permit.

RIPPLES ACROSS THE CHANNEL

While the police scour the streets of Paris for Azose, we may pause in our scrutiny of the French context to ask how the wartime treatment of Ottoman Jewish foreign nationals was unfolding across the British Channel and in the Crown colonies. This exercise is useful insofar as it further highlights the spectrum of wartime legal categories through which Ottoman-born Jews could travel and hints at that which was unique to the French case. As we shall see, British wartime policies towards the Ottoman born were modeled on those shaped in France. Their subtle differences highlight the asymmetrical makeup of the Ottoman Jewish émigré population in the two countries and the authorities' interpretation of the relative wartime threat these communities posed to the state. For these differences, legal standards towards Ottoman-born Jews developed in both cases at the intersection of imperial politics and private lives.

On the eve of the First World War, Great Britain's Ottoman Jewish community of nearly 4,000 was smaller than that of France with 8,000, but nonetheless was the second-largest Ottoman Jewish émigré community in Europe.[46] While the Ottoman-born Jewish community in France at this time consisted mostly of Ladino-speaking Jews from Ottoman Anatolia and the Balkans, in Britain the Ottoman Jewish émigré population was more diverse. In London and Manchester, cities home to the largest numbers of émigré Ottoman Jews in Britain, the community was made up of families from all provinces and erstwhile provinces of the empire, including Ottoman Mesopotamia, Egypt, Syria and Palestine, the Balkans, and Anatolia, as well as from various Ottoman successor states and émigré settings, including Egypt, Bulgaria, France, South Asia, and East Asia. This diversity, paired with the British Foreign Office's complex view of the communities involved, prompted the shaping of a convoluted policy towards the Ottoman born.

The war stoked anti-alien sentiment in Britain, precisely as in France, creating the pretext for the intensive monitoring, control, and expulsion of foreign nationals deemed "enemy aliens"—namely, those from Germany, Austria, the Ottoman Empire, and Bulgaria, including many Jews.[47] Ottoman-born Jews could easily have been interpreted to fall within this class. But keeping a close eye on developments in France, Britain's Foreign Office, Home Office, and police departments jointly shaped their own legal loophole that would exempt from categorization as "enemy aliens" approved Ottoman Jews who lived in Britain and her territories and were not naturalized British citizens.[48] This policy was akin, but not identical, to that which was pursued in France. One striking difference between the models was semantic; while the French Foreign Ministry protected "foreigners of Jewish nationality from the Levant," the British extended papers to "Ottoman subjects of Jewish nationality." One might think that the labeling of these classes provided evidence that greater precision would be applied in the British case—"Ottoman subjects," after all, was a more precise geopolitical classification than was the impressionistic designation "from the Levant." Yet, protecting Ottoman subjects en mass, as a single geopolitical unit, did not prove to be the ambition of the Home Office. Instead, British authorities made fine legal distinctions between Jews from

Ottoman Mesopotamia, Palestine or Syria, Salonica, and the Ottoman interior (including especially Istanbul and Izmir) based on their sense of these Jews' history and present-day threat. To this process we shall return momentarily.

A second crucial differentiation between the British and French strategies concerned whom the state turned to for assistance in the identification and documentation of Ottoman Jews—and just how centralized the process of surveillance that ensued was. The principal partner of the French state, as discussed, was the Alliance israélite universelle, an institution with proven credentials in the realm of international relations. Conspicuously, the Board of Deputies of British Jews, which arguably commanded a reputation similar to that of the AIU, did not emerge as the state's partner in this endeavor in Britain. Already overwhelmed by the internment of countless German Jewish foreign nationals, the Board of Deputies punted; and so it was that smaller, less established Zionist organizations in Manchester and London were charged with overseeing the collection of petitions appealing for recognition of the label "Ottoman subject of Jewish nationality" and with the task of recording supplicants' names, occupations, dates and places of birth, nationalities of parents, and lengths of residence in Britain. These organizations also worked to pair petitions with letters of reference, including one from London's Spanish and Portuguese Congregation or either of Manchester's two Sephardic synagogues.[49] (In the event that a Jewish foreign national was not a synagogue member, the Conjoint Foreign Committee of the Board of Deputies was permitted to testify to his or her honorability.) As per the 1914 British Nationality and Status of Aliens Act, the resultant paperwork was to be preserved by the individual and regularly submitted to the local police station.[50] Crucially, British authorities did not maintain painstaking vitas of all Ottoman Jewish foreign nationals, as did the French Foreign Ministry—hinting at the relative importance of centralized record keeping in the Britain and France. Even today, the surviving application forms for "Ottoman subjects of Jewish nationality" exist only in the archives of the Central Zionist Association, having migrated from London and Manchester to Jerusalem, with no copy seemingly preserved by the British state.

What prompted British officials to grant exemptions to Ottoman-born Jews? In Britain, as in France, this policy was not prompted by allosemitic sentiment on behalf of the authorities. On the contrary, the protection of Ottoman-born Jews followed the issuing of the so-called Aliens Restriction (Armenians, &c.) Order of 7 January 1915, which protected as friendly aliens those who could be "shown by satisfaction to be by race a Greek, Armenian, or Syrian, or a member of any other community well known as opposed to the Turkish regime, and to be a Christian."[51] In France, the issuance of a like policy excluding Ottoman Jews prompted an immediate critical response by the AIU. The leading Anglo-Jewish organization, the British Board of Jewish Deputies, did not rush to question the scope of the regime's policy. Preoccupied by the vulnerability of Jewish foreign nationals from Europe, the Board of Deputies' leadership was initially fearful of framing the internment and possible expulsion of the Ottoman-born as a Jewish question.[52] One of the earliest lonely voices of dissent was Rabbi Moses Gaster, chief rabbi of the Spanish and Portuguese Congregation in London, who ardently advocated the labeling of Ottoman Jews as friendly aliens.[53]

Rather than agitating to expand the 1915 order to include Ottoman-born Jews en masse, the Board of Deputies selectively chose a list of thirteen Baghdadi and Aleppan Jews on whose behalf they were willing to campaign.[54] The thirteen were chosen with class strategy in mind; each was a wealthy merchant who could refer to a well-off business partner willing to offer ample sureties on his behalf. But whom the Board of Deputies excluded from this list is at least as interesting as whom it chose to include. Conspicuously absent were any Jews from Salonica, Istanbul, or Izmir, as these cities were understood to be geographically more proximate to Ottoman authority and their residents might be assumed to harbor greater patriotism towards the empire with which Britain was at war. (Subsequent Home Office correspondence affirmed that its representatives did indeed believe this to be true.) In its earliest tangles with the Home Office over the question of Ottoman foreign nationals, the Board of Deputies was thinking tactically about how "Ottoman-born Jews" ought to be defined—and concluded, at least initially, that this should be a designation of strategy rather than law, lineage, or political geography.

After successfully obtaining state protection of the thirteen Baghdadi and Allepan Jews, representatives of the Board of Deputies returned to the Home Office with a more expansive claim. Ottoman Jews, they now argued, were "Turks by force of circumstances, and do not share in their political sympathies."[55] This formulation neatly echoed the aforementioned appeal of the Jewish merchant from Marseilles, who fictively represented France's Ottoman-born Jews as "victims of a nation that conquered them by force." Both statements overlooked the long history of Ottoman Jewish patriotism in order to craft designations that suited the exigencies of war.[56] Lucien Wolf, writer, activist, and tireless Board of Deputies representative, put it this way: Ottoman Jewish émigrés dwelling in Britain were "Turkish subjects by accident of birth."[57] To this formulation the Home Office relented, extending the 1915 Aliens Restriction (Armenians, &c.) Order in the spring of 1915 to cover "Jewish subjects of the Turkish Empire" on a case-by-case basis.[58]

This new formula ("Jewish subjects of the Turkish Empire") might have been interpreted expansively to include all Jews born within the boundaries of the Ottoman Empire. However, Home Office and Foreign Office representatives did not feel themselves able to apply a singular strategy to an emphatically manifold community. In weighing whether a given Ottoman Jewish subcommunity merited leniency in this time of war, British officials chose instead to calibrate each of these groups' historical relationship to the Ottoman Empire and contemporaneous attitude towards the war. The results were unscientific. Particular distrust was reserved for Jews from Salonica—who, internal memoranda of the Home Office and Foreign Office noted—had historically exhibited loyalty to the Ottoman Empire and distrust of Greece in the course of the Balkan Wars. Similarly suspicious were Jewish émigrés from Istanbul and Izmir, cities considered too proximate to Ottoman authority.[59]

Cognizant of these prejudices, individual Jewish petitioners (and representatives of the Zionist organizations of London and Manchester charged with filling out their appeals) designated nationality in creative fashion.[60] Jewish seekers of the designation "friendly aliens" represented themselves not simply as "Ottoman Jews" but as "Ottoman Spanish Jews," "members of the Constantinople settlement of Spanish and Portuguese Jews," "Smyrna and Constantinople Jews," "Syrian Jews (natives of Syria Palestine)," "Palestinian Jews," "British subjects (Spanish Descent)," "Ottoman, Italian Protected, Syrian by Marriage," and so on. Often, these labels deemphasized the imperial appellation "Ottoman" in favor of an Iberian lineage, European connection, or local fealty.[61] In other instances, an applicant's Arabness was emphasized, for this was imagined to draw the authorities' attention to the fact that Middle Eastern Jewish émigrés living in England could be conquered subjects of the Ottomans. This strategy was employed by twenty Jewish merchants of Baghdadi origin who signed a petition requesting "to be relieved of the stigma of being described and treated as alien enemies of a country that has become the country of their adoption." The petitioners emphasized that the signatories were loyal to the British Empire, "where many of them have lived since childhood," writing that "your Petitioners are in fact none of them of the Turkish race. They are all Jews and they are properly Arab Jews—their native tongue is Arabic. None of them speak the Turkish language."[62] This petition cleverly framed "Ottoman" as a category of force and chance rather than filiality and consensus.

Many applicants for the status of "friendly alien" found it a well nigh impossible to square personal histories with Home Office policy. This was particularly true of the population of British-dwelling, nonnaturalized Salonican-born Jewish émigrés like Vidal Coenca. Coenca, who emigrated to London prior to the war, had only one form of official paperwork in his possession. Having failed to file for Greek citizenship after 1913 as was his legal right, Coenca had only his Ottoman birth certificate to offer as proof of identity. In this, Coenca was akin to many Salonican Jewish émigrés living in Britain. Writing in the midst of the war, Lucien Wolf noted that "most of the Salonika Jews in this country knew nothing about this provision of the Treaty of Athens [which granted them the right to file for Greek citizenship] and imagined that, with the transfer of their birth place, their nationality was ipso facto changed."[63] These circumstances dictated that Coenca (and others like him) was recognized as neither Greek nor Ottoman—rendering it unclear whether he merited the title "friendly alien" (as a Greek national, at least prior to Greece's entry into the conflict) or "enemy alien" (as an Ottoman one) or should simply be considered a threat to Great Britain by dint of being an émigré Salonican Jew. As the Home Office continued to resist labeling Salonican Jews "friendly aliens" en masse, legal quagmires like this could reach resolution only through the submission of individual petitions. Following this method, Coenca was designated a friendly alien and spared internment.[64]

Others were not so lucky. An unknown number of Ottoman-born Jewish men were interned as enemy aliens even though they might have qualified as friendly ones.[65] For over three years, the Salonican-born Jacques Ascher Salem was imprisoned in Camp Douglas on the Isle of Man, gaining freedom only after he was able to marshal testimonies to his Ottoman origin and honorability from the grand rabbi of Salonica, Jacob Meir, and Moses Gaster, chief rabbi of the Spanish and Portuguese Congregation in London.[66] Other Jewish men of Ottoman origin were imprisoned for conducting trade with Britain's enemy—for example, by exporting textiles from Lancashire to Baghdad.[67] In the course of these men's internment, their mothers, sisters, wives, and daughters remained at home in Britain, struggling to keep businesses afloat and dutifully signing in at police headquarters, as the law dictated.[68] The register of aliens held by the Manchester Police Archive documents week after dizzying week of such activity, tracking the evolution of individuals' legal statuses over the course of the war and as Home and Foreign Office policy continued to mutate (figure 3.2).[69]

A final set of permutations in Britain's wartime definition of "Ottoman Jews" concerned those born in (or descended from) Ottoman Mesopotamia;

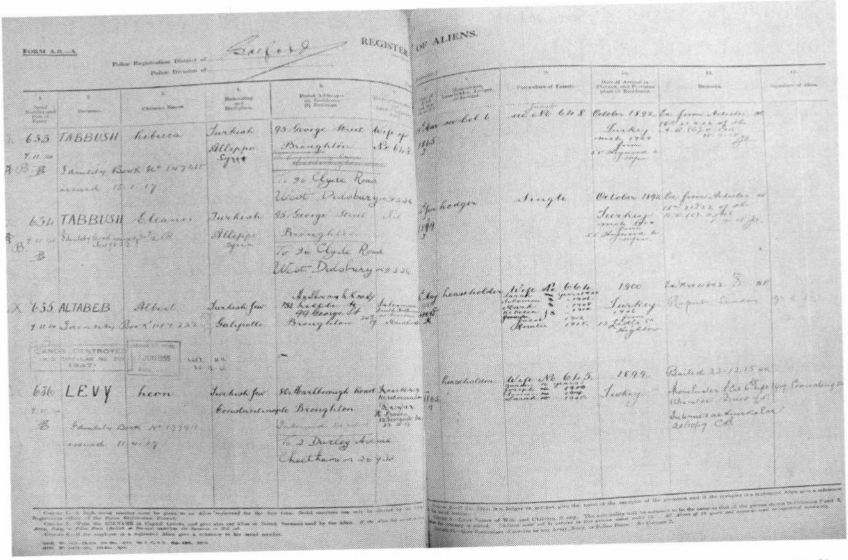

FIGURE 3.2 Page from the register of aliens maintained by the Greater Manchester Police during the First World War, 1914. In Great Britain, as in France, the Great War created a pretext for the intensive monitoring, control, and expulsion of "enemy aliens," including émigré Jews holding German, Austrian, Bulgarian, or Ottoman citizenship. British authorities made fine legal distinctions between Jews from Ottoman Mesopotamia, Palestine or Syria, Salonica, and the Ottoman interior (including, especially, Istanbul and Izmir) based on their sense of these Jews' history and the likelihood that they would pose a present-day threat. While some were interned as enemy aliens, others were labeled "Ottoman subjects of Jewish nationality" and friendly aliens. These Ottoman Jewish émigrés were required to register regularly with the police, as evidenced in this page from the Manchester register of aliens. Courtesy Greater Manchester Police Museum and Archive. "Register of Aliens," serial nos. 399–807, book 1, box X1, serial nos. 633–636, c. 7 November 1914.

it took shape as the war inched towards its conclusion. In the summer of 1917, some months after the British occupation of Baghdad, Home Office representatives at last relaxed their legal treatment of Baghdadi Jewish émigrés in Britain. At this moment, the Home Office chose to understand this émigré population not as historical Ottoman subjects but as present-day beneficiaries of British rule—and as would-be middlemen and -women of an emergent neo-imperial Britain. Anticipating a British postwar presence in the Middle East (and particularly British access to valuable natural resources in the region), Home Office officials now curried favor with the Baghdadi mercantile community already on its shores. A June 1917 order in council offer broke down earlier protective policies towards the Ottoman born, sparing Jews who were "by race a Jew" and "a native of Baghdad or any other place in Mesopotamia" from the designation "enemy alien."[70] Some Jews of Baghdadi origin were released from enemy alien camps as a result of this policy, though Jews from Salonica, Istanbul, and other cities in the interior remained under suspicion until the war's end.

Here our extended digression into British (and Baghdadi Jewish) history must be put on pause until the subsequent chapter, when we look backwards for precedent to this story and also anticipate its postwar afterlife. Before returning across the Channel to conclude our exploration of France's wartime legal regime and the particular history of Jacques Azose, the following conclusion must be emphasized. In Britain, as in France, significant numbers of Ottoman Jewish émigrés sought immunity from the label "enemy alien" and, hence, relief from threat of internment or expulsion. Here, authorities crafted a legal edifice for Ottoman Jewish foreign nationals evocative of that erected in France. In the British setting, however, Ottoman Jews were not viewed by the authorities as a single or singular community, but rather as a puzzle of subcommunities, each with its own historical relationship to the Ottoman Empire and hence to the ongoing war. Crucially, this policy ensured that a single Ottoman-born Jew could migrate through a spectrum of identities in the course of the war, shifting from émigré to foreign national to internee to friendly alien—shifts that revealed the authorities' sense of Ottoman Jewish history, wartime threat, and their own strategic ambitions.

LEGACIES OF PROTECTION

The protection of French-dwelling Ottoman Jews also took on new meanings as the war progressed, and especially as France anticipated an Allied victory. The shifts were various, and were at times in close dialogue with events in Britain. As the war advanced, the Foreign Ministry hoped that its generosity towards Ottoman Jews might be deployed to curry the favor of American Jews—and, by extension, the American public—in hopes of prompting the United States to join the Allied war effort. Presenting the Third Republic as America's philo-Semitic ally was also imagined to assuage the sting for American Jews of East European background of an alliance with Russia. The Alliance israélite universelle and Association cultuelle orientale were the conduits for these ambitions. The Association cultuelle orientale explicitly reached out to American Jewry on behalf of the administration, writing the Kehillah (Jewish community) of New York City in the spring of 1916 to tout the success of French policies towards Ottoman Jews and to encourage the Kehillah to voice its praise of the Third Republic.[71] The Alliance israélite universelle, too, orchestrated a campaign to influence Jewish opinion in neutral countries—and the United States, in particular—in favor of the Allies, boasting of the Third Republic's generosity towards the Ottoman-born.[72] When France's policy towards this population was shaped, the opinion of American Jewry was hardly of strategic interest. The course of the war changed this, and therefore the implications of the Foreign Ministry's erstwhile actions shifted too.

By 1916 and 1917, French interministerial dialogue also came to tout the humanitarian motives that underlined its wartime protection of Ottoman Jews and Christians. In a lengthy letter to the Minister of the Interior, the Minister of Foreign Affairs now proclaimed that the procedures were shaped out of a "loyalty to the traditions of our race and conscience," designed "not in the service of history, but in support of our effort to advance the liberation of the Ottoman yoke," and to promote greater freedom for "Syrians, Armenians, Levantine Jews, and others who are oppressed by the Turks."[73] The authorities considered the truth of these claims to be compounded as France opened its doors to refugees of the Armenian genocide and when viewed in comparison with the Ottoman Empire's treatment of its own "enemy aliens," on whom the regime began an assault in the late winter of 1914. Jews seeking papers from the Foreign Ministry echoed Republican language cannily, appreciating the symbolic cache of humanitarian need. One seeker of papers, an Ottoman-born Jewish peddler who had lived in Marseille for some twenty years, had the cheek to remind the Foreign Minister that the regime had extended favor to Ottoman Jews for the same reason that it extended good will to Armenians and residents of Alsace-Lorraine: because they were "victims of a nation that conquered them by force and caused them all measure of misery and trouble."[74] The irony of this formulation is manifold. Sephardic Jews were, in fact, the rare Ottoman subject populations to have migrated to the empire (rather than having been "acquired" through conquest); what's more, the late Ottoman Jewish press made continual laudatory reference to this fact, such that it became a cornerstone of Jewish anniversary celebrations of 1492, the infamous year in which Spain expelled its Jews.[75]

That many of the Ottoman Jews who appealed to France for special protection during the First World War had come, like Elia Levy, to "love France more than her own country" is believable enough. Not only had many of these individuals received a French education at the hands of the Alliance israélite universelle, but a great number had lived in France for decades by the war's outbreak. Less convincing are the claims of the Third Republic that it adopted its policies towards Ottoman Jews out of purely humanitarian motives. When so many subjects of countries at war with France were imprisoned or expelled, regardless of their sentiments towards France or personal history; when French-born women married to foreign men were denaturalized en masse; and when Algerian Muslims, though technically subjects of the republic themselves, were denied the rights accorded "full" French citizens, such Republican rhetoric was disingenuous at best.

Indeed, the realpolitik implications of the Foreign Ministry's wartime protection of Ottoman Jews came to the fore with time, lending truth to the claim that "modern humanitarianism was in symbiosis with colonialism."[76] As French designs on the eastern Mediterranean took shape in the course of war, the authorities came to see French-dwelling extraterritorial Ottoman merchants as useful allies (much as the British reimagined Mesopotamian Jews after their conquest of Baghdad). The Sykes-Picot agreement, which negotiated a postwar partition of Ottoman territory in the eastern Mediterranean by Britain, France, and (as a lesser player) Russia, and which Britain and France formally ratified in May 1916, announced the Third Republic's designs on Syria and Lebanon.[77] Keeping Ottoman Armenians, Jews, and Syrian Christians under state protection was perceived as abetting these plans (as was Britain's last-gasp protection of Mesopotamian Jews), anticipating a Triple Entente victory and the imminent dissolution of the Ottoman Empire. As the Foreign Minister argued, Jewish "Orientals with residential permits" had, prior to the war, proven important auxiliaries "in all branches of French industry and commerce" by engaging in direct commercial negotiations in the Mediterranean and by serving as indirect suppliers.[78] Their utility (according to regnant Foreign Ministry logic) promised only to grow as the war eroded trade between France and the Middle East. Whether or not there was truth to such claims, in the context of wartime geopolitical machinations, building goodwill with Mediterranean mercantile diasporas—Armenian as well as Jewish—came to be understood by Quai d'Orsay officials as one strand of a broader colonial strategy.

The last citizenship papers issued in France to a Jewish national of the Levant might well have been granted to Jacques Azose.[79] In 1920, the Paris Police Prefecture at last convinced that Azose was not a spy, granted the young man a passport that would carry him to Seattle, on which he was described as "a foreigner, of Jewish nationality from the Levant."[80] There is no evidence that the Foreign Ministry ever annulled this legal nomenclature. However, with the conclusion of the war, and ultimately the dissolution of the Ottoman Empire, the utility of the designation waned of its own accord. In the absence of specific legislation nullifying the classification, it is possible that the Parisian police approved Azose's request out of administrative negligence. Two years later, Azose could be found performing in the first Ladino-language play to be staged in Seattle: a dramatization of the Dreyfus affair, the scandal that gave life to anti-Semitic politics in France and nearly brought down the young Third Republic.[81] With anti-immigrant sentiment waxing in 1920s France, it is perhaps apt that the performance attributed Dreyfus' exoneration not to the triumph of justice but to divine intervention.

The shaping of a temporary classification for "foreigners of Jewish nationality from the Levant" (and "special protégés" more generally) provides evidence of the complex legal contortions that the leadership of the Third Republic was willing to undertake to advance its own shifting interests. More than anything, the French Foreign Ministry perceived Ottoman Jews living in France as symbols: as would-be middlemen in the eastern Mediterranean, as a lure that might attract the American Jewish public to the Allied cause, as worthy (and, significantly, trustworthy) subjects of French benevolence whose very existence exposed the despotism of Ottoman rule. The British Foreign Office and Home Office shared some of these perceptions, but applied them rather more selectively—privileging some Ottoman-born Jews over others and carefully subdividing this category to suit state priorities. It is a wonderful irony that the French Foreign Ministry, in seeking to advance these distinctly twentieth-century ambitions, developed a system of classification that awkwardly recycled Ottoman (or ostensibly Ottoman) social categories and gave new life in wartime France to relationships of protection that dated to the sixteenth century. Such complex legal calisthenics, as I have suggested, resembled those pursued in Algeria and French Protectorate Tunisia and Morocco: but their application in metropolitan France is arresting, shedding light on the inequities inherent in Third Republican notions of citizenship and on the spectrum of legal identities through which Jews in Europe could journey in the early twentieth century. Ottoman Jews living in France had come to occupy an extranational (and essentially early modern) legal niche in the course of the First World War; as we shall see in the conclusion, this mode of legal liminality proved fatal in the world war that followed.

CHAPTER 4

Protected Persons?

More than the presence of some 100 Taoist monks and priests, the performance of Chinese orchestras, the exchange of mourning gifts, the burning of paper figures in celebration of the spirit of the deceased, the kowtowing of visitors before pictures of the family, the draping of the funereal garden in white silk, the arrival of more than 3,000 gifts and 5,000 mourners—more, even, than the astonishing facts of Silas Aaron Hardoon's fortune, prominence, or cosmopolitan history—it was the wax effigy of the dead man with chopsticks in hand at this ostensibly Jewish funeral that riveted the international press.[1] When he died in the summer of 1931, Hardoon was called the richest foreigner in Shanghai, with an estate estimated at $150 million (figure 4.1). Like other young entrepreneurial Baghdadi Jewish men of his generation, Hardoon had made his way to China by way of India in the late nineteenth century.[2] In Bombay he worked for the mercantile firm of D. Sassoon and Company, a global operation owned by a Jewish family of Baghdadi origin that dealt in silk and cotton and monopolized the legal and highly lucrative transshipment of opium.[3] In Shanghai, Hardoon would live sixty years, amass a real estate empire in the city's International Settlement, meet and marry Liza Hardoon (neé Luosi Lirui and known by her Buddhist name, Luo Jialing)—a Eurasian Buddhist who may or may not have been the illegitimate daughter of a French Jewish father—adopt eleven children of diverse backgrounds, form deep ties with local Chinese politicians, merchants, and the educational elite, serve as life president of Beth-Aaron Synagogue, sit on the councils of the Shanghai Municipality, French Concession, and International Settlement, and, shortly before his death, will nearly the entirety of his fortune to his wife.[4]

FIGURE 4.1 A Jew of Baghdadi origin, Silas Aaron Hardoon (1851–1931) purportedly died the richest foreigner in Shanghai. Sixty years earlier, he had emigrated from Bombay in the employ of David Sassoon and Company—a global mercantile firm owned by a Baghdadi Jewish family—as a British protected person, a status he inherited from his father. In Shanghai, Hardoon built a fortune in real estate and enjoyed a forty-year marriage with Liza Hardoon (née Luosi Lirui and known by her Buddhist name, Luo Jialing), a Eurasian Buddhist woman to whom he willed his $150 million fortune.

But the eventful life of Silas Aaron Hardoon did not end with his death, in the wake of which there surfaced a series of claimants on the family estate: distant cousins—if they were cousins at all—carrying the Hardoon name and dwelling in Baghdad and across the Baghdadi Jewish diaspora, including Shanghai and Calcutta. The trials that followed, conducted in His Britannic Majesty's Supreme Court in Shanghai, pondered a complicated legal question: whether Hardoon's estate—and Hardoon himself, as a long-time resident of Shanghai, one-time Ottoman subject, British protected person, Baghdadi émigré, and out-married Jew—was subject to Chinese, British, Jewish, Iraqi, or private international law.

What was so absorbing about Hardoon's death and the controversy unleashed by it? Beyond the sensational quality of his life, the legal debates that followed his death became a test case for questions that reverberated through the Baghdadi, Mediterranean, and Middle Eastern Jewish diasporas in the early twentieth century, particularly in the wake of the First World War and the dismantling of the Ottoman Empire. As the empire gave way to nation-states and mandates, how was the significant population of extraterritorial Jews in colonial and semicolonial settings—émigré merchants and their families residing in entrepôts in India, Asia, the Middle East, and the Mediterranean Basin—to be legally defined by the state?[5] What place, and what political allegiances, would they seek for themselves once their extraterritorial status came into conflict with evolving national and international legal norms? In the British Empire specifically, what did it mean to acquire and lose the status of protected person: how would this process affect individual Jews or their communities?[6]

The testamentary battle over the Hardoon fortune emerged at the intersection of various environments of modern colonial encounter—Ottoman, Iraqi, and Indian, as well as British and Chinese. Thus, it invites a reading of what Priya Satia has called "intra-imperial sources and their imbrication."[7] At the moment the Hardoon trial unfolded, in the early 1930s, the Ottoman Empire no longer existed, but the British Empire was in the midst of an expansionist moment, a time of active and multivectored extension in the Middle East and in East and Southeast Asia (as elsewhere). And yet when it came to the malleable legal identity of the Baghdadi Jewish diaspora, these two empires (Ottoman and British) were live and mutually informing. Ironic as it might first appear, in the course of the legal struggle over the Hardoon estate, representatives of British interests defended the enduring integrity of certain legal categories born of the Ottoman context—in particular, the notion that after his death, Hardoon could be viewed as a British subject because, decades earlier, his father had been granted British protection while living in India as an Ottoman subject. This legal opinion, offered first by the Foreign Office and subsequently upheld by the court, went against the tide of British consular and foreign policy in East Asia, on the one hand, where, as of 1906, Baghdadi Jews were increasingly being denied or stripped of their protection; and of early interwar Iraq, on the other hand, where many Jews traumatized by the First World War and fearful of Iraq's postwar fate sought but were denied British naturalization.[8]

In undermining these general trends, the Hardoon trial proved three important things about Jews, British law, and imperialism in the decades between the late nineteenth century and interwar period. First, the spaces through which the Baghdadi Jewish diaspora moved in the nineteenth and twentieth centuries continued to inform its members' legal status as the twentieth century unfolded, even though growing numbers of this diasporic body had themselves never set foot in these spaces (in the case of the Ottoman Empire, Iraq, India, or Britain), or indeed after certain of these spaces had ceased to exist (in the case of the Ottoman Empire). Extraterritoriality was, for these individuals, a layered matter that was always in the process of accruing sediment from the various social, legal, and political contexts through which they and their families moved.

Second, the status of a wealthy individual—and the money he promised to deliver to the state in the form of an estate tax—could influence the rigidity or direction of British citizenship policy, or indeed undermine it altogether. Class was a mottling factor that differentiated the state's treatment of its protected subjects—and of those it had no interest in protecting—within and across discrete diasporic groups. From this point, a third insight naturally follows. Though by the interwar period the British Foreign Office sought to decouple the categories "British protected person" and "British subject," there remained occasions on which it was useful for both the state and the court to view these as coterminous entities. Thus, just as the British Empire continued to reinvent itself in the early decades of the twentieth century, so too did the essentially colonial category of British protected person persist into an era ostensibly marked by the global drift toward sovereignty and the associated nationalization of individuals.

THE MAKING AND UNMAKING OF A PROTÉGÉ: THE BAGHDADI JEWISH DIASPORA AND THE BRITISH STATE, IN SOUTH AND EAST ASIA

Shanghai was a dynamic and divided city in the early decades of the twentieth century. A treaty port, administratively it was divided into three sectors—the Chinese Municipality of Greater Shanghai, the International Settlement, and the French Concession—each with its own government, laws, and authorities. Although the city was majority Chinese, a diverse European expatriate community (and especially the British) held sway over its rule, with Baghdadi Jews, by and large an affluent population of real estate holders, tentatively accepted among them.[9]

At its height, the Baghdadi Jewish population of Shanghai likely numbered around eight hundred. "Baghdadi Jews" is convenient shorthand for this population because, given the alternatives, it is the most precise and historically accurate term.[10] This term tends to be applied to any Jewish descendant of Ottoman Mesopotamia, even though a portion of this émigré population had roots in other regional trading entrepôts, especially Basra and Muscat. Moreover, "Baghdadi" is a category that likely was not employed by Baghdadi Jews prior to the early twentieth century, when this diasporic population encountered poorer, Ashkenazi Jewish émigrés from the Russian Empire in places such as Shanghai.[11] Until roughly the 1860s, the Baghdadi Jewish diaspora, though multilingual, relied principally on Judeo-Arabic as a language of commerce and quotidian culture and upon Hebrew as a language of rabbinic high culture; over the course of the next decades, as the number of "Baghdadi Jews" born in South, East, and Southeast Asia and across the British Empire increased, the business records, personal correspondence, and newspapers circulated by this diasporic community appear to have gradually reverted to or were first penned in English.[12]

As in other commercial hubs of the Baghdadi and Middle Eastern Jewish diasporas, in Shanghai the Baghdadi Jewish population lived in political limbo in the late nineteenth and the earliest years of the twentieth century, having inherited what was essentially an early modern legal order. These Jews were Ottoman subjects by dint of birth. However, because the Ottoman Empire had no extraterritorial treaty with China that might ensure its subjects' protection, here (as in port cities in North Africa and the Eastern Mediterranean) émigré Jewish merchants were entitled to French protection by virtue of the capitulatory regime. Some sort of foreign protection was crucial to this largely mercantile population. In her study of the Baghdadi Jewish community of Shanghai, Maisie Meyer has suggested that British protection promised maximum social capital for this community, arguing that its members were allied with Britain aspirationally, politically, and linguistically.[13] This claim may overstate the case. Baghdadi Jews were hardly monogamous in their quest for official status, but instead shifted allegiances between foreign powers as suited, first and foremost, their interests, the prevailing political climate, the ebb and flow of markets, and the whim of individual bureaucrats who had the power to approve or deny their protection. Hardoon himself rotated between the French and British in Shanghai, representing both, at one time or another, on local political councils.[14] For this, the story of Hardoon and of the Baghdadi Jewish diaspora more generally was closely tied to that of the British Empire, through whose territories this individual and this population cycled.

While European protection was accessible to Hardoon and his peers as a result of centuries-old capitulations brokered with the Ottoman Empire, the status of "British protected person" was a rather younger institution—even if British protection, broadly conceived, had existed for some time. Created in the late nineteenth century, this category was availed by Royal Prerogative to people and places located outside the Crown's dominions that Britain had nonetheless promised to protect. It was accessible to Baghdadi Jewish émigrés such as Hardoon because, in the late nineteenth century, Britain and

France had agreed that Britain would extend protection to all Baghdadi Jews employed by D. Sassoon and Company and other British firms operating in South, Southeast, and East Asia.[15] With the passage of the British Protected Persons Order of 1934, this category would be reinvented again—this time to refer to persons who did not possess any other nationality but who belonged to British protectorates or to United Kingdom–mandated or trust territories other than Palestine and Transjordan.[16] By then, the classification had functioned elastically for several generations. Once Jewish merchants (and in some cases their families) were labeled protected persons, British consular agents in South, Southeast, and East Asia could and often did take a further step, registering them in local consuls as British subjects of the United Kingdom, colonies, and dominions. This despite the fact that technically, British protected persons were not British subjects; indeed, they would not be mentioned in British legislation concerning citizenship until the passage of the British Nationality Act of 1948, which labeled all British "subjects" of the United Kingdom or crown colonies "citizens," formally excluding protected persons from this category. Prior to the delineation of these categories, casual interpretation of the notion of protection was favored not only by British officials in Asia, nor were Jews the only beneficiaries. At least since the late nineteenth century, British authorities had voiced discomfort with the tendency of local consulates in the Ottoman dominions to "register as British subjects, persons who are not so by British law," a strategy that some feared would "some day [cause] some serious trouble" for the state.[17]

When it came to Shanghai's Baghdadi Jews, an individual's status as a British subject or protected person could often be traced back to the colonial laboratory of India. Although precise statistics evade the historical record, it appears that many, if not most, of the Baghdadi Jewish families living in Shanghai in the early twentieth century had come to China by way of India; and it was in South Asia that family patriarchs tended to receive the naturalization or protected status that would be handed down to subsequent generations (at least temporarily, for reasons we will continue to explore). This trend dated to the early 1870s, when the still-young Baghdadi Jewish population of India began to lobby aggressively—and by and large successfully—to be considered by the British state as European, white, and loyalist. As Joan Roland has shown, this ambition had much to do with the Baghdadi Jewish population's desire to be distinguished from the so-called "native" Jewish community of western India, the Bene Israel, whom immigrant Baghdadi Jews viewed as religiously impure and racially inferior; it also resonated with the ebb and flow of British imperial policy and the shifting ambitions of the Indian nationalist movement.[18] These intra-Jewish communal struggles in India, and more specifically the British naturalizations they produced, echoed elsewhere in Asia decades later, as British authorities traced a Baghdadi Jew's viability as a naturalized Briton or British protected person back to patriarchs' registration in India a generation or more earlier.

The case of the Ezra family is illustrative of this late-nineteenth- and early-twentieth-century bureaucratic pattern. Three generations of men, women, and children in this Baghdadi Jewish family received permission from the British consulate in Shanghai to add their names to the passport of the family patriarch, Edward Ezra, who was made a British subject in Poona (present-day Pune) in 1872 and was granted his first British passport in Shanghai in 1918. By the third generation, when the situation attracted the wary attention of the Foreign Office, officials were still registering Edward's grandson Cecil Ezra as British, even though they acknowledged him to be "the Shanghai-born son of the equally Shanghai-born son of an Iraqi father."[19] The case of the Ezras demonstrates the importance of India as a nursery for Baghdadi Jews' naturalizations across the British Empire. It also indicates that, at least for a time, the status of British protected person appears to have been interpreted both by British consular agents conducting such registrations in China and by the Jews who acquired it as potentially coterminous with naturalization. This "custom," in the words of the British Foreign Office's senior expert in Far Eastern affairs, F. A. Campbell, "has apparently, rightly or wrongly, existed for some time, [and] it was not thought necessary to disturb it."[20] Such officially sanctioned laxity, and the culture of extranationality it engendered, would become anachronistic as of 1906. This process reverberated in Britain's overseas possessions and among the Mediterranean and Middle Eastern Jewish communities that had long hitched their stars to British rule.

Consular practice was to become strict beginning in 1906, when the Ezras and other Baghdadi Jewish families like them found the political hospitality of British authorities in Shanghai tested and the side door to citizenship all but closed. Only a year after anti-alien legislation was adopted in Britain restricting migration, and perhaps in response to an accusation that American consuls in Shanghai, Canton, and Amoy had abused their juridical powers, the Foreign Office issued a China Order in Council that strictly instructed its consular agents overseas to cease renewing Baghdadi Jews' registration as British protected persons, particularly if they had inherited their status from a family patriarch without themselves having lived on British soil.[21] This order was meant to close the loophole that had been available to consular agents and Jewish applicants—what one consular agent described as "a misapprehension as to the exact terms under which Ottoman subjects should in certain circumstances be given British Protection."[22] Whereas the registration papers of the Baghdadi Jewish community in Shanghai had once been renewed automatically, now each application was reviewed independently, and previous approvals were understood to offer no precedent.[23]

The response was panicked and instantaneous. Beginning in 1906, intensifying during and after the First World War, and continuing for at least four decades, the British Foreign Office was peppered with letters from Baghdadi Jews residing in Shanghai who found themselves denied renewal of their registration papers, in some cases even after having received routine approval for decades or generations.[24] Children, wives, widows, and sisters proved particularly vulnerable to the contraction of administrative permissiveness, as their legal status rested on that of fathers, husbands, sons, and brothers, on whose passports or paperwork their own legal status was often recorded.[25] With respect to the Ezra clan, the Foreign Office determined that earlier extensions of British protection had been made in error, and future determinations of protection or citizenship could not be based upon them. Three generations of the extended Ezra family (including not only male applicants but their wives and children) were thus told that they could not piggyback on the Indian-based registration of the family patriarch. As one member of the British bureaucracy put it, "British nationality cannot be acquired by the mistake of any British Official, high or low."[26]

Among those confronting the tightening of British law was D. Silman Somekh, who in 1906 appealed to the British consulate in Shanghai after his request for renewal of his registration was denied. Born in Baghdad in 1872, Somekh "was sent to Bombay for an English education" at age seventeen. After seven years in India in the employ of D. Sassoon and Company, he followed the firm to Shanghai. "From the first time I came here I have been registered at the British Consul as a British subject," explained Somekh to the authorities. "For years past I have been a British Subject as my registration shows, [and] now to be told suddenly that I can be no longer is, to say the least, surprising."[27] The consulate viewed matters differently. Referring to Somekh baldly as "a Turkish subject," representatives of the crown concluded that he was "registered in error as a British subject." The resulting verdict: no longer an employee of D. Sassoon and Company, Somekh could no longer have British protection extended to him. Utilizing a strict interpretation of the legacy of Ottoman capitulations, the consulate determined that Somekh, "in common with other Ottoman subjects . . . should look to the French Consul-General for Protection."[28]

It was true that applicants for British registration *could* turn to the French for the paperwork they required, but this belied the complexity of the relationship between the Baghdadi Jewish émigré community in Shanghai and the British state. Extended as it sometimes was for generations, the status of British protected person marked the Baghdadi population racially and economically, framing elite members of this community as white, European, and bourgeois—members of the power structure in a city intricately organized around the presence of state powers. The conceptual value of protected status transcended Shanghai, resonating with the circuitous histories of Baghdadi Jews themselves. One thinks of Somekh in this regard, and the striking fact that he had traveled from Baghdad to India to "receive an English education"—a decision, one suspects, made not of abstract Anglophilism nor merely on economic grounds, but out of the desire to cannily utilize an imperial order.

Somekh was not alone in voicing desperation to the British consulate. After the British authorities threatened to attenuate protection over Simon Abraham Levy and his infant son, Levy—a native of Cairo who for six years had served D. Sassoon and Company in Hong Kong—described himself as "surprised and pained," and protested that

> since my boyhood I have been associated with the British authorities and have lived in a British Colony for a number of years and am imbued with British ideas [and so] you can understand how hard it must be for me to be told that I can no longer enjoy the protection of HBM [His Britannic Majesty's] Government and that I have now to seek protection of another power when my sympathies are entirely British.[29]

Nissim Jeremiah, a Baghdadi-born Jew who had "enjoyed the hospitality of His Britannic Majesty's kind protection" during thirty years' residence in Hong Kong, put things rather more tersely after his request for registration was denied by the British authorities in Shanghai; he felt himself, he wrote, to be "a lost man."[30] These were strategic statements, to be sure. But the authenticity of their message notwithstanding, they hint at the urgency with which Baghdadi Jews confronted a shifting political landscape. To those whom it benefited, British protection remained a coveted category well into the twentieth century, quasi-legal though this category may have been.

The 1906 China Order in Council restricting Baghdadi Jews' access to British protection might have faded in importance over time, with Jewish applicants in search of paperwork and the consuls in charge of granting it finding ways to circumvent the rule. Instead, global politics intervened to calcify it.

The First World War, the violence and deprivation that accompanied it, and, in the wake of the war, the confusion and anxiety that attended the dismemberment of the Ottoman Empire pushed many Jews in and from the region (and especially in Iraq) to seek British protection and naturalization; they, like other residents of the Middle East, were keenly sensitive to the elevated importance of passports and official paperwork in the interwar world. Although this story is too expansive to do justice to here, one example is striking: in May 1919, more than fifty prominent Baghdadi Jews, including the president of the Jewish Law Committee and the acting chief rabbi and president of the religious council, submitted a request for naturalization to Edwin S. Montagu, secretary of state for India. Bemoaning what they saw as the total "lack of unpreparedness" in Iraq for self-administration and fearing the creation of a government in Iraq led by Arabic-speaking Sunnis, the petitioners requested that they be "taken under the shield of the British Government and considered true subjects of His Majesty, holding themselves prepared to accept all obligations and rights of true British citizens," adding that they were "confident that their [Jewish] brethren in all Iraq will formulate the same desire."[31] The applicants' request was swiftly denied; had it been approved, legal precedent would have been established, permitting a broad swath of Jewish applicants—including, of course, those in Palestine—to follow suit, a situation that the British hardly wished to invite.[32]

With the number of requests for protection or naturalization by Baghdadi Jews in and outside of Iraq soaring, the British authorities in London intensified their scrutiny of applications by Baghdadi Jews in Shanghai and East Asia more generally, bringing to them a skepticism born of both administrative confusion and anti-alien sentiment. Thus, for example, some in the Foreign Office falsely assumed that the Aliens Act of 1914 mandated that the children of British subjects naturalized in India could not inherit their father's or grandfather's legal status, rendering earlier instances of naturalization (as one representative put it) merely "of local effect"; a few years later, the Foreign Office advised its representatives in the region that "no Ottoman subject engaged by a British firm in China should be accorded British protection unless he has a claim to such treatment on some other ground," a thinly veiled reference to Baghdadi Jewish employees of the offices of D. Sassoon and Company.[33] Similarly, while beginning in 1925 it seemed possible that Iraqi Jewish émigrés could ground their requests for paperwork in a treaty signed by Britain and the five-year-old state of Iraq that promised Iraqis (as defined by Article 8 of the Iraqi Nationality Law) British consular and diplomatic protection, this possibility was undercut by a subsequent Order in Council that called for more strenuous review of applications for the necessary paperwork.[34]

At the same time, tolerance among theorists of international law for the system of capitulations—the legal bedrock on which so many Mediterranean Jewish merchants' relationship with Britain and France was constructed—had fallen into disfavor by the interwar period; in the words of Norman Bentwich, former attorney general for Palestine and at the time the most prominent scholar of the theme, capitulations were "out of accord with the system of the modern world," in which, in his view, all polities ought to share "one goal—a single system of law, a single system of courts; absence of privilege and [absence of] discrimination in favour of the foreigner."[35] Given that his own rulings in Palestine in the early 1920s had strategically conformed to Ottoman law in order to sanction the expropriation of Palestinian (Muslim) land, this was an uneasy position for Bentwich to maintain.[36] It would seem that his particular vision of Zionism (albeit nuanced and sympathetic with the notion of binationalism as it was) was subtly intertwined with his desire to see eradicated a legal system that inadvertently privileged Jews of Middle Eastern or Mediterranean origin.[37]

Despite the hardening of legal and consular standards, British representatives could be swayed in favor of particular applicants or their families, with class and social status proving to be crucial credentials for would-be protected persons or naturalized Britons. Such was the case with the Elias family. Baghdadi-born brothers Reuben Bey Elias and Joseph Rahmin Elias moved to Bombay (in 1872) and Shanghai (in 1881) with their father, an employee of D. Sassoon and Company. The Elias brothers registered at times with the French consulate (in 1881 and again from 1885 to 1905) and at times with the British (in 1882 and from 1905 to 1908). This pattern seemed to cause offense to neither consulate—indeed, each granted papers to the brothers with the permission of the other—until 1908, when pressure was being placed upon British consular agents to view such situations as irregular. And yet the British consul general in Shanghai, Pelham Warren, hesitated before denying the brothers' request. "It appears to be my duty [to refuse] their application," he wrote his superiors. Warren's hesitation may have been based on his knowledge of the Eliases' special place in the fabric of Jewish Shanghai. Joseph Rahmin (known to the Baghdadi Jewish community as Yosef Rahamim) was, after all, a pivotal member of Shanghai's Baghdadi Jewish community, the only *mohel* (performer of circumcisions) and *shohet* (ritual slaughterer) trained in Baghdad according to Baghdadi rites. Perhaps it was for this reason that

Warren viewed the Eliases' history sympathetically even though, on the face of it, it was technically no less controversial than Nissim Jeremiah's. Concluded Warren, "There are sufficient grounds to justify me . . . again renewing their certificates as British Protected Persons."[38]

Not surprisingly, class also mattered. Along with his brother Elias Aaron and sister Sophie Aaron, Silas Aaron Hardoon had been registered as a British protected person since 1896 because their father had been naturalized in India some years earlier as an employee of D. Sassoon and Company. By 1907, the Foreign Office concluded that the Hardoon siblings "are not British Subjects and ought not in the first instance to have been registered as such." Aware that a revocation of a legal relationship with the Crown would be damaging to the family, the Foreign Office agreed to recognize the siblings as British subjects despite their previous error "as an act of grace and favour."[39] This was no selfless act of generosity: the British authorities were interested in ensuring that the British state would administer Silas Aaron's estate after his death, for should Hardoon cease to be classified as a British subject or protected person, "the loss to the treasury . . . would be very considerable."[40] (Indeed, oversight of Hardoon's fortune eventually yielded the British Exchequer the sum of £500,000 in duties.)[41] If money could buy protection for some, poverty could forestall it for others. When reflecting on the growing number of requests for registration by Baghdadi Jews, one British consul general mused with relief (and possibly scarcely concealed contempt) that the state was under little pressure to extend English law to the "considerable body of Sikhs" employed by the Municipal Police Force in China, "owing to the fact that they are not possessed of any great means, [and therefore] personal cases affecting them do not often come before the Court. The estates of those who die without relatives in China are remitted to India to be dealt with."[42] To put it another way, the British Foreign Office was highly self-interested in its consideration of registration requests. Class could throw a wrench into the administrative cogs or grease the necessary wheels because individual consuls exercised great power in determining (and sometimes even writing or rewriting) British protection and naturalization laws on the ground, case by case, and according to their own understandings and predilections. More specifically, class could interrupt the general trend to deny Baghdadi Jews' subjecthood—an arrangement that aided some Jewish applicants in Shanghai and other colonial hubs across Asia and the Mediterranean.[43] This built a great deal of fungibility into the system, for what privileges a consul could grant he could also take away, not only in an applicant's lifetime but even after the applicant's death.

Indeed, death did not necessarily conclude the story of an émigré Baghdadi Jew's legal status. One could, after all, be stripped of nationality postmortem if and when one's status was deemed retroactively illegitimate, or if and when one's child, grandchild, widow, or sister was told that he or she could no longer "inherit" this status. In part, the trials that surrounded the Hardoon estate were sensational for this very reason: because in weighing the proper means by which to disperse the estate, they evaluated the legal status of Baghdadi Jews in Shanghai—and, to a lesser extent, of Baghdadi, Mediterranean, and Middle Eastern Jews across the Crown's colonies—in court, and before an international audience.

PROTECTED PERSON? CONTESTING
THE HARDOON FORTUNE

In September 1931, seven members of the Baghdadi branch of the Hardoon family, represented by one who resided in Shanghai, submitted an Arabic-language petition to the Iraqi minister of foreign affairs. The document read:

> Early in June last there died in the City of Shanghai a person named Salih (nick-named Silas) son of Harun Hardun. Salih, who died without leaving a child, was a Baghdadi and a member of our Hardun family. He left many legal heirs, and we are among them. We are informed that Liza Hardun, a Chinese, has laid her hand on the big fortune that the deceased had left claiming that he was her husband and that he had bequeathed all his property to her. We know nothing about her matrimonial relation with him . . . It is unreasonable and against the relations that had existed between our family and the deceased to bequeath his property to a woman from whom he had no offspring and to forget his relatives and kinfolk. Therefore [Silas Aaron Hardoon's] will must have been falsely made. As this question is prejudicial to our rights as legal heirs, we consider that we are badly in need of the protection of our government.[44]

In June 1932, the trial spawned by the Hardoons' petition began in Shanghai, in HBM Supreme Court for China. It would last nearly nine months, drawing upon a battalion of witnesses and international legal talent, captivating and polarizing observers locally and beyond (figure 4.2).

The counsel for the plaintiffs, who were joined at the last minute by a Bombay-based claimant on the estate, argued that according to Iraqi law, Liza Hardoon was entitled to either none or only a small fraction of her late

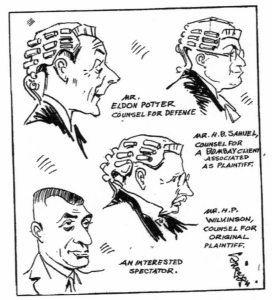

FIGURE 4.2 After the death of Silas Aaron Hardoon, a "galaxy of legal talent" battled over the Hardoon estate in His Britannic Majesty's Supreme Court for China, Shanghai. The case tested the complicated status of British Protected Persons of Baghdadi Jewish background, distilling a broad legal encounter well captured in these juxtaposed caricatures by Sadajou. *Israel's Messenger* (Shanghai), 1 July 1932, 15.

husband's estate, and that in the absence of biological children, the remainder ought to be divided among Silas Aaron Hardoon's (ostensible) kin in Iraq. They justified this determination by submitting that Hardoon was beholden to the law of his domicile of origin; he was, they advanced, initially an Ottoman, and hence an Iraqi citizen for the duration of his life and at the time of his death.[45] His British naturalization, they maintained, had violated both British and international law. British law did not allow one to "shake off a domicile of origin" by residing in another country—particularly one that was extraterritorial, with no real sovereignty of its own. Having never dwelled on British soil, the plaintiffs maintained, Hardoon was never entitled to the naturalization he circuitously acquired; indeed, the granting of this naturalization impinged both on the laws of Iraq and on certain forms of international law.[46] (In the skeptical words of the defense, Hardoon's "registration was a compliment to his personal worth. Registration did not confer nationality.") Given, furthermore, that the National Chinese Government had ruled in 1918 that when faced with a conflict of laws, the principle of nationality governed, the estate ought to be distributed according to Iraqi law—entitling Liza Hardoon to but a quarter of the inheritance and Silas Aaron Hardoon's next of kin to the remainder. To substantiate these claims, the Baghdadi Hardoons appealed to the Iraqi minister of foreign affairs and high commissioner, whose offices, "intent" on the case, confirmed that Silas Aaron was an Iraqi subject and that international law guaranteed that a deceased foreigner's estate would be governed by the laws of personal status in effect in his country of origin.[47]

The arguments offered by the counsel for the plaintiffs and the Iraqi minister of foreign affairs were, on one level, self-serving: all stood to gain financially should the Hardoon estate be granted to the appellants and thus be distributed in and taxed by the Iraqi state. And yet more than greed was involved. All of these parties were also engaging a complex and delicate question that animated the Iraqi public sphere (and the region more generally) in the years after the First World War and the establishment of the British mandate, and, increasingly, as "independence" from the mandate neared: the question of who precisely was or ought to be an Iraqi, and how national identity should be understood to align with or diverge from religious and sectarian identities. These debates were far from abstract; they would determine who would be allowed to return to and remain in Iraq, who would be exiled from it, and where its boundaries should be drawn.[48] Iraqi Jews were animatedly involved in this conversation; and for this community, as for so many others, this question was inflected by varied historical relationships to the Ottoman, British, and Iraqi authorities. Suffice it to say that at the moment the future plaintiffs in the Hardoon trial solicited the support of the Iraqi minister of foreign affairs (in September 1931), Iraqi Jews were expressing widespread enthusiasm for the new British-backed Iraqi regime—envisioning and (at least for the moment) successfully framing themselves as "Arab Jews" and full-fledged Iraqis.[49] These sentiments inflected the demands of the Hardoon family, seeking as they were to bring an émigré back into the legal fold of the Iraqi and Iraqi Jewish body politic. It is all the more striking then that the Hardoon cousins' 1931 petition to the Iraqi government was balanced by comparable appeals by the same parties to the British high commissioner for Iraq. Upholding the authority of Iraqi law, it seems, did not obviate the need to hedge one's political bets. Even, or perhaps especially, at a moment in which a transition of power (that is, the fulfillment of the mandatory promise of sovereignty) was eagerly anticipated, the strategic pursuit of protection remained vital.

Internal British Foreign Office correspondence, seemingly ignorant of these nuances, acknowledged that Hardoon had initially been "registered wrongly as a British subject," which meant that "under [the] strict letter of law it is open to the Iraqi Government to claim that Mr. Hardoon was [an] Iraqi national."[50] At the same time, both the government and the defense argued vigorously that he "must be regarded as a person to whom jurisdiction of His Britannic Majesty's Court extends." Curiously, the fact that Hardoon's father had been naturalized in India did not prove the backbone of the defense.[51] Instead, they based their claim on the Foreign Office's previously cited 1907 dispatch registering Hardoon as a British subject "as an act of grace and favour," and on the 1925 China Order in Council, which declared the category of British subject to include protected persons.[52] What is more, they elaborated that Ottoman subjects who had been born in Iraq but were not habitually resident in Iraq were, in the wake of the Iraqi Nationality Act, obliged either to formally request that nationality or to forsake it; thus, by not pursuing Iraqi citizenship, Hardoon was announcing himself as British.[53] Finally, the defense argued that British protected subjects residing in China "with knowledge and tacit consent of Chinese authorities would fall under British Courts' jurisdiction by sufferance."[54]

The plaintiffs' accusations reached further into the legality of the Hardoons' marriage, probing the relevance of the pair's Jewishness—or lack thereof—to their national affiliation. Maintaining that there was no evidence that Liza Hardoon had converted to Judaism, the plaintiffs charged that a Jewish marriage between the pair could not legally have taken place—an argument substantiated by the lack of a *ketuba* (Jewish marriage contract). Given further that the Hardoons had registered their marriage with the British civil authorities only in August 1928, the plaintiffs insisted that the pair were not legally joined, and that therefore Liza Hardoon had no claim upon Silas Aaron's estate. The defense countered that the Hardoons' marriage had taken place when Shanghai's Jewish community was still young and when records were not maintained.[55] In any case, they argued, Liza and Silas Aaron had long been accepted as a married couple by the community, the synagogue, authorities, and even the Jewish journal of Shanghai, *Israel's Messenger*, which had long referred to the pair as husband and wife. (This fact did not inhibit the journal from siding against Liza Hardoon as the trial progressed.) Continued Liza Hardoon's counsel, the Hardoons were philanthropists of Shanghai's Baghdadi synagogue, they had brought their adopted children up as Jews, and (the controversy about the use of Buddhist rituals during the observances notwithstanding) Silas Aaron Hardoon's funeral had been overseen by the Hevra Kadisha (Jewish Burial Society). Finally, Liza Hardoon's counsel argued that the Hardoons' long history of cohabitation, and the associated "presumption of marriage which arises under English common law," was evidence of their union.[56]

That the British court appeared to be deliberating on the extent of the Hardoons' individual and joint credibility as Jews caused what one observer called "intense indignation" on the part of a faction of Shanghai's Jewish community.[57] The editor of *Israel's Messenger*, N. E. B. Ezra, proved a particularly vocal and biting critic of the court's apparent foray into Jewish law. "Marriage by reputation is an unknown thing among Jewish and Muslim communities," wrote Ezra. "Jewish opinion is not divided on this point."[58] While technically Ezra was correct that Jewish and Muslim law did not sanction "marriage by reputation" (as British law did in certain circumstances), other observers were more invested in the production of new norms rather than the reassertion of traditional ones. Thus the Jewish Communal Organization of Shanghai, which the British authorities deemed "in a position to speak for Jews of British nationality," insisted that in all matters of personal law (including those pertaining to marriage, dissolution of marriage, inheritance, and wills), it was their preference to have the law of England extended to them.[59]

Analyzing the Hardoon case for the *Law Journal*, Norman Bentwich took a different view. Bentwich argued that when it came to matters of marriage, divorce, and succession, British protected persons residing in Shanghai and other Chinese treaty ports ought not to be subject to English law, which might "not be suitable to the rights in marriage of, say, Hindoos or Moslems," but rather to "religious laws prescribed by their domicile of origin."[60] From Bentwich's perspective, this legal approach, in addition to being "in conformity with reason and convenience," had the advantage of shielding "British subjects of polygamous race or religion" from standards ill-suited to them. This was a progressive stance in its way, although undeniably it also protected the British state from thorny legal questions about the state's sanction of subjects involved in polygamous (or so-called "potentially polygamous") marriages, a topic that would come to a head in the years after 1945.[61] In any case, when it came to Baghdadi Jewish émigrés who were also British protected persons, Bentwich's arguments raised as many questions as they resolved, for the religious laws proscribed by their domicile of origin were not Jewish but Islamic. As the British government was informed in a lengthy and sharp dispatch from the Iraqi Legal Drafting Department, in matters of succession, Jewish subjects followed the provisions of shari'a (Islamic law); whether Jewish, Christian, or Muslim, they were from a legal perspective Iraqis first and foremost.[62]

One would expect plaintiffs and defense to differ. And yet the range of opinions was breathtaking. All the parties—the Iraqi government, the Jewish religio-cultural establishment of Shanghai, Hardoon's fellow Baghdadi Jewish protected persons, and an influential Anglo-Jewish theorist of international law—proposed radically different answers to the question of what legal system Silas Aaron Hardoon (and, by extension, his estate) was beholden to. Far from merely weighing the legality of his marriage or religious status then, the trial that followed the magnate's death raised questions of broad concern. When it came to personal law, at what point did the authority of the Jewish community cease and that of the modern state begin? With respect to Mediterranean and Middle Eastern Jews specifically, was the state's respect for the legal authority of Jewish communities over matters deemed internal—long a hallmark of state policy in the Ottoman terrains—imperiled by the rising power of national legal systems (Iraqi as well as British) and the international codes that guided them? What or who had the authority to affirm the legality of identities—documents? individuals? the community? the state?

Judge Grain's judgment, which found in favor of Liza Hardoon, rested on three arguments. First, he opined that regardless of whether Hardoon was by birth Iraqi, he had chosen China as his permanent home. That, submitted the judge, "is the essence of the acquisition of domicile." Hardoon had lived in China for fifty-seven years, leaving only once to vacation in Japan; he had purchased property in China, had been buried there, and had "had no intention of returning to Baghdad and in fact never went back, even for a visit, after he left it when a boy."[63] Second, citing legal precedents that spanned the reach of the British Empire, Grain maintained that the sovereignty of China had granted Great Britain the right to administer its own law in its own courts, and more specifically that the testamentary estates of British subjects domiciled in China were to be governed and administered by British law. Finally, he suggested that as a British protected subject, Hardoon was British from the perspective of the law. Stated Grain's judgment: "I am of the opinion that under the China Order in Council, 1925, British protection is sufficient to make a person a British subject so far as the jurisdiction and the laws applied to this Court are concerned. That there are not two classes, 'British subject,' and 'British protected person'; they are one and the same for the purpose of applying the British law of the Court."[64] On the basis of these arguments, Grain determined Hardoon's will to be "good and valid," and found in favor of the defendant, with costs.

Although Judge Grain's verdict settled a round of claims on Silas Aaron Hardoon's fortune, in the long run it resolved neither the fate of the family estate nor the national status of Baghdadi Jewish émigrés in China. The British Foreign Office continued to field challenges to the distribution of Hardoon's fortune for some time, a fact that caused a British bureaucrat based in Baghdad to despair that there was "no evidence to show that [Hardoon's] relatives

have not given up hope . . . in this contentious and somewhat sordid case."[65]
Most subsequent challenges to the estate came to naught, as, for example, did
a 1936 inquiry from a Syrian lawyer representing claimants in India.[66] But one,
lodged by a Baghdadi Jew by the name of Khan Bahadur Ezra Saleh Hardoon,
found its way again to HBM Supreme Court in China in 1937. The judge overseeing this second Hardoon estate trial, Penrhyn Grant Jones, found in favor
of Liza Hardoon for a second time, in what the *North China Herald* deemed
"one of the most important, and certainly one of the longest judgments ever
given in H. M. Supreme Court for China."[67] Jones's judgment was in some
sense but an expansion on and conceptual deepening of Grain's, delivered
five years earlier. Arguably this second judgment was deemed so crucial because it widened the implications of the Hardoon fracas. What Jones made
clear in his judgment that Grain had left rather more murky was that if distant
cousins or the Iraqi government could lay claim to Hardoon's fortune after his
death, then any Briton of immigrant origin—indeed, any national subject of
immigrant origin—living in an extraterritorial zone was similarly vulnerable
to denaturalization at the hands of international courts in the wake of his or
her death. This decision conceptually transformed Hardoon from a liminal
Baghdadi Jewish protected person to a prototypical Briton, indeed, a vehicle
for British benevolence, which had (in Grain's words) rescued Hardoon from
"the contempt of the Ottomans for the unbelievers and of the Chinese for the
Western barbarian." Argued Grain, these parties "were probably ignorant of
[Hardoon's] existence before his death; they certainly afforded him no protection in life and in life he proffered them no allegiance."[68] Extraordinarily
wealthy Baghdadi Jewish protected persons, it would seem, had the potential
to be resuscitated in the eyes of the court, serving not as a damaging hangover
of the colonial order, but as a barometer of the success of Britain's enlight-
ened foreign policy. Their success raises the more general question of whether
Mediterranean and Middle Eastern Jews served as a litmus test in instances
when colonial, national, and international laws collided.

Grain's judgment, like Jones's, seems to have had little effect beyond the
Hardoon estate when it came to how the Foreign Office treated Shanghai's
Baghdadi Jews who sought registration papers.[69] As late as 1948, the national
status of members of the Hardoon family, of Silas Aaron Hardoon himself,
and of British protected persons in China of Ottoman descent more generally
was still perplexing the British Foreign Office, prompting one British official to
muse that "the whole question of BPPs [British protected persons] in China
should be gone into. It is of considerable practical importance for the Consular

Office in Shanghai and elsewhere in China and the present position seems alarmingly vague."[70] Many officials in the British Foreign Office hoped that the notion of the British protected person would be rendered legally more precise; others maintained that the state required a whole new way to classify this body of individuals. One bureaucrat offered, "[British protected persons] are really protégés in the true meaning of the French term. I have found no term that satisfies me, but I suggest 'a person enjoying British protection.' I think this is a term which could be put on a passport."[71] Although the United Kingdom had given up its rights to extraterritoriality for nondiplomatic persons in China five years before these notes were penned, the vexing liminality of the Baghdadi Jewish diaspora lingered on for the state, evading terse legalistic categorization and even what some felt to be a duly British categorization.

Baghdadi Jews were hardly the only protégés who acquired, lost, or negotiated for the status of British protected person in China (or elsewhere). Nonetheless, as the twentieth century unfolded, Baghdadi Jewish applicants for protection or naturalization, who once might have been afforded more latitude, seemed to stick with increasing persistence in the craw of British officials, particularly those in London. Why this should be so is difficult to say with precision; studying this group comparatively (with regard, for example, to Armenians or the aforementioned Sikhs employed in Shanghai's Municipal Police who were the butt of a consul general's humor) might yield more definitive conclusions in this regard. But a number of preliminary theories arise. Perhaps the relatively small number of Baghdadi Jewish émigrés made them a visible target of increasingly punctilious bureaucrats. Perhaps because many of these Jews were wealthy, they (and, more pointedly, whatever estates they might generate) were less easy to dismiss than other protected persons dwelling in China with whom they could be compared. Perhaps because their émigré path stretched through India, their legal status, which reflected multiple colonial histories, was particularly difficult to parse. Or perhaps when the First World War came to its bloody end and the Arab provinces of the Ottoman Empire were carved into mandates, émigré Baghdadi Jews seeking protection from the British state threatened, from the perspective of the officials who held the power to grant or deny their requests, to set a dangerous legal precedent that reached far beyond the boundaries of Shanghai or East Asia, into mandatory Iraq, Palestine, and beyond. Whatever the causes of their vexatious stature, Baghdadi Jewish émigrés in East Asia were caught in an extended multigenerational struggle for legal clarity with the British state. All of this played out in court and before an international audience in the various testamentary battles that followed the death of Silas Aaron Hardoon.

THE PERSISTENCE OF EMPIRE

Twice in the 1930s, the British Supreme Court in Shanghai determined that Silas Aaron Hardoon was a Briton. And yet the conditions of his postmortem naturalization at the hands of the court were nothing if not colonially conditioned. Hardoon was, after all, the son of a father born in Baghdad and naturalized in India, himself Ottoman-born, a British protected person (a status extended in violation of British law), a sixty-year extraterritorial resident of a treaty port city, and not even a one-time traveler to Britain. The British Supreme Court did not misread Hardoon's history. Rather, the judgment emanating from this authority provided evidence of the enduring and extraordinarily malleable nature of British protected person as an ambiguous but nonetheless significant legal category of the early twentieth century. This category has been neglected by scholars of Jewish, British, colonial, and legal studies heretofore, but understanding how it was extended, revoked, petitioned for, and transformed promises to deepen—and no less to intertwine—our historical understanding of modern Jews, evolving norms of international and national law, and the reshaping of European imperialism in the wake of the First World War.

While Hardoon is as idiosyncratic a historical character as one could imagine, the principal question that arose in the aftermath of his death was salient for Britain and Iraq, for international legal observers, and for extraterritorial Mediterranean and Middle Eastern Jews living in Aleppo, Java, Shanghai, Tripoli, and beyond. Could an ambiguous legal category of identity inherited from the colonial era survive a time of ostensible global nation-building? What the Hardoon testamentary trials indicated was that well into the interwar period, the status of British protected person, rather like European imperialism itself, could be selectively renamed and recast, serving at one and the same time as a stepping-stone to citizenship for certain holders of wealth and connections and a mark of dispossession for others. Perhaps it does not strain the limits of interpretation to say that in this regard, these phenomena were not so very different from the effigy of Silas Aaron Hardoon that so captivated the international press in the wake of this man's extraordinary funeral. Then, as now, there was something compelling and complex about a substance (wax), status (protégé), and political project (imperialism) that was eminently malleable, capable of being reconstituted and remolded, assuming ever new faces and hybrid cultural forms, shifting its shape without ever altogether melting away.

Conclusion: Aftershocks

My grandfather, Victor Abrevaya, born in Ottoman Çanakkale but a child of the Bronx, was always afraid of returning to Turkey. Perhaps he was aware of Turkey's 1938 Passport Law, which prohibited former Turkish citizens from entering Turkey even if they held the passport of another country.[1] Or perhaps he was haunted by the memory of his own father, Solomon Abrevaya, an ardent Freemason and Young Turk who (as far as the family can discern) fled the empire with his wife Luna and young son amidst the countercoup of 1909.[2] No matter. Victor—known to wear a fez to "Turkish night celebrations" at Los Angeles' Sephardic Temple Tifereth Israel, where he "performed" his "Oriental heritage," in Julia Phillips Cohen's evocative formulation—would not return, despite having close relatives in Turkey.[3] His American passport, acquired in New York City, listed him as Turkish born. Were he to visit Turkey, might his exit be denied? Could the (antipatriotic) sins of father be revisited on son?

Passports, papers, passes, permits, stamps—means of documenting, tracking, and policing—became important to so many people and places in the early twentieth century. In Stefen Zweig's words, quoted in the epigraph of this book, they are the "petty trifles, always merely trifles" that bear evidence of the madness that allowed "human values [to] sink more rapidly than those of currency" in the heady interwar period. As the words of the Viennese-born Zweig make clear, legal documents were as vexing to Ashkenazi Jews as to Mediterranean and Middle Eastern Jews—and, of course, equally as treasured and troublesome for non-Jews as for Jews. But a unique, forgotten history is nonetheless commanded by those Ottoman-born and Ottoman-descended Jews whose legal identities were grounded at the intersection of the capitulatory regime and the passport regime; at a time of transition from empire to nation-state and a moment of juncture between heartland and diaspora. This legal transition was immensely complex to navigate because it coincided with wars and mass migration, as well with the dismemberment of the Ottoman Empire, the expansion of European neoimperialism, and the emergence of new states (including mandate and protectorate regimes) at their intersection.

The echoes of the capitulatory regime rang through the twentieth century, hardly diminishing with the formal abolition of the institution of protection with the Treaty of Lausanne. In this conclusion I briefly trace the reflection of a few such historical sound waves.

In the face of the widespread denaturalization of European Jewry in the course of the Second World War, it is perhaps surprising that there should be a history of wartime extraterritoriality to tell. Yet legal identity did, in fact, determine the fortune of individual Sephardi Jews and, in cases, entire Jewish communities from the erstwhile Ottoman territories (figure C.1). The results were not unidirectional. The fact of being an extraterritorial Jew could render one extraordinarily vulnerable or, conversely, entitle one to preferential treatment, making the difference between life and death. True to the case studies we have explored in the preceding pages, Sephardi Jews' wartime tangles with legal identity followed no code. In their diversity, they indicate the enduring complexity of extraterritoriality as a legal niche and lived experience for Jews and their descendants well into the mid-twentieth century.

We begin review of this subject with the same site at which this book began: the heart of the Ladino cultural heartland, Salonica. On the day the deportation of Salonican Jewry began, in early February of 1943, 860 Jewish foreign nationals lived in the city, including 511 Jews with Spanish papers, 281 with Italian citizenship, 39 with Turkish, 6 with Portuguese, 15 with Argentinian, Swiss, Hungarian, or Bulgarian papers, and 8 "enemy citizens" (presumably holders of French, British, or American papers).[4] Though the genocide of European Jewry was yet unfolding, German authorities were determined, at this point in the war, to avoid alienating neutral and Allied nations. Thus Germany granted overseeing countries the opportunity to "repatriate" their foreign nationals from areas under German control.[5] (As in previous chapters, the word "repatriation" demands quotation marks, as many of the Jews in question had never set foot in the country whose passport they carried.) With this determination, various pathways emerged for Salonica's foreign Jews.

FIGURE C.1 Ink and water color selection from Andrea Ventura's "The Hôtel Meina." Despite the widespread denaturalization of European Jewry in the course of the Second World War, legal identity and an extraterritorial inheritance determined the fortune of individual Sephardi Jews. France's Vichy regime deported foreign-born Jews and stripped citizenship from many Ottoman-born women and men who had recently been naturalized as French citizens. Spain rescued hundreds of Jewish holders of Spanish passports after their deportations; but Portugal resisted coming to the aid of Jews in Greece who held "provisional Portuguese protection" until nearly the war's end. Small numbers of Mediterranean and Middle Eastern Jews who possessed Italian citizenship were "repatriated" to Italy from France, Belgium, or Holland—though some (like those pictured here) were subsequently forced to confront the extension of the Final Solution to Italy. All told, individual experiences of the war did not conform to general trends. © Andrea Ventura.

German and Spanish authorities now began an agonizing back and forth over the future of the Spanish Jews caught in the Third Reich. As Spain vacillated in its determination to aid this vulnerable population, and as Germany and Spain debated who would pay for "repatriation" were Spain to encourage this course, Germany prepared to send Salonica's Spanish Jews to the Bergen-Belsen concentration camp, sparing them (in deference to their foreign status) from Auschwitz, where the vast majority of Greek Jews were sent for near certain death. Even before this plan could be actualized, Spain's diplomat in Salonica, Sebastián de Romero Radigales, arranged for 150 Spanish nationals to flee Salonica for Athens. German representatives boarded the remaining Spanish nationals of the city onto trains destined for Bergen-Belsen. With their deportation, Salonica was rendered officially devoid of Jews.[6]

Still the administrative fugue continued. Even before the deported Jews reached Bergen-Belsen, the Spanish Foreign Ministry agreed to accept them as "repatriates." The details of repatriation would take over six months to iron out (during which the Jews remained interned), after which Spain "repatriated" the group with a degree of fanfare that arguably exceeded the circumstances. In Athens, meanwhile, the Spanish nationals from Salonica who earlier found safe haven now found their status in flux. After Italy's surrender to the Allies in the autumn of 1943, Athens fell to German hands. As the deportation of Italian Jews began, German authorities initiated a search for foreign Jews, yielding some 1,300 Greek, Italian, Spanish, and Portuguese paper holders. Of this larger group, a total of 367 Spanish nationals were sent to Bergen-Belsen, again with Radigales' intervention.[7] (For his efforts to protect Spain's Jews, Yad Vashem recently named Radigales a "Righteous among the Nations."[8]) Nehama, the Salonican Jewish intellectual critical of his community's rush on foreign papers whom we encountered in the first chapter, was among these deportees. In an ironic twist, Nehama proved to be one of a small minority of Salonican Jews who were spared the death camps due to his last-dash acquisition of foreign protection.[9]

The Portuguese administration of Prime Minister António de Oliveira Salazar was also slow and selective in opening its doors to its protégés from Salonica. While Portugal granted entry to Jews from Hungary, the Netherlands, and Vichy France by labeling them "Portuguese" in the course of the war, it resisted coming to the aid of documented "Portuguese" Jews in Greece until nearly the end of the conflict, in the face of many personal petitions for safe haven.[10] In the interest of breaking with a mandate set in 1912–13 by the young Portuguese Republic, Salazar exhibited greater tolerance of Jews who had no historical relationship to Portugal then he showed those who held "provisional [Portuguese] registration" and, indeed, had once been embraced by Portugal. This despite the fact that the Nazi regime notified Portuguese authorities of the deportation of Jews from Greece and Italy before the fact, granting Salazar the opportunity to "repatriate" Jewish holders of Portuguese papers or, at least, to request that the German authorities transport these Jews to a concentration camp in Germany rather than a death camp in the east.[11] In 1943, however,

Salazar's regime was unmoved, adhering fastidiously to the Foreign Minster's recent determination that Portugal reject the nationality claims of Jews who acquired Portuguese protection in Salonica in or after 1913.

Some perished in the Nazi death camps as a result of Salazar's inflexibility, including the Benveniste family from Kavalla. In March 1943, Saloman and Flora Benveniste, together with their son Moise and his wife Lucie, were taken from Kavalla to Bulgaria's Gorna-Dzhumaya transit camp and thence (under the oversight of Bulgarian authority) by train to Lom, a port city on the Danube River. Even as this horrific journey was under way, a family member in Lisbon notified the Red Cross in Geneva of the Benvenistes' plight. The Red Cross contacted Portuguese representatives in Switzerland, warning them (incorrectly, as it turns out) that the family was soon to be sent to Upper Silesia [Auschwitz], and these Portuguese officers in turn began an inquiry into the Benvenistes' history. The intelligence gathered was not enough to deter Foreign Minister Eduardo Vieira Leitão. Unmoved by the fact that the Benvenistes were (in the words of the Portuguese mission in Switzerland) "Jews of Portuguese nationality" [*israelitas, de nacionalidade portuguêsa*] or by the fact that the administration had acceded to saving other Jews with more tenuous ties to Portugal, Leitão concluded that the Benvenistes' claims to nationality were groundless. On 18 March 1943, the Benvenistes were deported to Treblinka, where they perished.[12]

Other "Portuguese Jews" from Greece were deported from elsewhere in Europe. Nineteen such women and men, ten of whom were born in Salonica, were arrested by the SS in Athens on 25 March 1944. The Spanish Consulate in Athens was called upon to affirm their Portuguese papers, which it did—presumably, given the short time this task required, without recourse to deep investigation.[13] A week later, the legal identity of (and Portugal's disinterest in) this population established, the German authorities deported the nineteen.[14] That Portugal would reverse its policy towards Greek Jews a few months later (in June 1944) as a result of American pressure could not undo the experience of these Sephardi Jews, nor that of other Salonican Jewish holders of provisional Portuguese registration who shared their fate.

Small numbers of Mediterranean and Middle Eastern Jews who possessed Italian citizenship were "repatriated" to Italy from France, Belgium, and Holland in late 1942 or early 1943—some of these women and men were subsequently forced to confront the extension of the Final Solution to Italy.[15] Among the very first Jews killed on Italian soil in the course of the Second World War were Salonican émigrés descended from Frankos (Ottoman Jews possessing

European citizenship). A portion of these families had emigrated from Greece to Italy prior to the war; others had fled there in the summer of 1943 with the help of Lucillo Merci, an Italian official who, from his station in Salonica, granted them the Italian papers required to retreat southward in the face of the Nazi onslaught.[16] Five days after the armistice between the Allied forces and Italy in September 1943, a number of these families gathered north of Milan, in and around the town of Meina on Lake Maggiore. Alas, the region around the lake was occupied by the SS, which initiated an aggressive hunt for Jews. Among those caught up in the resulting sweep were twenty individuals staying in a hotel owned by Alberto and Eugenia Behar, a Franko couple from Salonica. The Behars' guests included various Salonican Frankos, including members of the Fernandez Diaz, Mosseri, Torres, Nahum, Modiano, and Pompas families (figure C.2). The SS confined the guests to the hotel until, one by one, they were taken to the nearby lake, shot, and thrown into the water with stones round their necks.[17] These murders attenuated the family line of some of the last descendants of the quintessential early modern Ottoman Jewish protégés.

In France, Ottoman-born Jews found themselves more vulnerable than native-born French Jews to German genocidal policies (and Vichy French practices), regardless of whether they held French citizenship or had a protégé past. Many of the Ottoman-born Jews we followed in chapter 3 were naturalized as French citizens in the interwar period, mostly in the wake of Turkey's 1935 regulation that declared Turkish and Ottoman-born citizens who had not returned to the country between 1924 and 1927, and had not renewed their passports, to be Turkish nationals no longer.[18] Other Ottoman-born Jews living in France were formally stateless and continued to rely on the *laissez-passer* or resident permits as their principal form of state-issued documentation through the interwar period (just as many Ottoman-born Jews who lacked citizenship papers and lived in Great Britain continued to rely, well into the 1920s, on Home Office travel permits when they journeyed abroad).[19] With the outbreak and advance of the Second World War, this choice proved irrelevant. While the Vichy regime protected most of its native-born Jewish citizens, it stripped citizenship from many French men and women who were recently naturalized, ultimately deporting them, along with foreign-born Jews, to the Nazi death camps.[20] Insofar as it amalgamated naturalized and nonnaturalized foreign-born Jews, this act of the Vichy regime dissolved what legal boundaries existed *between* Ottoman Jewish immigrants in France. With this homogenization, protégé histories lost all meaning or value in the eyes of the law.

FIGURE C.2 Ink and water color selection from Andrea Ventura's "The Hôtel Meina." Among the Jewish holders of foreign papers to find themselves under Nazi occupation were descendants of Salonica's Frankos [Ottoman Jews possessing European citizenship]. Having fled Greece for Italy, a number of these families gathered in and around the town of Meina on Lake Maggiore, when the area was occupied by the SS. When the SS initiated an aggressive hunt for Jews, those caught up in the sweep included twenty guests of a hotel owned by a Franko couple from Salonica. The SS confined the guests to the Hôtel Meina until taking them to the nearby lake, where they were shot and thrown into the water. These murders attenuated the family line of some of the last descendants of the quintessential early-modern Ottoman Jewish protégés. © Andrea Ventura.

Like so many European Jews who faced denaturalization, social death, and deportation in the period of the Second World War, Ottoman-born Jews living in France still clung, desperately, to the promise latent in legal documentation. In this, Bension Haim Yaco Soulam and Rebecca Soulam (née Bensasson) were typical. This Ottoman-born couple had come to France in the interwar period not as protégés but as Ottoman subjects—subsequently failing (or choosing not) to renew their papers with the Turkish authorities. As a result of this accident (or choice), the Turkish consulate would not recognize the pair as Turkish nationals deserving of repatriation in the course of the Second World

War.[21] Thus Yaco was interned in Drancy, an internment camp located in a northeastern suburb of Paris that was designed to house France's foreign Jews. (Later, Drancy became the primary transit camp for all of French Jewry.) From Drancy, Yaco wrote his wife letters in a combination of French and Ladino, one of which is quoted in the epigraph to this book. Yaco's letters, peppered with elaborate coded messages and instructions, included the advice that the couple's children hold fast to proof of their French nationalization as a form of insurance more dear than money or jewels. Citizenship, Yaco believed, was solid, inviolate; precious objects were transitory, for "they take it all anyway."[22] How wrong he was. Along with countless Jews of Ottoman origin, Yaco was deported from Drancy to Auschwitz, where he perished. Rebecca remained in Paris for a time until she was forced to follow her husband. As France deported the majority of its native-born Jews, Yaco's advice to his children proved useless. Miraculously, however, the Soulam children survived the war in hiding, only to be reunited with Rebecca (who survived typhus as well as the horrors of Auschwitz) after the war.

At the end of the day, individual experiences of the war did not conform to general trends. Some Southeastern European Jewish holders of foreign papers were murdered during the occupation process; others were swept up in deportation efforts without the protector state's involvement, or in the face of statist disinterest or inaction. Protection could prove to be an asset, but it could also prove to be irrelevant, or even a liability.

After the war, the fact of having been an extraterritorial Jew under the protection of a foreign power continued to accrue repercussions for some survivors. Since at least 1958, a group calling itself Union de los subditos Españoles de Grecia por sus reclamaciones ante Alemania [the Union of Spanish Subjects of Greece Seeking Claims against Germany] began appealing to a number of major Jewish philanthropies with the complaint that Jewish survivors from Greece who held Spanish protection during World War II were being denied their share of material claims paid by Germany to Spain in the wake of the war.[23] The group's representatives argued in an appeal of 1962 that the survivors (then living in Greece and Israel) had been cheated by the Spanish government, which allocated its claims from Germany without regard to this unique class of Spanish Jews.[24] This complaint was factually thin but nonetheless identified a loophole in the then-extant logic of German reparations. As one official explained in response to the Union de los subditos Españoles de Grecia por sus reclamaciones ante Alemania, negotiations between the German Federal Republic and Spain had stalled before a bilateral agreement pertaining to the allocation of claims was reached; moreover, because Germany did not pay reparations to individuals (only to states or the Claims Conference), extraterritorial Spanish Jews victimized in the course of the war had no recourse to indemnification.[25]

Looking beyond the Second World War and its aftermath, the legacy of the capitulatory regime extended further still into the twentieth century in the form of a legally pluralistic institution created in Egypt in 1876—the mixed court system. The mixed court system was created in the Ottoman era to adjudicate cases involving the considerable number of foreigners in Egypt, and it remained intact through the British Protectorate period (1882–1956), experiencing a "precarious life and slow death" until its abolition in 1949.[26] Through this period, the Jewish community of Egypt included a significant number of European protégés and citizens; in 1948, an astonishing 30,000 Jews out of a total Egyptian Jewish population of 75,000–80,000 held foreign citizenship.[27] Understandably, the mixed courts of Egypt adjudicated an extraordinary number and range of court cases concerning Jewish litigants.[28]

Though the mixed court system was not always demonized by Egyptian critics, in time Jews' reliance on the mixed court system would prove one factor in fueling an association in the minds of many Egyptian nationalists between Jews, foreign privilege, British colonial authority, and the unequal distribution of wealth in Egypt. This association was solidified after the outbreak of the Suez/Sinai War of 1956, during which Britain, France, and Israel coordinated an assault on Egypt. In response, the regime of Gamal Abdel Nasser initiated various affronts against Egyptian Jews. Some 1,000 Jews, half of whom were Egyptian citizens, were detained; 13,000 British and French citizens, including many Jews, were expelled along with an additional 500 Jews who were not foreign nationals; and the government nationalized the assets of British and French citizens (among other activities). After the war, Jews were subjected to unofficial pressure to leave Egypt, and it is estimated that as many of one third of the prewar Jewish population complied.[29] In a nationalizing Egypt, Jewish protégés had assumed a menacing symbolic potency.

The assault on Egypt's foreign nationals, and the resulting "dispersion of Egyptian Jewry," as Joel Beinin has put it, generated—or, better put, rekindled—new sets of memories about the importance and hazards of extraterritoriality for Middle Eastern Jews. Perhaps no better example can be found than in André Aciman's fictionalized memoir, *Out of Egypt*, which is also cited in the epigraph to this book. As Aciman's young narrator watches the events of 1956 unfold in his childhood home of Alexandria, one family member in particular seems to embody the fantastic hopes and devastating defeats of the family—the narrator's Uncle Vili.[30] At times pro-Egyptian, at times pro-Italian, at times pro-British, Vili was a fabulist, but one who nonetheless succeeded in shaping his own destiny through negotiations with citizenship: negotiations that hued to a logic that was frantic and savvy, both. Late in the twentieth century, Mediterranean and Middle Eastern Jews were continuing to harbor extraterritorial dreams, even in the face of political nightmares.

In the writing of Patrick Modiano, winner of the 2014 Nobel Prize for Literature, extraterritorial history yields a spectral inheritance. While Modiano himself is French born and raised, his father was a Livornese Jew from Salonica. Resident in Paris when the Vichy regime began its sweep for Jewish foreign nationals, the elder Modiano evaded arrest and spent the war as a black marketeer associated—in what form, precisely, he never told his son—with the French Gestapo. His evocation frequents Modiano's stories: here as an Italian Jewish photographer released from Drancy at the intervention of the Italian Consulate, there as a father figure rescued from detention and deportation by racketeer friends.[31] In Modiano's writing, extraterritoriality, danger, and questionable morality blur, exerting an inexorable force upon the present.

This book has surveyed the histories of myriad Jews like the fictional Vili, whose acquisition of foreign papers proved a means of navigating the protracted transition from imperial to neoimperial and national realities, through migration, wartime violence, and border changes. Of the conclusions it has reached, four warrant emphasis here.

First, for Ottoman-born Jews and their descendants who sought, acquired, or lost the protection of the states of Europe in the late nineteenth and early twentieth centuries, citizenship was not a possession one held or lacked. The protégé status was, instead, a flexible legal state whose value fluctuated over time and place. Persistence, felicitous timing, luck, class, gender—all were factors that could allow one to parlay protection into citizenship. On the other hand, one's protected status could expire, or be revoked, audited, legally circumscribed, or ignored by the state. For all of these reasons, to study the institution of protection is to understand European citizenship in ways familiar to historians of gender and colonialism, but novel to Jewish historians—as a legal spectrum along which individuals and states traveled in various unpredictable directions.

Second, as much as the protégé status put Ottoman Jewish women and men in legal relationships with Ottoman and successor state authorities and the states of Europe, and as much as Jewish protégés brought myriad polities into fraught dialogue, protection was a local affair. Protégé relationships were dynamic. They hinged on interactions with consuls and vice-consuls in Ottoman, European, and émigré centers—notwithstanding the existence of state laws and policies concerning capitulatory subjects. Precisely because these laws were imprecise, inconsistent, and shifting, it fell to local officials to work out their meaning through practice, thereafter awaiting possible correction, censorship, or audit. It is no surprise that the resulting strategies (and, indeed, precise legalese) employed by local officials were manifold, which in turn impeded the ability of the state to formulate and enforce legal superstructures. Jewish holders and seekers of the protégé status found this chaotic landscape difficult to navigate, but they—like Aciman's Uncle Vili—could locate opportunity in tumult: playing consuls (or even states) off one another, using their class status to advantage, exploiting loopholes, combatting official stasis with determination. These dynamics may render a comprehensive history of the legal institution of protection elusive, but, by the same token, they allow for the telling of transimperial, transnational, and global history in a strikingly intimate tone.

Third, this study has illuminated the intertwined nature of European, Ottoman, Middle Eastern, and Jewish histories. Relationships of protection, the movement of protégés (sometimes voluntary, sometimes forced), and a seemingly endless archival stream crosscut and intertwined these histories. Since the early modern period, the capitulatory regime had the effect of extending Europe's influence into the Ottoman Empire, creating subjects insulated from Ottoman law (at least to a degree). In the late nineteenth and early twentieth centuries, migration, war, border changes, and the collapse of the Ottoman Empire brought protégés (and, with them, Ottoman histories and law) into the heart of Europe—influencing policies domestic to France and Great Britain. These developments appear abstract, but they were lived by women and men who were Europeans, Ottomans, Middle Easterners, *and* Jews.

Fourth and finally, extraterritoriality was a reverie. Protection was, of course, a tangible legal state for Middle Eastern, Mediterranean, and Southeastern European Jews. But the protégé status was also a vessel into which many parties—nationalists, socialists, localists, imperial loyalists, representatives of states, consular officials, émigrés—deposited their own ambitions, fears, and fantasies.

These emotions are resurging today as Spain and Portugal again seek to ingather their scattered Sephardi subjects. Predictably, the range of responses is broad. Some seekers of naturalization are enthusiastic, others cautious. Yet other eligible candidates are offended by the states' imposition of fees, linguistic requirements, and conditions, or confused as to what this legal possibility might portend for themselves or their children. There are descendants of Muslims expelled from Medieval Iberia who feel their histories have been ignored; Muslim commentators in Turkey who interpret the Jewish embrace of Spain as a sign of disloyalty.[32] These emotions are familiar to the student of history. The reawakening of this maelstrom—the bombast, zeal, strategy, caution, offense, confusion, injury, and resentment—is achingly familiar, testimony to the enduring symbolic and material force of an extraterritorial dream.

ACKNOWLEDGMENTS

For many years, in the course of a visit to a great many archives, I have been haunted by extraterritorial dreams. Ottoman-born Jewish protégés and their descendants make an appearance in an astonishing range of documentary repositories—in archives of all the foreign ministries of Europe's "capitulatory nations," of consulates across the Mediterranean, Middle East, and Europe, of various police headquarters, and of global Jewish philanthropies the world over. Within these collections, one can find elements of protégé history in archival folders relating to commerce, law, regional and global conflict, refugees, politics, and migration, to name but a few categories among many. Not surprisingly, protégés (and all they represent) also figure in family archives, memoirs, literature, and the popular press. Such documentary abundance is the historian's fantasy and fear.

How fortunate I have felt, then, to have so many generous colleagues offering help, guidance, correctives, and succor. My first debt is to my colleagues at the Mosse Program in History at the University of Wisconsin, Madison, who invited me to present the George L. Mosse Lectures in the autumn of 2014. This extraordinary honor provided me the opportunity to weave together many years of research and reflection on the complex subject of extraterritoriality. In Madison, John Tortorice, Tony Michels, Mary Louise Roberts, Simone Schweber, and Giuliana Chamedes, among others, proved extraordinarily generous hosts and erudite interlocutors. The life history—and genius—of George Mosse has informed my thinking about extraterritoriality; not only because Mosse himself experienced the trauma of statelessness, but insofar as his own groundbreaking conflation of historical scales (macro and micro, geopolitical and familial, intimate and diplomatic) has inspired these inquiries.

Aron Rodrigue has been the most steadfast, unflagging interlocutor when it came to this project—fielding, over many years, innumerable questions, reading countless drafts, and encouraging me to persist in a topic equally ubiquitous and elusive to the Sephardi historian. That he has done so with unstinting good humor and joy makes him the rarest, most precious scholarly friend. My work on this project coincided with a wonderful, long collaboration with Julia Phillips Cohen. My sense of Ottoman and Middle Eastern Jewish history has expanded infinitely in dialogue with Julia, who generously read and commented upon this manuscript in its entirety, with tremendous erudition and care: for all this I am immensely grateful. David N. Myers, a most stimulating colleague, offered erudite comments on this project at various crucial stages, while Jessica Marglin delivered insightful reflections on the completed work.

Others were generous enough to read sections of the manuscript and offer invaluable insights based on their own expertise: for their wisdom, kindness, and friendship, I thank Orit Bashkin, Olga Borovaya, Jeffrey Culang, James Gelvin, Joshua Schreier, and Todd Shepard. Devin Naar and Paris Papamichos Chronakis deserve special credit not only for reading my drafts, but for their willingness to indulge my endless questions about Salonican Jewish history (and so much more) as they readied their own, path-breaking works for publication. Jordanna Bailkin is still the speediest, most sage reader one could ask for: her astonishing twenty-four-hour-turnaround commentary always prompts insights and amazement. Steven Zipperstein continues to serve as an unstinting mentor and conversation partner. Twenty some years (and counting) of conversation and companionship with Ra'anan Boustan, Cecile Kuznitz, Tony Michels, Ken Moss, and Eddy Portnoy continues to be crucial. My loyal writing group has indulged various bits of this project in various stages of gestation: to Chris Chism, Barbara Fuchs, Hannah Landecker, and Carla Gardina Pestana, my warmest appreciation.

An alphabet of colleagues and friends offered reading suggestions, advice, and conversation as the project progressed. Much appreciation is due, in this regard, to Sebouh Aslanian, Joel Beinin, Aviva Ben-Ur, David Biale, Michelle Campos, Jeffrey Culang, Dina Danon, Nathaniel Deutsch, Marc Michael Epstein, Darcie Fontaine, Michal Friedman, Eyal Ginio, Harvey Goldberg, Will Hanley, Ali İğmen, Maureen Jackson, Abigail Jacobson, Dalia Kandiyoti, Mary Dewhurst Lewis, Caroline Libresco, Zachary Lockman, Devi Mays, Susan Miller, Marina Rustow, Steven Sage, Benjamin Schreier, Daniel Schroeter, Zvi Shiloni, Reeva Simon, Susan Slymovics, Julia Clancy Smith, and Lynn

Thomas. Others offered invaluable company and hospitality in the course of my research travels, including Giovanna Bertazonni and Andrea Coscelli; Mark and Dinah Sounigo Diwan; Luisa Ferreira; Gregory and Sophie Katz; and Sarah, Jak, Betsy, and Mert Penso.

Crucial financial support for this project came from a National Endowment for the Humanities Fellowship; a Faculty Research Grant by the UCLA Faculty; and the Maurice Amado Chair at UCLA. Early recognition was extended by the North American Conference of British Studies, which awarded me the 2012 Walter D. Love Article Prize for an essay that seeded many of the ideas for (as well as the last chapter of) this book.

I feel myself immensely privileged to serve UCLA as a faculty member, and am deeply grateful to so many members of this institution, including (in addition to those already mentioned) Andy Apter, Sebouh Aslanian, Aomar Boum, Lia Brozgal, Greg Cohen, Robin Derby, Jessica Goldberg, Gil Hochberg, Lynn Hunt, Chris Kelty, Benjamin Madley, Norma Mendoza-Denton, Teo Ruiz, and Todd Presner. That I am so honored as to hold the Maurice Amado Chair in Sephardic Studies at this institution is icing on an already delicious cake—my gratitude to the Maurice Amado Foundation Board, and to Elaine Lindheim and Pam Keizer in particular, is unending.

Various graduate students at UCLA assisted with aspects of this project, helping me collect, sort through, and translate a morass of documentary material. Ceren Abi, Rachel Deblinger, Lela Gibson, Alma Heckman, Shir Alon, Morgan Guzman, Nadav Molchadsky, and Cassia Pagen Roth—I am grateful to all of you for sharing your time and expertise. Sam Wetherell gathered precious documents in the National Archives of the United Kingdom that I had missed, while Sabrina Donati drew upon her bottomless knowledge of the Italian Foreign Ministry Archive, sharing material I never could have obtained on my own.

Librarians, archivists, and institutional representatives the world over helped me wend my way through this multi-sited archival project. I wish to offer special thanks to those, too numerous to acknowledge in full, who went out of their way in offering aid, including Claude Kuperminc and Rose Levy, Director and Archivist (respectively) at the Archive of the Alliance israélite universelle, Paris; Yochai Ben-Ghedalia and Eli Ben-Yosef, Director and Archivist (respectively) at the Central Archives for the History of the Jewish People, Jerusalem; Thomas Just, Director of Archives at the Österreichisches Staatsarchiv, Vienna; Manuela Franco, Anabela Isdiro, and Margarida Lages of the Instituto Diplomático, Lisbon; Pablo Martín Asuero, Director of the Cervantes Institute, Istanbul; D. Pablo Benavides Orgaz, General Consul of Spain in Istanbul; and Devin Naar and Ty Alhadeff of the Sephardic Studies Digital Collection, University of Washington, Seattle. Last but not least, various individuals were magnanimous in availing material and memories from family archives, including Hazzan Isaac (Ike) Azose; Monique Reisner; Alan and Hilary Salem; Jackie Slutzky; Esme Solomons; Eugénie, Florence, Laurent, and Sabbeta Souolam; and Sivan Toledano. Special appreciation goes to Andrea Ventura for allowing me to reproduce selections from his stunning series "The Hôtel Meina" in my conclusion.

Portions of this book were presented to the Center for European Studies, Harvard University; the Center for Law, History and Culture at USC's Gould School of Law; the Graduate Faculty of Humanities, Kyushu University, Fukuoka, Japan; the Center for Middle East Studies at the University of California, Santa Barbara; the School of Law at the University of Lund, Sweden; and the Program in Jewish Studies at the University of Colorado, Boulder. For their hospitality and engagement at these events, I offer special thanks to Phyllis Albert, Peter Gordon, and Mary Dewhurst Lewis; Nomi Stolzenberg, Ariela Gross, Mary Dudziak, and Hilary Schor; Cynthea Bogel and John Stevenson; Dwight Reynolds and Erika Rappaport; Matilda Arvidsson, Per Nilsén, and Jan Schwartz; and David Shneer, Nan Goodman, Liora Halperin, and Sasha Senderovich (respectively). Versions of chapters 3 and 4 were published in article form in *Past & Present* and the *American Historical Review*, and I warmly thank the editors, copyeditors, and anonymous readers of these journals for the tremendous care and wisdom they applied to my articles. What a pleasure to work with the incomparable University of Chicago Press team yet again—to David Brent, Ellen Kladky, Michael Koplow for their efficiency, vision, professionalism, and kindness: my warmest thanks.

My last and most profound debt, as always, is to my family. Lorrie and Al Levin, incomparable neighbors; Joan Abrevaya, close to the heart even if a bit farther from home; Rebecca Luna Stein, Andrew Janiak, and Saul and Isaac Janiak Stein, truly the greatest partners in crime; my parents, Richard and Carole Stein, in appreciation of their ceaseless support, good humor, and model. The last and most profound words of thanks are always due Fred Zimmerman and Ira and Julius, the finest companions, who have exuberantly joined me in tracing the thread of Jewish history to and through countries too numerous to mention.

ABBREVIATIONS

AHD: Instituto Diplomático, Ministério dos Negócios Estrangeiros, Arquivo-histórico diplomático, Lisboa

AIU: Archives de l'Alliance israélite universelle, Paris

AJA: The Jacob Rader Marcus Center of the American Jewish Archives, Cincinnati

AMAE: Archives du ministère des Affaires étrangères, Paris, La Courneuve

APP: Archives de la Préfecture de police, Paris

ASDMAE: Archivio Storico Diplomatico del Ministero degli Affari Esteri, Rome

BL: British Library, London

CAHJP: Central Archive for the History of the Jewish People, Jerusalem

CZA: Central Zionist Archive, Jerusalem

GMPMA: Greater Manchester Police Museum and Archive, Manchester

ICRC: International Committee of the Red Cross Archives, Geneva

JDC, JERUSALEM: Joint Distribution Committee, Jerusalem

JDC, NEW YORK: Joint Distribution Committee, New York

LMA: London Metropolitan Archives, London

LNA: League of Nations Archives, Geneva

TNA: The National Archives of the United Kingdom, Kew

UWLSC: University of Washington Libraries Special Collections, Seattle

YIVO: YIVO Institute for Jewish Research, New York

NOTES

INTRODUCTION

1. International coverage of these developments has been extensive. See, for example, Ceylan Yeginsu, "Sephardic Jews Feel Bigotry's Sting in Turkey and a Pull Back to Spain," *New York Times*, 26 May 2015; "Portugal to Grant Citizenship to Descendants of Persecuted Jews," *Guardian*, 29 January 2015; Associated Press, "Portugal to Offer Citizenship to Descendants of Persecuted Jews," *Haaretz*, 11 March 2015; "Portugal Plans to Grant Sephardic Jews Citizenship," *Haaretz*, 17 April 2014; "Portugal to Offer Passports to Sephardic Jews," *Jewish Daily Forward*, 16 February 2014; Isabel Kershner and Raphael Minder, "Prospect of Spanish Citizenship Appeals to Descendents of Jews Expelled in 1492," *New York Times*, 13 February 2014. As concerns the recent bill passed by the Spanish Parliament, see "Spain: Citizenship Plan for Sephardic Jews," *New York Times*, 6 June 2014; "Spain Approves Bill Granting Citizenship to Sephardic Jews," *Haaretz*, 6 June 2014; J. D. Arden, " 'The Sephardim Are Coming, the Sephardim Are Coming!,' " *16th Street, The Blog of the Center for Jewish History*, viewed 31 July 2015. By one account in the contemporary Turkish press, fully half of the extant Jewish community of Istanbul has submitted paperwork in pursuit of Spanish citizenship: Erkan Arkut, "5000 Musevi Vatandaşımızın Göç Etmek Istemesi Türkiye İçin Felaket . . . ," *HaberKıta*, 2 March 2015.

2. Among the array of scholarly works on these themes are Jane Caplan and John C. Torpey, eds., *Documenting Individual Identity: The Development of State Practices in the Modern World* (Princeton: Princeton University Press, 2001); Andreas Fahrmeir, *Citizens and Aliens: Foreigners and the Law in Britain and the German States, 1789–1870* (New York: Berghahn Books, 2000); Will Hanley, "Papers for Going, Papers for Staying: Identification and Subject Formation in the Eastern Mediterranean," in *A Global Middle East; Mobility, Materiality, and Culture in the Modern Age, 1880–1940*, ed. Liat Kozma, Avner Wishnitzer, and Cyrus Schayegh (London: I. B. Tauris, 2014); Claude Moatti and Wolfgang Kaiser, eds., *Gens de passage en Méditerranée de l'antiquité à l'époque moderne: procédures de contrôle et d'identification* (Paris: Maisonneuve & Larose, 2007); Gérard Noiriel, ed., *L'identification: Genèse d'un travail d'état* (Paris: Berlin,

2007); Uğur Ümit Üngör, *The Making of Modern Turkey: Nation and State in Eastern Anatolia, 1913–1950* (Oxford: Oxford University Press, 2011); James C. Scott, John Tehranian, and Jeremy Mathias, "The Production of Legal Identities Proper to States: The Case of the Permanent Family Surname," *Comparative Studies in Society and History* 44, no. 1 (2002); John Torpey, *The Invention of the Passport: Surveillance, Citizenship, and the State* (Cambridge: Cambridge University Press, 2000). A splendid bibliography of the existing literature may be found at http://identinet.org.uk/bibliography/.

3. Here I frame "extraterritoriality" not in a strict or static legal sense, but as a phenomenon experienced differently by different groups in different arenas at different moments in time. Explorations of extraterritoriality and the institution of consular protection in the modern period that provide a comparative context include Julia Clancy-Smith, "Women, Gender, and Migration along a Mediterranean Frontier: Pre-Colonial Tunisia, c. 1815–1870," *Gender and History* 17, no. 1 (2005); Clancy-Smith, *Mediterraneans: North Africa and Europe in an Age of Migration, c. 1800–1900* (Berkeley: University of California Press, 2011); Maya Jasanoff, "Cosmopolitan: A Tale of Identity from Ottoman Alexandria," *Common Knowledge* 11, no. 3 (2005); Jessica Marglin, "The Two Lives of Mas'ud Amoyal: Pseudo-Algerians in Morocco, 1830–1912," *International Journal of Middle East Studies* 44, no. 4 (2012); Marglin, "In the Courts of the Nations: Jews, Muslims, and Legal Pluralism in Nineteenth-Century Morocco" (Ph.D. dissertation, Princeton University, 2012); Marglin, "The Extraterritorial Mediterranean," presented at Middle East Studies Conference (Washington, D.C., 2014); Ziad Fahmy, "Jurisdictional Borderlands: Extraterritoriality and 'Legal Chameleons' in Precolonial Alexandria, 1840–1870," *Comparative Studies in Society and History* 55, no. 2 (2013); Will Hanley, "When Did Egyptians Stop Being Ottomans? An Imperial Citizenship Case Study," in *Multilevel Citizenship*, ed. Willem Mass (Philadelphia: University of Pennsylvania Press, 2013); Hanley, "Papers for Going, Papers for Staying"; Hanley, "Foreignness and Localness in Alexandria, 1880–1914" (Ph.D. dissertation, Princeton University, 2007). On the related notion of "territoriality," see Charles S. Maier, "Consigning the Twentieth Century to History: Alternative Narratives for the Modern Era," *American Historical Review* 105, no. 3 (2000).

4. Within this motley group were a number of Jewish theorists of international and capitulatory law, including Henri Bonfils, Norman Bentwich, Nasim Sousa, and Shlomo Yellin.

5. Norman Bentwich, "The End of the Capitulatory System," *British Yearbook of International Law* 89 (1933).

6. A resident of Alexandria who was assigned British registration in 1897, Peradon lost her protégé status in 1898 after it was determined to be "false." When Peradon died, her nationality was considered indeterminate. TNA FO 847/28, File 16, "Re V. Peradon."

7. The "New Christians" of Bayonne were protected by a series of sixteenth-century patent-letters issued by the French king guaranteeing their residency rights. Frances Malino, *The Sephardic Jews of Bordeaux: Assimilation and Emancipation in France* (Tuscaloosa: University of Alabama Press, 2003).

8. As Will Hanley has demonstrated, the range of paperwork issued to those traveling through the Mediterranean was, in itself, tremendous; see Hanley, "Papers for Going, Papers for Staying."

9. United States Department of State, *Capitulations of the Ottoman Empire. Report of Edward A. Van Dyck, Consular Clerk of the United States at Cairo, Upon the Capitulations of the Ottoman Empire since the Year 1150* (Washington, DC: Government Printing Office, 1881), 7–8.

10. Cihan Artunç, "The Price of Legal Institutions: The Protégé System and Beratlı Merchants in the Eighteenth-Century Ottoman Empire," *Journal of Economic History* 75/3 (September 2013).

11. Susan Pedersen, *The Guardians: The League of Nations and the Crisis of Europe* (Oxford: Oxford University Press, 2015), especially part I; Pedersen, "The Meaning of the Mandates System: An Argument," *Geschichte und Gesellschaft* 32, no. 4 (2006); Pedersen, "Back to the League of Nations," *American Historical Review* 112, no. 4 (2007); Ronen Shamir, *The Colonies of Law: Colonialism, Zionism, and Law in Early Mandate Palestine* (Cambridge: Cambridge University Press, 2000). Norman Bentwich also addressed this issue in the period under discussion in, among other sources, Norman Bentwich, "Palestine Nationality and the Mandate," *Journal of Comparative Legislation and International Law* 21, no. 4 (1939); Bentwich, "The Legal System of Palestine under the Mandate," *Middle East Journal* 2, no. 1 (1948). I am also building here on Isabel Hull's ambition to restore international law as a crucial component of the First World War and its contemporary and subsequent interpretation; see Isabel V. Hull, *A Scrap of Paper: Making and Breaking International Law during the Great World War* (Ithaca: Cornell University Press, 2014).

12. On the notion of legal pluralism generally, see Lauren Benton, *Law and Colonial Cultures: Legal Regimes in World History, 1400–1900* (Cambridge: Cambridge University Press, 2002); John Griffiths, "What Is Legal Pluralism," *Journal of Legal Pluralism* 24 (1986); Sally Engle Merry, "Legal Pluralism," *Law and Society Review* 22, no. 5 (1988).

13. The quotation is from Laura Tabili, "Outsiders in the Land of Their Birth: Exogamy, Citizenship, and Identity in War and Peace," *Journal of British History* 44 (2005). Also relevant: Julia Phillips Cohen, *Becoming Ottomans: Sephardi Jews and Imperial Citizenship in the Modern Era* (Oxford: Oxford University Press, 2014); Adrian Favell, *Philosophies of Integration: Immigration and the Idea of Citizenship in France and Britain* (New York: Palgrave, 1988); Nicoletta F. Gullace, *The Blood of Our Sons: Men, Women, and the Renegotiation of British Citizenship during the Great War* (New York: Palgrave Macmillan, 2003); Linda Kerber, *No Constitutional Right to Be Ladies: Women and the Obligations of Citizenship* (New York: Hill and Wang, 1999); Mary Dewhurst Lewis, *The Boundaries of the Republic: Migrant Rights and the Limits of Universalism in France, 1918–1940* (Stanford: Stanford University Press, 2007); Patrick Weil, *How to Be French: Nationality in the Making since 1789*, trans. Catherine Porter (Durham: Duke University Press, 2008).

14. I refer here to the way in which the possession or lack of citizenship (and, by extension, the fact that one lived in a nation-state or empire) has been used diagnostically by some Jewish historians to predict or infer the nature of Jews' political activism, philanthropy, gendered practices, and so on. To cite but a few of the relevant sources, with an emphasis on the broadly schematic: Pierre Birnbaum and Ira Katznelson, *Paths of Emancipation: Jews, States, and Citizenship* (Princeton: Princeton University Press, 1995); Pierre Birnbaum, *Jewish Destinies: Citizenship, State, and Community in Modern France*, trans. Arthur Goldhammer (New York:

Hill and Wang, 1995); Paula Hyman, *Gender and Assimilation in Modern Jewish History* (Seattle: University of Washington Press, 1995); Ezra Mendelsohn, *On Modern Jewish Politics* (Oxford: Oxford University Press, 1993). Rather more nuanced treatments, upon which this study builds, include Michelle Campos, *Ottoman Brothers: Muslims, Christians, and Jews in Early Twentieth-Century Palestine* (Stanford: Stanford University Press, 2010); Cohen, *Becoming Ottomans*; Eric Lohr, *Russian Citizenship: From Empire to Soviet Union* (Cambridge: Harvard University Press, 2012); Joshua Schreier, *Arabs of the Jewish Faith: The Civilizing Mission in Colonial Algeria* (Piscataway: Rutgers University Press, 2010); Sarah Abrevaya Stein, *Saharan Jews and the Fate of French Algeria* (Chicago: University of Chicago Press, 2014).

15. The relevant case studies are too many to reference in full; one thinks of the complex legal subdivisions imposed by France upon colonial subjects, or of European women forced to sacrifice their nationality due to their marriage to foreign-born men, or of the many individuals who lived or traveled at the intersection of regions, states, and empires, sometimes using this liminality to their legal advantage. In addition to work already cited, see Elisa Camiscioli, "Intermarriage, Independent Nationality, and the Individual Rights of French Women: The Law of 10 August 1927," *French Politics, Culture, and Society* 17, no. 3–4 (1999); Kerber, *No Constitutional Right to Be Ladies*; Emmanuelle Saada, *Empire's Children: Race, Filiation, and Citizenship in the French Colonies* (Chicago: University of Chicago Press, 2012); Todd Shepard, *The Invention of Decolonization: The Algerian War and the Remaking of France* (Ithaca: Cornell University Press, 2006), especially chapter 1.

16. Especially Julia Phillips Cohen, "Between Civic and Islamic Ottomanism: Jewish Imperial Citizenship in the Hamidian Era," *International Journal of Middle East Studies* 44 (2012); Cohen, *Becoming Ottomans*; Lois C. Dubin, *The Port Jews of Habsburg Trieste: Absolutist Politics and Enlightenment Culture* (Stanford: Stanford University Press, 1999); Mary Dewhurst Lewis, *Divided Rule: Sovereignty and Empire in French Tunisia, 1881–1938* (Berkeley: University of California Press, 2013), especially chapters 1–3; Benjamin Nathans, *Beyond the Pale: The Jewish Encounter with Late Imperial Russia* (Berkeley: University of California Press, 2002), especially part 1; Aron Rodrigue, "From *Millet* to Minority: Turkish Jewry," in *Paths of Emancipation: Jews, States, and Citizenship*, ed. Pierre Birnbaum and Ira Katznelson (Princeton: Princeton University Press, 1995); Schreier, *Arabs of the Jewish Faith*; Stein, *Saharan Jews and the Fate of French Algeria*.

17. In their legal inbetweenness, extraterritorial Ottoman-born Jews (and their diasporic-born children) are evocative of many other liminal subjects of empire, including translators, missionaries, midwives, and native bureaucrats. In this important respect, their histories complicate our understanding of power relations in the colonial arena. Useful in framing my thinking in this regard were Timothy Burke, *Lifebuoy Men, Lux Women: Commodification, Consumption, and Cleanliness in Modern Zimbabwe* (Durham: Duke University Press, 1996); Linda Colley, "Going Native, Telling Tales: Captivity, Collaborations, and Empire," *Past and Present* 168 (2000); Catherine Hall, *Civilising Subjects: Colony and Metropole in the English Imagination* (Chicago: University of Chicago Press, 2002); Nancy Rose Hunt, *A Colonial Lexicon: Of Birth Ritual, Medicalization, and Mobility in the Congo* (Durham: Duke University Press, 1999); Jasanoff, "Cosmopolitan: A Tale of Identity from Ottoman Alexandria." Evocative, too, is the case of the Lascar seamen who were employees of the East India Company and settled in Britain as early as

the seventeenth century, and whose status became a source of anxiety for the state in the interwar years; see Michael H. Fisher, "Excluding and Including 'Natives of India': Early-Nineteenth-Century British-Indian Race Relations in Britain," *Comparative Studies of South Asia, Africa, and the Middle East* 27, no. 2 (2007); Shompa Lahiri, "Patterns of Resistance: Indian Seamen in Imperial Britain," in *Language, Labour, and Migration*, ed. Anne J. Kershen (Aldershot, UK: Ashgate, 2000); Lahiri, "Contested Relations: The East India Company and Lascars in London," in *The Worlds of the East India Company*, ed. H. V. Bowen, Margarette Lincoln, and Nigel Rigby (Woodbridge: D. S. Brewer, 2002); Norma Myers, "The Black Poor of London: Initiatives of Eastern Seamen in the Eighteenth and Ninteenth Centuries," in *Ethnic Labour and British Imperial Trade: A History of Ethnic Seafarers in the UK*, ed. Diane Frost (London: F. Cass, 1995).

18. The first such treaty was signed by sultan Suleiman I in 1535, with France. Feroz Ahmad, "Ottoman Perceptions of the Capitulations 1800–1914," *Journal of Islamic Studies* 11, no. 1 (2000); J. B. Angell, "The Turkish Capitulations," *American Historical Review* 6, no. 2 (1901); Maurits H. van den Boogert, *The Capitulations and the Ottoman Legal System: Qadis, Consuls, and Beratlis in the 18th Century* (Leiden: Brill, 2005); P. M. Brown, *Foreigners in Turkey: Their Juridical Status* (Princeton: Princeton University Press, 1914); Fatma Müge Göçek, *East Encounters West: France and the Ottoman Empire in the Eighteenth Century* (Oxford: Oxford University Press, 1987), 97–103; Alexander H. de Groot, "The Historical Development of the Capitulatory Regime in the Ottoman Middle East from the Fifteenth to the Nineteenth Century," *Oriente moderno* 23, no. 3 (2003); Halil İnalcık, "Imtíyāzāt—the Ottoman Empire," in *The Encyclopedia of Islam* (Leiden: Brill, 1960–2000); Umut Özsu, "Ottoman Empire," in *The Oxford Handbook of the History of International Law*, ed. Bardo Fassbender et al. (Oxford: Oxford University Press, 2012); Özsu, "The Ottoman Empire, the Origins of Extraterritoriality, and International Legal Theory," in *The Oxford Handbook of the Theory of International Law*, ed. Florian Hoffmann and Anne Oreford (Oxford: Oxford University Press, 2015); Francis Rey, *La protection diplomatique et consulaire dans les échelles du Levant et de Barbarie* (Paris: L. Larose, 1899); Nasim Sousa, *The Capitulatory Regime of Turkey: Its History, Origin and Nature* (Baltimore: Johns Hopkins University Press, 1933).

19. Daniel Goffman, *The Ottoman Empire and Early Modern Europe* (Cambridge: Cambridge University Press, 2002), especially chapter 6.

20. As Maurits H. van den Boogert has explored with exacting detail, the Ottoman authorities succeeded in overseeing, regulating, and constraining the capitulatory regime from the sixteenth to at least the late eighteenth century, notwithstanding the Porte's awareness that representatives of the capitulatory nations were profiting off the sale of grants of privilege and otherwise violating the terms of the capitulations. Van den Boogert notes that the Ottoman grip on the capitulatory regime was sufficiently tight to allow the revocation and numerical reduction of protégés when circumstances so demanded. Van den Boogert, *The Capitulations and the Ottoman Legal System*, 115. Van den Boogert signals an inherited historiographic tendency to inflate the numbers of *beratlı*, particularly relative to Aleppo—where, it has long been claimed, over 1,500 non-Muslims held *berat* certificates in 1793 alone. For a cognate critique of the extant literature, based on archival sources, see Artunç, "The Price of Legal Institutions." For the contested figure, see Charles Issawi, "The Transformation of the Economic Position of Millets in

the Nineteenth Century," in *Christians and Jews in the Ottoman Empire: The Functioning of a Plural Society*, ed. Benjamin Braude and Bernard Lewis (New York: Holmes & Meier Publishers, 1982).

21. The term *Franko* has an elastic definition in Ladino, used in a variety of fashions, both adjectivally and as a noun; the evolution of its meaning over time awaits inquiry. The term *Grana* no doubt had a similarly elastic meaning in the Arabophone context. My thanks to Olga Borovaya for her erudite commentary on this theme.

22. Francesca Trivellato, *The Familiarity of Strangers: The Sephardic Diaspora, Livorno, and Cross-Cultural Trade in the Early Modern Period* (New Haven: Yale University Press, 2009), 103. See also Haim Gerber, *Crossing Borders: Jews and Muslims in Ottoman Law, Economy, and Society* (Istanbul: ISIS, 2008), 185–94; Minna Rozen, "Contest and Rivalry in Mediterranean Maritime Commerce in the First Half of the Eighteenth Century: The Jews of Salonika and the European Presence," *Revue des études juives* 147 (1988).

23. Giacomo Saban has offered evidence that the Franko community of Istanbul appealed for protection to the Italian Embassy in 1862, basing their claim on the fact that they maintained Italian as a language of the home and synagogue, while the nationality of most "brothers" of the community was already Italian. Giacomo Saban, "À propos de la communauté juive italienne de Constantinople," *Revue des études juives* 158, no. 1–2 (1999): 95. See also Saban, "I trattati di pace della primar guerra mondiale, il problema della cittadinanza e le leggi razziali fasciste," *Mondo contemporaneo*, no. 3 (2012). The legal transformations of the Franko population continued under the rule of Benito Mussolini. For the broader context, see Sabina Donati, *A Political History of National Citizenship and Identity in Italy, 1861–1950* (Stanford: Stanford University Press, 2013).

24. The quotation is drawn from AIU Tunisie I. C. 4, letter by D. Cazès to Alliance israélite universelle, Paris, 31 October 1892, cited in Aron Rodrigue, *Jews and Muslims: Images of Sephardi and Eastern Jewries in Modern Times* (Seattle: University of Washington Press, 2003), 156. The particular relationship forged by the Livornese Jewish merchants of North Africa and consular authorities are discussed further in Minna Rozen, "Les Marchands juifs livournais à Tunis et le commerce avec Marseille à la fin du XVIIe siècle," *Michael* 9 (1985); Rozen, "Contest and Rivalry"; Daniel J. Schroeter, *The Sultan's Jew: Morocco and the Sephardi World* (Stanford: Stanford University Press, 2002), 41. On the distinctions drawn between the Franko and Judeo-Spanish community of Istanbul, see Saban, "À propos de la communauté juive italienne de Constantinople." On the Frankos' role as modernizers, see Orly C. Meron, "Sub Ethnicity and Elites: Jewish Italian Professionals and Entrepreneurs in Salonica (1881–1912)," *Zakhor: Rivista di storia degli ebrei d'Italia* 8 (2005); Esther Benbassa and Aron Rodrigue, *Sephardi Jewry: A History of the Judeo-Spanish Community, 14th–20th Centuries* (Berkeley: University of California Press, 2000), 72–82; Aron Rodrigue and Sarah Abrevaya Stein, *A Jewish Voice from Ottoman Salonica: The Ladino Memoir of Sa'adi Besalel a-Levi* (Stanford: Stanford University Press, 2012), xxiii–xxv. Aron Rodrigue's ongoing work on the Jewish community of Rhodes will flesh out our knowledge of this history in crucial ways.

25. This was not the case in every instance. In 1905 and 1907, Shakir Khoury Bey, chief interpreter to the British army in Egypt, appealed to the British Home Office for naturalization.

By this point, the Syrian-born Khoury had served the British for twenty-five years, but he and his family continued to exist, legally speaking, as Ottoman subjects. In Khoury's [possibly calculating] view, this raised the possibility of Turkish retribution, should circumstances arise. TNA HO 144/795/131471, "Nationality and Naturalisation: Khoury, Shakir, from the Ottoman Empire. Resident in Cairo."

26. Eyal Ginio, "Jews and European Subjects in Eighteenth-Century Salonica: The Ottoman Perspective," *Jewish History* 28/3–4 (2014). The same could be said of the Republic of Ragusa (Dubrovnik) and Morocco, whose histories I cannot attempt to do justice to here. On these settings, see Ivana Burdelez, "Jewish Consuls in the Service of the Republic of Dubrovnik," in *Diplomacy of the Republic of Dubrovnik*, ed. Svjetlan Berkovic (Zagreb: Ministry of Foreign Affairs of the Republic of Croatia, Diplomatic Academy, 1998); Marglin, "In the Courts of the Nations"; Daniel J. Schroeter, *The Sultan's Jew: Morocco and the Sephardi World* (Stanford: Stanford University Press, 2002), especially chapter 7. On the dragoman population writ large, see Roderic H. Davison, "The French Dragomanate in Mid-Nineteenth Century Istanbul," in *Istanbul et les langues orientales*, ed. Frédéric Hitzel (Montreal: L'Harmattan Inc., 1997); Alexander H. de Groot, "Dragomans' Careers: The Change of Status in Some Families Connected with the British and Dutch Embasses at Istanbul 1785–1829," in *Friends and Rivals in the East: Studies in Anglo-Dutch Relations in the Levant from the Seventeenth to the Early Nineteenth Century*, ed. Alastair Hamilton, Alexander H. de Groot, and Maurits H. van den Boogert (Leiden: Brill, 2000); E. Natalie Rothman, *Brokering Empire: Trans-Imperial Subjects between Venice and Istanbul* (Ithaca: Cornell University Press, 2011); Rothman, "Intepreting Dragomans: Boundaries and Crossings in the Early Modern Mediterranean," *Comparative Studies in Society and History* 51, no. 4 (2009); Christine Philliou, "Mischief in the Old Regime: Provincial Dragomans and Social Change at the Turn of the 20th Century," *New Perspectives on Turkey* 25 (2001). For more on the Jewish constitution of the consular corps and dragoman population in 1915 Salonica, see Meron, "Sub Ethnicity and Elites," 187n40.

27. The literature on the capitulations and the associated economic relationship between the Ottoman Empire and Europe is extensive, including: Fatma Müge Göçek, *East Encounters West*; Daniel Goffman, *Izmir and the Levantine World, 1550–1650* (Seattle: University of Washington Press, 1990); Goffman, *Britons in the Ottoman Empire, 1642–1660* (Seattle: University of Washington Press, 1998); Goffman, *The Ottoman Empire and Early Modern Europe*; Halil İnalcık and Donald Quataert, eds., *An Economic and Social History of the Ottoman Empire*, 2 vols., vol. 1 (Cambridge: Cambridge University Press, 1997); İnalcık, "Imtíyāzāt—the Ottoman Empire"; van den Boogert, *The Capitulations and the Ottoman Legal System*; Alexander Wood Renton, "The Revolt against the Capitulatory System," *Journal of Comparative Legislation and International Law* 15, no. 4 (1993). On the exceptional case of Egypt, see Nathan J. Brown, "The Precarious Life and Slow Death of the Mixed Courts of Egypt," *International Journal of Middle East Studies* 25, no. 1 (1993).

28. Ottoman efforts to abolish the capitulations took shape in 1856, 1862, 1867, 1871, and 1914—on this topic, the best survey is Sousa, *The Capitulatory Regime of Turkey*. On the distrust of Ottoman protégés by the authorities, see Isaiah Friedman, "The System of Capitulations and Its Effect on Turco-Jewish Relations in Palestine, 1856–1897," in *Palestine in the Late Ottoman*

Period: Political, Social, and Economic Transformations, ed. David Kushner (Jerusalem: Yad Izhak Ben-Zvi; Leiden: Brill, 1986); Ginio, "Jews and European Subjects." Freidman has noted that this distrust focused on cities with a large protégé population, such as those in Palestine, which had boasted a particularly legally pluralistic community of Jews (as well as Christians) since the mid-eighteenth century. As Friedman notes, this demographic fact fueled Ottoman distrust of Jewish immigrants in Palestine well before the Zionist movement took hold.

29. Matthew Elliot, "Dress Codes in the Ottoman Empire: The Case of the Franks," in *Ottoman Customs: From Textile to Identity*, ed. Suraiya Faroqhi and Christoph K. Neumann (Istanbul: Eren, 2004).

30. Roderic Davison, "Ottoman Diplomacy at the Congress of Paris (1856) and the Question of Reforms," in *VII. Türk Tarih Kongresi, Ankara 25–29 Eylül 1970, bildiriler* (Ankara: TTK Basımevi, 1973); Özsu, "Ottoman Empire"; Özsu, "The Ottoman Empire."

31. Benbassa and Rodrigue, *Sephardi Jewry*, 70; Cohen, *Becoming Ottomans*, 8–9; Kemal Karpat, *The Politicization of Islam* (New York: Oxford University Press, 2001), 73–78; Umut Özsu, *Formalizing Displacement: International Law and Population Transfers* (Oxford: Oxford University Press, 2015), 24–27, 31–32; Rodrigue, "From *Millet* to Minority."

32. Among the classic works that explore these themes are Donald Quataert, "The Age of Reforms, 1812–1914," in *An Economic and Social History of the Ottoman Empire*, ed. Halil İnalcık and Donald Quataert (Cambridge: Cambridge University Press, 1994); İnalcık, "Imtíyāzāt—the Ottoman Empire"; Charles Philip Issawi, *The Economic History of Turkey, 1800–1914* (Chicago: University of Chicago Press, 1980); Şevket Pamuk, *The Ottoman Empire and European Capitalism* (Cambridge: University of Cambridge Press, 1987); Reşat Kasaba, *The Ottoman Empire and the World Economy: The Nineteenth Century* (Albany: State University of New York Press, 1988).

33. Palmira Brummett, *Image and Imperialism in the Ottoman Revolutionary Press, 1908–1911* (Albany: Syracuse University Press, 2000), 171–80.

34. Shlomo Yellin, *Les Capitulations et la juridiction consulaire* (Beirut: Selim E. Mann, 1909), 15. My thanks to Michelle Campos for sharing her notes on this difficult-to-locate source. For more on Yellin's extraordinary personal history, see Campos, *Ottoman Brothers*, 1–2.

35. While the torture and killing of Damascene Jews accused of ritual murder became an international cause célèbre, less is known of the blood libel of Rhodes. In the course of this scandal, the European consuls of Rhodes conspired in persecuting the island's Jews (commercial rivals whose undoing would benefit European interests) with the assistance of the pasha of Rhodes. After a harsh blockade was imposed upon the Jewish community of Rhodes and two prominent members of the community (including the rabbi and the Danish dragoman) were tortured violently, word of the events in Rhodes reached the chief rabbi in Istanbul, Haim Moses Fresco. Pointing to the recently promulgated Hatt-ı Şerif of Gülhane, Fresco appealed to the Sublime Porte, which intervened to stop the assault. On the Damascus blood libel, see, among other sources, Jonathan Frankel, *The Damascus Affair: "Ritual Murder," Politics, and the Jews in 1840* (Cambridge: Cambridge University Press, 1997). For two first-hand accounts of the Rhodes blood libel—one translated from Ottoman Turkish by Kürşad Akpınar and prepared for publication by Olga Borovaya, the other translated from German and introduced by Olga Borovaya—see Julia Phillips Cohen and Sarah Abrevaya Stein, eds., *Sephardi Lives: A Documentary History, 1700–1950* (Stanford: Stanford University Press, 2014), 109–15.

36. İrade Mesail-i Mühimme 1007, Başbakanlık Osmanlı Arşivi (Istanbul). An English-language translation of the Ottoman Turkish text by Kürşad Akpınar, which was prepared for publication by Olga Borovaya, appears in Cohen and Stein, *Sephardi Lives*, 115–18.

37. Vangelis Constantinos Kechriotis, "The Greeks of Izmir at the End of the Empire: A Non-Muslim Ottoman Community between Autonomy and Patriotism" (Ph.D. dissertation, University of Leiden, 2005), 60.

38. Kemal H. Karpat, *Ottoman Population, 1830–1914* (Madison: University of Wisconsin Press, 1985), 75; Karpat, "The Ottoman Emigration to America, 1860–1914," *International Journal of Middle East Studies* 17 (1985); Karpat, "Jewish Population Movements in the Ottoman Empire, 1862–1914," in *The Jews of the Ottoman Empire*, ed. Avigdor Levy (Princeton: Darwin Press, Inc., 1994); Selim Deringil, "Some Aspects of Muslim Immigration into the Ottoman Empire in the Late 19th Century," *Al-Abhath* 38 (1990).

39. Timothy Winston Childs, *Italo-Turkish Diplomacy and the War over Libya: 1911–1912* (Leiden: Brill, 1997), 84–85, 120–25; Avram Galante, *Histoire des juifs de Turquie*, 9 vols. (Istanbul: ISIS, 1985–86). Among those expelled was Aaron de Yosef Hazan of Izmir, editor of the Ladino periodical *La Buena Esperansa* and dragoman for the Italian embassy in his city.

40. Campos, *Ottoman Brothers*; Cohen, *Becoming Ottomans*; Cohen, "Between Civic and Islamic Ottomanism."

41. Aviva Ben-Ur, *Sephardic Jews in America: A Diasporic History* (New York: New York University Press, 2009), chapter 1; Devi Mays, "Transplanting Cosmopolitans: The Migrations of Sephardic Jews to Mexico, 1900–1934" (Ph.D. dissertation, Indiana University, 2013); Devin Naar, "From the 'Jerusalem of the Balkans' to the Goldene Medina," *American Jewish History* 93, no. 4 (2007); Yitzchak Kerem, "The Influence of Anti-Semitism on the Jewish Immigration Pattern from Greece to the Ottoman Empire in the Nineteenth Century," in *Decision Making and Change in the Ottoman Empire*, ed. Cesar E. Farah (Kirksville, MO: Thomas Jefferson University Press, 1993); Karpat, "Jewish Population Movements"; Karpat, "The Ottoman Emigration to America, 1860–1914."

42. For a wide-reaching glimpse of the politicization of Sephardi Jewry during this period, see Benbassa and Rodrigue, *Sephardi Jewry*, chapter 4.

43. As Rosanes describes, the cholera outbreak lead to an intrafamilial lawsuit that in turn required the intervention of the Prussian consul, under whose legal aegis the family stood. To avoid adjudication at the hands of the consul—whom Rosanes was certain would side against him—Rosanes sought the intervention of the local Austrian consulate, and, when those efforts failed, attempted to acquire Ottoman nationality. The Prussian consul, outraged, managed to rebuff Rosanes' efforts, but the episode highlighted the essential fungibility of the protégé relationship. Unpublished memoir of Abraham Rosanes, Private Collection of Sivan Toledo. For an English-language excerpt of the memoir, translated by Matt Goldish, see Cohen and Stein, *Sephardi Lives*, 126–32. A comparable example may be identified in the history of Jacob Lasri, a Maghribi Jewish merchant based in Oran who, in the face of the transition from Ottoman to French rule in Algeria, navigated between the French and British consulates, obtaining the protection of each as strategy and timing dictated. Joshua Schreier, "From Mediterranean Merchant to French Civilizer: Jacob Lasry and the Economy of Conquest in Early Colonial Algeria," *International Journal of Middle East Studies* 44, no. 4 (2012).

44. In 1924 the percentage of "aliens" working as licensed prostitutes in Alexandria reached 41. Under what circumstances these women made their way to the sex trade, and whether they came to Alexandria for the purpose of selling their bodies, is unclear from available sources. League of Nations, *Report of the Special Body of Experts on Traffic in Women and Children* (Geneva: Publications of the League of Nations, 1927), 64, table B. Warm thanks to Nefertiti Takla for this pointing me to this source.

45. Behar-Menahem's appeal to the Spanish consulate in Istanbul, dated 24 February 1913, is cited in Pablo Martín Asuero, "The Spanish Consulate in Istanbul and the Protection of the Sephardim (1804–1903)," *Quaderns de la Mediterrània* 8 (2007): 176. On Jews' experience of the Siege of Edirne, see Eyal Ginio, *The Social and Cultural History of Ottoman Society during the Balkan Wars (1912–1913)* (forthcoming), chapter 7; Avigdor Levy, "The Siege of Edirne (1912–1913) as Seen by a Jewish Witness: Social, Political, and Cultural Perspectives," in *Jews, Turks, Ottomans: A Shared History, Fifteenth through the Twentieth Century*, ed. Avigdor Levy (Syracuse: Syracuse University Press, 2002).

46. Such was the case with Abram J. Asseo, a Salonican Jew who acquired Austro-Hungarian citizenship only to lose it, in 1912, after failing to renew his passport. HHStA, Konsulatsarchiv Saloniki, 419.

47. On Jewish expressions of Ottoman patriotism, see Campos, *Ottoman Brothers*; Cohen, *Becoming Ottomans*; Cohen, "Between Civic and Islamic Ottomanism."

48. Karpat, *Ottoman Population, 1830–1914*, statistical appendix I.16.B, 169. These figures are admittedly evasive, as discussed by a number of scholars, including Fuat Dundar, "Empire of Taxonomy: Ethnic and Religious Identities in the Ottoman Surveys and Census," *Middle Eastern Studies* (2015); Stanford Shaw, "The Ottoman Census System and Population, 1831–1914," *International Journal of Middle East Studies* 9 (1978); Servet Mutlu, "Late Ottoman Population and Its Ethnic Distribution," *Turkish Journal of Population Studies* 25 (2003).

49. Kasaba, *The Ottoman Empire and the World Economy*, 72. Some two thousand "little citizens" of Italy made up the Franko community in Istanbul in 1938, when the regime of Benito Mussolini stripped citizenship from those who came to Italy (or lived in lands annexed by Italy) in or after 1919; the application of this law was, however, not carried out in a uniform fashion outside the boundaries of Italy. Saban, "À propos de la communauté juive italienne de Constantinople"; Saban, "I trattati di pace della primar guerra mondiale."

50. Hanley, "Foreignness and Localness in Alexandria," 273–74.

51. At this time, Jerusalem was home to 1,400–1,600 American, 4,000–5,000 Austrian, 500 British, more than 1,000 French, and 770 German subjects, and an unknown number of Russian subjects. Campos, *Ottoman Brothers*, 62, 268n16; Justin McCarthy, *The Population of Palestine: Population History and Statistics of the Late Ottoman Period and the Mandate* (New York: Columbia University Press, 1990), esp. table 1.4d; Friedman, "System of Capitulations."

52. Turan Kayaoğlu, *Legal Imperialism: Sovereignty and Extraterritoriality in Japan, the Ottoman Empire, and China* (Cambridge: Cambridge University Press, 2010), 1.

53. On the elusive nature of Ottoman census data, see Dundar, "Empire of Taxonomy"; Shaw, "The Ottoman Census System and Population, 1831–1914"; Ipek Yosmaoğlu, "Counting Bodies, Shaping Souls: The 1903 Census and National Identity in Ottoman Macedonia," *International Journal of Middle East Studies* 38, no. 1 (2006).

54. On those converts who vexed European and Ottoman authorities, see Selim Deringil, *Conversion and Apostasy in the Late Ottoman Empire* (Cambridge: Cambridge University Press, 2012), see especially chapter 2; Deringil, *The Well-Protected Domains: Ideology and the Legitimization of Power in the Ottoman Empire, 1876–1909* (London: I. B. Tauris, 1998), especially chapter 3.

55. Examples of Algerian Muslims who hedged their legal bets by maintaining French protection while living in Ottoman domains arise elsewhere: Deringil, *The Well-Protected Domains*, 54–55; Friedman, "System of Capitulations," 283.

56. TNA, FO 881/9245, "Corres. National Status and Registration in the Ottoman Dominions of Persons of British Descent," note by H. P. A. to [William Edward] Davidson [Legal Advisor to the Foreign Office], 12 June 1895.

57. Further complicating Houri's case was the fact that his great-grandfather acquired his own protection by claiming to be Maltese—a fact that the Foreign Office questioned. This is not the only instance of state paranoia about the so-called "false Maltese," whether Jewish or non-Jewish, as the number of Maltese protégés skyrocketed across the colonies of Great Britain and France, in North Africa, in particular. See, for example: Lewis, *Divided Rule*, chapter 4; Clancy-Smith, *Mediterraneans*, chapter 2.

58. TNA, FO 881/9245, letter by T. H. Sanderson to Sir P. Currie, 10 August 1895.

59. Ibid.

60. Manchester Jewish Museum Archive, 2010.45.3, "Passport of A. Hamwee." Hamwee's *laissez-passer* allowed him to obtain authorization from the French consulate in Alexandretta to travel to Marseilles in 1876; and was confirmed again by the Ottoman consulate in Manchester in 1882. I speculate that this is the case of Abraham Hamwee (1848/1845–1913), whose personal and familial details are outlined in Lydia Collins, *The Sephardim of Manchester: Pedigrees and Pioneers* (Manchester: Shaare Hayim, the Sephardi Congregation of South Manchester, 2006), 232–35.

61. The Law of Nationality rendered all residents of the empire eligible for Ottoman citizenship, while mandating that a child of an Ottoman father who acquired foreign citizenship would remain Ottoman. This law also clarified how foreigners—including Ottoman-born Christian and Jewish protégés—could become Ottoman citizens. Campos, *Ottoman Brothers*, 62–64; Ibrahim Serbestoğlu, *Osmanlı Kimdir? Osmanlı Devleti'nde tabiiyet sorunu* (Istanbul: Yeditepe Yayınevi, 2014), 65–77. Earlier thwarted attempts to hedge the power of protégés took the form of late eighteenth-century edicts designed to ferret out illegitimate dragomans and protégés, and the creation of an Ottoman-sponsored merchant class—the Avrupa tüccarı. This innovation found initial success in Aleppo, where Jews dominated the novel niche, but failed elsewhere and even in Aleppo quickly flagged. Bruce Masters, "The Sultan's Entrepreneurs: The Avrupa Tuccaris and the Hayriye Tuccaris in Syria," *International Journal of Middle East Studies* 24, no. 4 (1992).

62. Through the nineteenth century and into the early twentieth there were, it is true, ongoing instances of successful Ottoman resistance to foreign governments that claimed legal jurisdiction over Ottoman subjects. When Italian authorities sought to defend their legal sovereignty over the Yeni family of Salonica in the early twentieth century, for example, Ottoman representatives succeeded in staving them off. But in other instances, it was the Ottomans who found

themselves thwarted. Such was the case when Ottoman administrators in Salonica sought, in a symbolically resonant episode, to assert legal sovereignty over the Asseo family in the 1880s. This Sephardi family had roots in Ragusa, but its extended members had inherited Austro-Hungarian protection from Mordechai Asseo, a patriarch who had served as dragoman to the Habsburg consulate in Salonica in the 1830s. When the Ottoman authorities questioned the Asseos' legal right to Austro-Hungarian citizenship, Habsburg representatives commenced an elaborate investigation. What they found is that the Ottoman inquiry had been initiated despite the fact that the Asseos had unfailingly registered with Habsburg authorities, had never been asked to pay the requisite poll tax due non-Muslim Ottoman subjects (the *cizye*), and had never fallen under the jurisdiction of the Ottoman court. The attempt to re-Ottomanize the Asseos, Habsburg representatives argued, was not so much legalistic as opportunistic; the assault on the Asseo family began, they pointed out, shortly after the establishment of the controversial Austro-Hungarian trade council in Salonica, on which no less than thirteen members of the Asseo family sat. This body was controversial insofar as it was a blatant arm of Habsburg interest. Since securing the right, in 1883, to connect Vienna to Salonica by railroad—thereby providing a coveted outlet to the Aegean Sea and the promise of greater economic influence in the Balkans—the Habsburg monarchy was itching to bolster its presence in the Ottoman port city. After marshaling a fantastic paper trail attesting to the Asseos' historic relationship with the Habsburg monarchy, the Austro-Hungarian consulate succeeded in rebuffing Ottoman claims upon the family. HHStA, Vienna, Konsulatsarchiv Saloniki, 419, "Concerning the death of the de-facto Austrian Hungarian Citizen Bohor [Behor] Samuel Asseo, who died in Salonika 21 January 1893"; see especially letter from the Imperial and Royal Austrian Hungarian Embassy in Istanbul to the Imperial and Royal General Consulate in Salonika, 29 August 1887. On the Yeni family, see ASMAE, box 86 folder 1 and box 201 folder 3.

63. Rıfat Bali, *Cumhuriyet yıllarında Türkiye Yahudileri: Bir Türkleştirme Serüveni (1923–1945)* (Istanbul: İletişim, 1999); Benbassa and Rodrigue, *Sephardi Jewry*, 89–105; K. E. Fleming, *Greece: A Jewish History* (Princeton: Princeton University Press, 2008), chapter 5; Mays, "Transplanting Cosmopolitans," 189–90; Rodrigue, "From *Millet* to Minority." As already mentioned, under the rule of Benito Mussolini, Italian citizenship was stripped in 1938 from the so-called little citizens of Italy who came to Italian territory (or who lived in lands that were annexed by Italy) after 1919.

64. Sarah Shields has argued that the Treaty of Lausanne signaled the ascendance of religion as a legal category that served, at times, as a proxy for nationality. Other historians have proposed that this "resort" to religion essentially recast the millet system, thereby proving the impossibility of pinning down the nationality of former Ottoman subjects. Sarah D. Shields, *Fezzes in the River: Identity Politics and European Diplomacy in the Middle East on the Eve of World War II* (Oxford: Oxford University Press, 2011); Renée Hirschon, *Crossing the Aegean: An Appraisal of the 1923 Compulsory Population Exchange between Greece and Turkey* (New York: Berghahn Books, 2003). See also Umut Özsu, "Fabricating Fidelity: Nation-Building and the Greek-Turkish Population Exchange," *Leiden Journal of International Law* 24 (2011).

65. Bali, *Cumhuriyet yıllarında Türkiye Yahudileri*, 77–84.

66. Rogers Brubaker, "Unmixing of Peoples," in *After Empire: Multiethnic Societies and Nation-Building, the Soviet Union and the Russian, Ottoman, and Habsburg Empires*, ed. Karen

Barkey and Mark Von Hagen (Boulder, CO: Westview Press, 1997); Umut Özsu, " 'A Thoroughly Bad and Vicious Solution': Humanitarianism, the World Court, and the Modern Origins of Population Transfer," *London Review of International Law* 1 (2013); Özsu, *Formalizing Displacement*; Özsu, "Fabricating Fidelity."

67. I could find no evidence of a systematic consideration of Ottoman Jews seeking the *heimatlosen* status in the face of the empire's retraction or collapse in either the International Committee of the Red Cross Archives, Geneva, or the League of Nations Archives, Geneva. Further investigation would be required, however, before definitive declarations along these lines could be reached. I will return in greater length to the histories of these Armenian and Russian Jewish refugees in chapter 2, at which point relevant sources shall be cited.

68. The notion of minority protection, developed in the nineteenth century by the Concert of Europe and refined after the Paris Peace Treaty of 1919, failed to offer much legal insulation to formerly Ottoman Jews who took on the citizenship of a successor state—just as it did not safeguard Armenian Christians in 1915, Christians and Muslims subject to population exchanges in 1923, and the innumerable subjects of European imperialism across the Middle East and the globe. On the growth, over the course of the nineteenth and early twentieth centuries, of the notion of legal internationalism that underpinned the national minority treaties, see Mark Mazower, *Governing the World: The History of an Idea, 1815 to the Present* (New York: Penguin Books, 2013). On the fallible legal logic that justified the 1923 population transfers, see Özsu, *Formalizing Displacement*. On the Armenian genocide, see Taner Akçam, *The Young Turks' Crime against Humanity: The Armenian Genocide and Ethnic Cleansing in the Ottoman Empire* (Princeton: Princeton University Press, 2012); Üngör, *The Making of Modern Turkey*, chapter 2; Raymond H. Kévorkian, *The Armenian Genocide: A Complete History* (New York: I. B. Tauris, 2011).

69. TNA, HO 144/11658, "Naturalisation: Souhami, Joseph, from the Ottoman Empire (Spanish Jew)." Souhami, by his own admission a French protégé "from the time of my birth," emigrated to Britain in 1914, was registered by the French consulate in London in March 1923, was granted a French passport by that office a year and a half later, acquired a Nansen passport by the British Home Office in August of the same year, and obtained British naturalization in March 1926. The quotation is drawn from the cited file, and from a sheet of questions entitled "Questions to be answered by an applicant for a certificate of naturalization" dated 2 September 1929. Souhami was naturalized by Great Britain as an "Ottoman (Spanish Jew)," a designation that allowed, in the 1920s and 1930, for the naturalization of at least sixty Ottoman-born Jews of Sephardi descent. On this fascinating legal development, see Aviva Ben-Ur, "Identity Imperative: Ottoman Jews in Wartime and Interwar Britain," *Immigrants & Minorities: Historical Studies in Ethnicity, Migration, and Diaspora* 33, no. 2 (2014).

70. TNA HO 144/7336, "Nationality and Naturalisation: Coenca, Vidal," and HO 334/105/14617, "Naturalisation Certificate: Vidal Coenca." Coenca had journeyed to England with his brother Maurice, who also found himself denied Turkish and Greek nationality once in England. The unique phrasing of Vidal Coenca's appeal, however, was not duplicated in that of his brother. TNA HO 144/7732, "Nationality and Naturalisation: Coenca, Maurice."

71. TNA HO 144/11685, "Nationality and Naturalisation: Sassoon, José Vital."

72. TNA HO 144/11685, "Nationality and Naturalisation: Sassoon, José Vital."

73. My thanks to Devin Naar for this information.

CHAPTER 1

1. AHD 3PA12 M312, "Diversos: Consulta do Consul G. em Paris sobre se deve renovar a inscrição consular de Leon Mitrami, Maurice Yacoel e Edgard Kasari e proceder a inscrição de Mair de Botton e seu filho Alfredo Archer de Botton como cidadãos portugeses," letter by general director of administrative services to the Foreign Minister, 2 November 1935.

2. On Salonica and global commerce, see Benjamin Braude, "The Rise and Fall of Salonica Woolens, 1500–1650: Technology Transfer and Western Competition," *Mediterranean Historical Review* 6, no. 2 (1991); Edhem Eldem, "French Trade and Commercial Policy in the Levant in the Eighteenth Century," *Oriente moderno* 18, no. 79 (1999); Rozen, "Contest and Rivalry"; Simon Schwarzfuchs, "The Salonica 'Scale'—the Struggle between the French and the Jewish Merchants" [in Hebrew], *Sefunot* 15 (1981); Nikos Svoronos, *Le commerce de Salonique au XVIIIe siècle* (Paris: Presses universitaires de France, 1956).

3. The history of Salonican Jewry has commanded growing interest of late. While much literature on this topic will be cited in the pages that follow, here I acknowledge recent scholarship that has been particularly influential to this project: Fleming, *Greece: A Jewish History*; Devin Naar, "Jewish Salonica and the Making of the 'Jerusalem of the Balkans,' 1890–1943" (Ph.D. dissertation, Stanford University, 2011); Aron Rodrigue and Sarah Abrevaya Stein, eds., *A Jewish Voice from Ottoman Salonica: The Ladino Memoir of Sa'adi Besalel a-Levi* (Stanford: Stanford University Press, 2012). (Notably, Naar has traced the shaping of the nomenclature "Jerusalem of the Balkans," framing it as a term with a precise and temporally late history.) Ongoing work by Paris Papamichos Chronakis promises to enrich our understanding of this history yet further. Paris Papamichos Chronakis, "The Jewish, Greek, Muslim and Donme Merchants of Salonica, 1882–1919: Class and Ethnic Transformations in the Course of Hellenization" (in Greek) (Ph.D. dissertation, University of Crete, 2011). Foundational scholarship by Rena Molho, Minna Rozen, and (in an earlier generation) Isaac Emmanuel, Joseph Nehama, and Abraham Recanati will be cited in time. On Jews and protégés in eighteenth-century Salonica, see Ginio, "Jews and European Subjects."

4. On Jewish experiences of the Balkan Wars, see N. M. Gelber, "An Attempt to Internationalize Salonika, 1912–1913," *Jewish Social Studies* 17, no. 2 (1955); Ginio, *The Social and Cultural History of Ottoman Society*; Eyal Ginio, "Mobilizing the Ottoman Nation during the Balkan Wars (1912–1913)—Awakening from the Ottoman Dream," *War in History* 12 (2005); Eyal Ginio, "'Ottoman Jews! Run to Save Our Homeland!'—Ottoman Jews in the Balkan Wars" [in Hebrew], *Pe'amim* 105–6, no. 23 (2005/2006); Mark Levene, "'Ni Grec, ni Bulgare, ni Turc'—Salonika Jewry and the Balkan Wars, 1912–1913," *Simon Dubnow Institute Yearbook* 2 (2003); Rena Molho, "The Jewish Community of Salonika and Its Incorporation into the Greek State, 1912–19," *Middle Eastern Studies* 24, no. 4 (1988); David Recanati, *Zikhron Saloniki: gedulatah ve-hurbanah shel Yerushalayim de-Balkan* (Tel Aviv: Ha-Va'ad le-hotsaat sefer Kehilat Saloniki, 1972). On the war more generally, see Richard C. Hall, *The Balkan Wars 1912–1913: Prelude to the First World War* (London: Routledge, 2000). Special thanks to Eyal Ginio for sharing his work in progress.

5. On the growing appeal of Zionism, see David A. Recanati, "La maccabi-epoca heroica en Salonique," in *Zikhron Saloniki: gedulatah ve-hurbanah shel Yerushalayim de-Balkan, ha-'Orekh* (Tel Aviv: Ha-Va'ad le-Hotsaat Sefer Kehilat Saloniki, 1971); Rena Molho, *Salonica and*

Istanbul: Social, Political, and Cultural Aspects of Jewish Life (Istanbul: ISIS, 2005), 165–201; Esther Benbassa, "Presse d'Istanbul et de Salonique au service du sionisme (1908–1914): les motifs d'une allégeance," *Revue historique* 560 (1986). On the allure of socialism, see Yitzhak Ben-Zvi, "Ha-tnua ha-sotsialistit be-Saloniki," in *Saloniki, 'ir' va-em be-Yisrael* (Tel Aviv: Makhon le-heker Yahadut Saloniki, 1967); Avraam Benaroya, "A Note on the Socialist Federation of Saloniki," *Jewish Social Studies* 11, no. 1 (1949); Paul Dumont, "A Jewish, Socialist, and Ottoman Organization: The Workers' Federation of Salonica," in *Socialism and Nationalism in the Ottoman Empire, 1876–1923*, ed. Mete Tunçay and Erick J. Zürcher (New York: British Academic Press, 1994); Gelber, "An Attempt to Internationalize Salonika"; Joshua Starr, "The Socialist Federation of Saloniki," *Jewish Social Studies* 7 (1945). On support for the internationalization of Salonica, see Gelber, "An Attempt to Internationalize Salonika"; Molho, *Salonica and Istanbul*; Molho, "The Jewish Community of Salonika"; Recanati, *Zikhron Saloniki*, 324–26; Fleming, *Greece: A Jewish History*, 68–72.

6. Naar, "From the 'Jerusalem of the Balkans' to the Goldene Medina," see especially 445. At the same time, Jews from satellite towns (particularly in Ottoman Macedonia) immigrated to Salonica. "The Balkan Wars and the Jews," *American Jewish Yearbook* 15 (1913–14): 192–93.

7. Orly C. Meron, *Jewish Entrepreneurship in Salonica, 1912–1940* (Brighton, UK: Sussex Academic Publishing, 2011), 33–38.

8. Though reliable figures are difficult to come by, Joseph Nehama's estimates appear reasonable: Austro-Hungary registered 80 men on behalf of their families (representing a total of some 1,000 individuals), Spain registered 175 men on behalf of 850 family members, while Portugal registered some 1,200. AIU Fonds Grece IG3, letters by Joseph Nehama to the AIU 28 May 1913 and 8 December 1913.

9. Naar, "Jewish Salonica," 22, and n75.

10. Matilde Rosillo Morcillo, "La communidad sefardita de Salónica: cuestíon del reconocimiento de la nacionalidad española. Desde el final de las guerras balcánicas hasta la segunda guerra mundial," *Sefárdica* 17 (2008); P. Risal, *La ville convoitée, Salonique* (Paris: Perrin et cie, 1918), 255, quoting Nehama.

11. Miriam Bodian, *Hebrews of the Portuguese Nation: Conversos and Community in Early Modern Amsterdam* (Bloomington: Indiana University Press, 1997); *Dying in the Law of Moses: Crypto-Jewish Martyrdom in the Iberian World* (Bloomington: Indiana University Press, 2007); Yosef Yerushalmi, *From Spanish Court to Italian Ghetto: Isaac Cordoso, a Study in Seventeenth-Century Marranism and Jewish Apologetics* (New York: Columbia University Press, 1971); Benjamin R. Gampel, ed., *Crisis and Creativity in the Sephardic World, 1391–1648* (New York: Columbia University Press, 1997), especially contributions by Yosef Kaplan and Thomas Glick.

12. Trivellato, *The Familiarity of Strangers*, 240–41. I exclude here the significant population of New Christians who remained in Portugal or conducted commercial transactions across its territories.

13. Ginio, "Jews and European Subjects."

14. Lewis, *Divided Rule*, see especially chapter 3.

15. Ibid., 3, 42.

16. For an exploration of the legal status of Jews in Tunisia at this time, see ibid., especially chapter 3. See also Matthias Lehmann, "A Livornese "Port Jew' and the Sephardim of the

Ottoman Empire," *Jewish Social Studies* 11, no. 2 (2005); Lionel Lévy, *La nation juive portugaise: Livourne, Amsterdam, Tunis, 1591–1951* (Paris: Harmattan, 1999); Rozen, "Les Marchands juifs livournais."

17. AHD 3PA12M312, "Inspeções in Levante, Inspector Jorge Roza de Oliveira," letter by de Oliveira to the Foreign Minister, 10 January 1937 with appendix, "Inscrições no Consulado de Portugal em Tunis." Of the Morinaud Law, Sfax-based Alliance israélite universelle teacher Vitalis Danon observed that "the law was applied so poorly and in such a narrow spirit that the majority of the applications were rejected, dismissed *sine die*, and now it is in a slow trickle that French nationality is granted to Tunisian Jews—scarcely four or five families a month in all of Tunisia." AIU Tunisie II.C.5, Vitalis Danon to the Alliance israélite universelle, Paris, 18 February 1932. Cited in Rodrigue, *Jews and Muslims*, 225.

18. Ángel Fernández Pulido, *Españoles sin patria y la raza sefardí* (Madrid: Estab. Tip. de E. Teodoro, 1905). Further attention to this story has been given by, among others, Michael Alpert, "Dr. Angel Pulido and Philo-Sephardism in Spain," *Jewish Historical Studies* 40 (2005); Haim Avni, *Spain, the Jews, and Franco* (Philadelphia: Jewish Publication Society of America, 1982); David N. Bunis, "Modernization and the Language Question among Judezmo-Speaking Sephardim of the Ottoman Empire," in *Sephardi and Middle Eastern Jewries: History and Culture in the Modern Era*, ed. Harvey E. Goldbert (Bloomington: Indiana University Press, 1996); Stacy N. Beckwith, ed. *Charting Memory: Recalling Medieval Spain* (New York: Garland Publishing, Inc., 2000); Paloma Díaz-Más, *Sephardim: The Jews from Spain* (Chicago: University of Chicago Press, 1992); Michal Friedman, "Recovering Jewish Spain: Politics, Historiography and Institutionalization of the Jewish Past in Spain (1845–1935)" (Ph.D. dissertation, Columbia University, 2012); Alisa Meyuhas Ginio, "Reencuentro despedida: Dr. Ángel Pulido Fernández y la diáspora sefardí," in *España e Israel. Veinte años después*, ed. Raanan Rein (Sevilla: Fundación Tres Culturas del Mediterráneo, 2007); Ginio, "The Sephardic Diaspora Revisited: Dr. Ángel Pulido Fernández (1852–1932) and His Campaign," in *Identities in an Era of Globalization and Multiculturalism: Latin America and the Jewish World*, ed. Judit Bosker Liwerant et al. (Leiden: Brill, 2008); Joshua Goode, *Impurity of Blood: Defining Race in Spain, 1870–1930* (Baton Rouge: Lousiana State University Press, 2009); Martine Lemoine, "El Doctor Pulido y los 'Españoles sin patria,'" *El Olivo* 9 (1970); José Antonio Lisbona Martín, *Retorno a Sefarad: La política de España hacia sus judíos en el siglo XX* (Barcelona: Riopiedras, 1993); Naar, "Jewish Salonica," 125–26. As these and other scholars have noted, the Spanish romance with Sephardic Jews predated this episode. However, thanks to Pulido's efforts, a philo-Sephardic circle of Spanish intellectuals emerged in the early twentieth century, with the senator at its gravitational center. Other intellectuals important to the movement included the Marquis Isidoro de Hoyos. For an articulate criticism of Pulido's efforts, penned by a Sephari lawyer, journalist, and publisher in Izmir in 1904 and translated by Julia Phillips Cohen, see "Should Sephardi Jews Reconcile with Spain: A Jewish Lawyer from Izmir Reflects," in Cohen and Stein, *Sephardi Lives*, 206–07.

19. Bunis, "Modernization and the Language Question," 229–30. Among the Sephardi intellectuals with whom Pulido maintained a correspondence was Joseph Nehama, whose voice we shall return to throughout the course of this study.

20. For example, Pulido, in tandem with the Iraqi-born Jewish scholar Abraham Shalom Ya-huda and a number of other Spanish intellectuals, pleaded with the French and Italian Foreign Ministries in 1916 to consider Turkish-born Jews within their borders as friendly aliens. AMAE CPC, 1897–1918 [nouvelle série], vol. 968, "Ottomans en France," "Dossier général, 1916, fév–août," petition by Senator Pulido, A. S. Yahuda, et al. to the president du conseil, 29 June 1916. As Haim Avni has pointed out, despite a flurry of short-term interest in Pulido's efforts, ulti-mately the Spanish right proved ascendant. Avni, *Spain, the Jews, and Franco*, 29.

21. AIU Fonds Grece ID 3, appendix to letter by Joseph Nehama to AIU president (Benedict) of 8 December 1913 written by Spanish consul in Salonica and dated 23 November 1912.

22. The talks were written by the Spanish ambassador to Istanbul, the Marquis de Prat de Nantouillet. AIU Fonds Grece ID 3, letter by Joseph Nehama to AIU president (Benedict) of 12 December 1912.

23. "Spain Seeks Return of Sephardic Jews," *New York Times*, 2 February 1913.

24. AIU Fonds Grece XVI E 202, letters by Joseph Nehama to AIU president (Benedict) of 18 December 1912.

25. In December 1913, Joseph Nehama sent to the Alliance israélite universelle office in Paris a copy of a letter written in November 1912 by the Spanish consul in Istanbul to the Greek authorities, in which this policy was articulated. After President Benedict requested of Nehama proof of Spain's advances to the Jews of Salonica, Nehama noted that he could only provide a copy of this single document, as the original—and various other documents attesting to the situation—had been confiscated by the Greek authorities, presumably in the course of 1913. AIU Fonds Grece ID3, appendix to letter by Joseph Nehama to AIU president (Benedict) of 8 De-cember 1913 written by Firma Prat, the Spanish consul in Salonica, and dated 23 November 1912. The number 850 is derived from Nehama's letter. Further confirmation of this history, based upon the archives of the Spanish consulate of Istanbul, is offered in Asuero, "The Spanish Consulate in Istanbul."

26. Asuero, "The Spanish Consulate in Istanbul," 176. The most influential contemporary report on the atrocities of the Balkan Wars, commissioned by the Carnegie Foundation, was published in 1914. The Carnegie Foundation, *International Commission to Enquire into the Causes and Conduct of the Balkan Wars* (Paris: Carnegie Foundation, 1914). Coverage of the vio-lence against Jews also proliferated through the popular press, notably in the *Jewish Chronicle* of London. On the violence of the war and the controversial Carnegie report, see Ginio, *The Social and Cultural History of Ottoman Society*.

27. HHStA, Vienna, Konsulatsarchiv Saloniki, 417, folder 6: Naturalization of Felix Haim Amar. My thanks to Devin Naar for his assistance in helping me to understand the historical nuances of these sources; here I echo one of the central points of his forthcoming book, that the Jewish Community of Salonica continued to assert legal authority over the city's Jews until the Second World War, acting like a state, and in keeping with a longer Ottoman tradition.

28. Manuela Franco, "Uma influencia portuguesa no Levante? A diplomacia ao serviço da propaganda do prestígio da República," *Política Internacional*, no. 26 (2002); Joao Medina and Joel Barromi, "The Jewish Colonization Project in Angola," *Studies in Zionism* 12, no. 1 (1991);

Avraham Milgram, *Portugal, Salazar, and the Jews,* trans. Naftali Greenwood (Jerusalem: Yad Vashem, 2011), 92–96.

29. "Le Portugal et la colonization juive," *Le Jeune-Turc,* 14 July 1912; "Le Portugal et l'Espagne veulent les juifs," *L'Aurore,* 14 July 1912; "Portugal et Turquie," *Le Jeune-Turc,* 16 September 1912.

30. Mesquita also noted, in correspondence with his superiors in Lisbon, that he had no hand in the publication or content of the coverage of this affair in the Ottoman Jewish press. AHD CAIXA 780, "Consulado de Portugal en Constantinople, Serie B," Alfredo de Mesquita to FM, 14 July 1912.

31. AHD CAIXA 780, "Consulado de Portugal en Constantinople, Serie B," Albert Algrante to Portuguese consul in Istanbul [Mesquita], 4 June 1912.

32. AHD CAIXA 780, "Consulado de Portugal en Constantinople, Serie A," Portuguese consul, Istanbul [Mesquita] to FM, 19 November 1912. Mesquita based his appeal to the Foreign Minister on the argument that although the Condois had not lived in Portugal for at least one year (as per the requirements associated with new citizens by Article 20 of the Portuguese Civil Code), Elie Condoi had served Portugal as a "competent and zealous" employee who had "affirmed at every opportunity an intelligent respect for Portuguese interests." On the evolution of Portuguese nationality laws, see Maria Joannis Baganha and Constança Urbano de Sousa, "The Portuguese Nationality Law," in *Acquisition and Loss of Nationality,* ed. Rainer Bauböck et al. (Amsterdam: Amsterdam University Press, 2006).

33. AHD 3PA12 M312, "O Consul G. em Paris pede autorisação para renovar a inscrição e conceder passaporte a Isaac Beja, natural de Salónica," letter by Maurice Yacoel to the Foreign Minister, 31 July 1935. Missir's subsequent reconstructions of the consular events in Salonica in 1912–13 elided his role in initiating the flood of registrations that would follow; no doubt this is because, at the time of his later writing, the practice of registering Levantine Jews had already come under scrutiny by the Foreign Minister's office. AHD 3PA12 M312, "Inspeções em Levante, Inspector Roza de Oliveira," letter by J. D. Missir to Foreign Minister Brederode, 23 April 1923.

34. TNA FO 286/682, "Foreign Office: Consulate and Legation, Greece (formerly Ottoman Empire)," letter by British Consul Wratislav to Consul Granville, 26 February 1919. My warm thanks to Paris Papamichos Chronakis for alerting me to this correspondence.

35. Ibid.

36. AHD 3PA12M100, "Israelitas de origem portuguesa, residents em Salonica que pretendem adquirir a nacionalidade portuguesa," letters by Consul Alfredo Mesquita to the Foreign Minister, 6 February 1913 and 11 March 1913; telegrams by Consul Alfredo Mesquita to the Foreign Minister, 6 February 1913, 18 February 1913, and 25 February 1913, and the three telegrams of 11 March 1913.

37. AHD 3PA12M100, "Israelitas de origem portuguesa, residents em Salonica que pretendem adquirir a nacionalidade portuguesa," letter by Consul Alfredo Mesquita to the Foreign Minister, 6 February 1913.

38. Ibid.

39. Coined by Artur Sandauer, a Polish-Jewish literary scholar, the term *allosemitism* refers to sentiments towards Jews that are neither inherently hostile (as with anti-Semitism) nor

inherently friendly (as with philo-Semitism), but which situate the Jew, obsessively, as an am-
bivalent other. I am indebted to Julia Phillips Cohen for this line of analysis. See also Zygmunt
Bauman, "Allosemitism: Premodern, Modern, Postmodern," in *Modernity, Culture and "the
Jew,"* ed. Bryan Cheyette and Laura Marcus (Stanford: Stanford University Press, 1998).

40. AHD 3PA12M100, "Israelitas de origem portuguesa, residents em Salonica que pretendem adquirir a nacionalidade portuguesa," telegram by the Foreign Minister to Consul Alfredo
Mesquita, 12 March 1913 and follow-up telegram of 15 March 1913. The policy of granting "provisional registration" adhered to Section 27 of Portugal's Consular Code. Milgram, *Portugal,
Salazar, and the Jews*, 232.

41. AHD 3PA12M100, "Israelitas de origem portuguesa, residents em Salonica que pretendem adquirir a nacionalidade portuguesa," letter by the Foreign Minister to Consul Alfredo
Mesquita, 23 April 1913.

42. AHD 3PA12M100, "Israelitas de origem portuguesa, residents em Salonica que pretendem adquirir a nacionalidade portuguesa," telegram by Consul Alfredo Mesquita to the Foreign
Minister, 10 July 1913.

43. The children included Levy de Botton, Isidor de Botton, José de Botton, Saloman/
Salomão de Botton, Sam de Botton, Albert de Botton, Jaques de Botton, Maurice de Botton,
Acher/Alfredo de Botton, Henri de Botton, and at least one sister, Matilde de Botton.

44. Matilde de Botton acquired a passport in Istanbul in 1915, Ascher/Alfredo de Botton
obtained one in Rio de Janeiro in 1929, Isidor and Saloman/Salomão de Botton and their wives
obtained passports in Rome in 1917 and 1918, while S. de Botton acquired two passports, both in
1918—one from the consul in Milan and the other from the consul in Barcelona. José de Botton
obtained Portuguese citizenship for his wife, Rita Misrachi (the denaturalized French citizen)
in Rome in 1918; at the same time Isidoro's wife Olga Hassen obtained Portuguese protection,
along with another of Mair's daughter in-laws, Flora. AHD 2PA57M63, "Emissão de passa-
portes pelos Consulados de Portugal e varios Israelitas de origem portuguesa," Pr. 130/1935,
"Diversos: Consulta do Consul G. em Paris sobre se deve renovar a inscrição consular de Leon
Mitrami, Maurice Yacoel e Edgard Kasari e proceder a inscrição de Mair de Botton e seu filho
Alfredo Archer de Botton como cidadãos portugeses," letter by Mair de Botton to Foreign Ministry, 19 June 1935, and Portuguese consul in Paris to the Foreign Minister, 10 April 1935. According to French law, the wife of S. de Botton, Rita Misrachi, would have been denaturalized upon
her marriage to a foreigner. On this gendered history, see Camiscioli, "Intermarriage, Independent Nationality, and the Individual Rights of French Women'"; Lewis, *The Boundaries of the
Republic*; Catherine Raissiguier, *Reinventing the Republic: Gender, Migration, and Citizenship
in France* (Stanford: Stanford University Press, 2010); Weil, *How to Be French.*

45. The list includes the consuls of Salonica, Istanbul, Milan, Rome, Barcelona, Paris, and
Rio de Janeiro.

46. One member of the de Botton family, Abram Salomon, was appointed guardian (by a
district court in Josefstadt, Austro-Hungary) of five children orphaned by Mordochai Boher
and Anna Asseo—Salonican natives who had taken on Austro-Hungarian citizenship. Yet other
de Bottons would subsequently acquire Spanish and British citizenship. For the Austrian case,
see HHStA, Vienna, Konsulatsarchiv Saloniki, 419, estate documents of Mordochai Asseo. For
the Spanish: Pablo Martín Asuero, *El consulado de España en Estambul y la protección de los*

sefardíes entre 1804 y 1930 (Istanbul: Editorial ISIS, 2011). For the British: TNA HO 144/13505, "Nationality and Naturalisation: Coenca, Joe de Botton." On the longer history of Mediterranean Jews jockeying among the European powers for protection, see Marglin, "The Two Lives of Mas'ud Amoyal"; Schreier, "From Mediterranean Merchant to French Civilizer"; Sarah Abrevaya Stein, "Protected Persons? The Baghdadi Jewish Diaspora, the British State, and the Persistence of Empire," *American Historical Review* 116, no. 1 (2011).

47. AHD 3PA12 M312, "Diversos, Resumo do processo no 170, 1927, acerca da situação dos israelitas de origem portuguesa que pretendem adquirir a nacionalidade portuguesa; Exposição (Contencioso, processo geral sobre nacionalidade)," letter by Consular Inspector Roza de Oliveira to Foreign Minister [Brederode], 5 December 1936; letter by J. D. Missir to Foreign Minister [Brederode], 23 April 1926. See also AHD 3PA12M100, "Israelitas de origem portuguesa, residents em Salonica que pretendem adquirir a nacionalidade portuguesa," letter by Portuguese Consul Mesquita to the Foreign Minister, 3 November 1913.

48. AHD 3PA12M100, "Israelitas de origem portuguesa, residents em Salonica que pretendem adquirir a nacionalidade portuguesa," Letter by Portuguese Consul Mesquita to the Foreign Minister, 15 July 1915. On the legal protection offered Sephardi Jews by the Spanish consulate in Istanbul: Asuero, *El Consulado de España.*

49. Mesquita was picking up here on a thematic thread that weaves through this climactic moment of regional and Jewish history. The competitive waving (or not waving) of flags preoccupied many observers invested in the remapping of Salonica and the Balkans more generally. Joseph Nehama noted that when the Greeks annexed Salonica, Greek residents of the city adorned their homes with the colors of Greece, while Jewish homes remained self-consciously unadorned. Cited in Rodrigue, *Jews and Muslims*, 236–38. At other moments in time, others chose to express other forms of patriotism through the waving of other flags. See, for example, Devin Naar's reading of Leon Sciaky's adoration of the French *tricolore* and Eyal Ginio's discussion of Ottoman patriotism expressed in the form of flag waving: Ginio, "Mobilizing the Ottoman Nation," 164; Naar, "From the 'Jerusalem of the Balkans' to the Goldene Medina," 452. Julia Phillips Cohen has provided a rich and broad contextualization for these phenomena; Cohen, *Becoming Ottomans.*

50. AHD CAIXA 780, "Consulado de Portugal en Constantinople, Serie A," Portuguese consul, Istanbul [Mesquita] to FM, 12 January 1914. For more on Danon, see Julia Phillips Cohen and Sarah Abrevaya Stein, "Sephardi Scholarly Worlds: Towards a Novel Geography of Modern Jewish History," *Jewish Quarterly Review* 100, no. 3 (2010); Dina Danon, "Abraham Danon, la vie d'un *maskil* Ottoman, 1857–1925," in *Itinéraires sépharades*, ed. Esther Benbassa (Paris: Presses de l'Université Paris-Sorbonne, 2010).

51. For local coverage of the event, see "Le Portugal et les Juifs," *L'Aurore*, 12 January 1914; "Le Portugal, l'histoire, l'actualité," *Le Jeune-Turc*, 12 January 1914.

52. Child dependents were obligated to register anew when they came of age. See, for example, AHD 2PA50M40, "Judeus Listas incrições da França (1)," "Relatorio sobre as incrições de Estambul," 31 December 1938, 8. Rachel Benhamias, a widow, was granted protection as a dependent of her son, Paul Salomon, as were numerous other widowed mothers. AHD 2PA50M40, "Judeus Listas incrições da França (1)," "[Undated] Liste des Familles se trouvant inscrites dans les registres matriculaires de ce consulat [Salonica]." Marriage was not the only

cause of joint registration. For reasons that remain a mystery, the Abram brothers, Isaac and Joseph, shared a registration number though they were adults when they acquired Portuguese protection in Salonica.

53. AHD 2PA50M40," Judeus Listas incrições da França (1)," papers of the Benveniste family.

54. AHD 2PA50M40," Judeus Listas incrições da França (1)," registration certificate for Esther Algrante, 10 January 1912.

55. AIU Fonds Grece ID3, letter by Joseph Nehama to the AIU, 28 May 1913.

56. AIU Fonds Grece ID3, letter by Joseph Nehama to the AIU, 8 December 1913.

57. "Exploiters Deceive the Jews of Salonica," *Nea Imera*, 21 April 1913. My warm thanks to Paris Papamichos Chroankis for translating this source for me. Of the various reprints referred to in this chapter, one has been confirmed. *Macedonia* published the same piece on 21 April 1913, 2.

58. The original article erroneously refers to the body responsible for granting Jews Austro-Hungarian citizenship as the "Austrian Chamber of Commerce." In fact, no such institution existed in Salonica.

59. The contemporary Greek city of Thessaloniki was known historically by many names, including Saloniki in vernacular Greek, Hebrew, and German; Selânik in Ottoman and modern Turkish; Salonicco in Italian; Salonique in French; Solun in South Slavic languages; Sărună in Aromanian (Vlach); and variously as Saloniki, Salonika, Saloniko, Salonik, Selanik, Tesaloniki, and Thesaloniki in Ladino. As Devin Naar has noted, the new, Hellenized appellation "Thessaloniki" was so controversial to the city's Jews that many refused to call the city as such until a 1937 Greek law mandated the change. Naar, "From the 'Jerusalem of the Balkans' to the Goldene Medina," 450.

60. Mark Mazower, *Salonica, City of Ghosts: Christians, Muslims, and Jews 1430–1950* (New York: Vintage, 2006), 301–4. See also Maria Vassilikou, "Post-Cosmopolitan Salonika—Jewish Politics in the Interwar Period," *Simon Dubnow Institute Yearbook* 2 (2003).

61. AHD 3PA12M100, "Israelitas de origem portuguesa, residents em Salonica que pretendem adquirir a nacionalidade portuguesa," telegram by Consul Alfredo Mesquita to the Foreign Minister, 10 July 1913; Letters by Alfredo de Mesquita to the Foreign Minister, 25 July 1913 and 25 November 1913. In a letter preserved in the same file, the Foreign Minister denied Mesquita's address to seek an audience in Athens along with his peers: Letter by the Foreign Minister to Portuguese Consul Alfredo de Mesquita, 10 December 1913.

62. AHD 3PA12M100, "Israelitas de origem portuguesa, residents em Salonica que pretendem adquirir a nacionalidade portuguesa," Letter by Haim and Levy Perez to the Foreign Minister, 25 November 1913.

63. Mazower, *Salonica, City of Ghosts*, pp. 305–18.

64. If Consul Arditti's account is to be trusted, the Greek authorities themselves were inconsistent in assessing the reach of consular authority. In his view, the Greek state seemed more inclined to respect the legal authority of the Austro-Hungarian and Spanish consuls than that of Portugal. To Arditti, this was less a reflection of the legal limits of provisional protection than a sign that the Greek state was weighing the relative influence of the embassy or consul involved. AHD PA12M100, "Israelitas de origem portuguesa, residents em Salonica que pretendem

adquirir a nacionalidade portuguesa," letter by Portuguese Consul Arditti to the Foreign Minister, 17 August 1916. See also his subsequent letter of 10 November 1917. On another occasion, Arditti wrote of successfully forestalling the arrest of a number of Portuguese "foreign nationals" who resisted the conscription efforts; in the same file, letter by Portuguese Consul Arditti to the Foreign Minister, 26 June 1917.

65. AHD PA12M100, "Israelitas de origem portuguesa, residents em Salonica que pretendem adquirir a nacionalidade portuguesa," letter by Portuguese Consul Arditti to the Foreign Minister, 26 June 1917.

66. AHD PA12M100, "Israelitas de origem portuguesa, residents em Salonica que pretendem adquirir a nacionalidade portuguesa," letter by self-proclaimed representatives of the Portuguese colony of Salonica to the Portuguese Consul in Salonica, 4 December 1916. See also, in the same file, the letter by the Portuguese Consul in Salonica to the Foreign Minister, 5 December 1916. The delegation was to consist of Jacques Benzonana, a holder of Portuguese papers, and Zacharia Naar, a lawyer and Spanish subject.

67. AHD PA12M100, "Israelitas de origem portuguesa, residents em Salonica que pretendem adquirir a nacionalidade portuguesa," letter by the Foreign Minister to Portuguese Consul in Barcelona, 28 May 1917.

68. AHD PA12M100, "Israelitas de origem portuguesa, residents em Salonica que pretendem adquirir a nacionalidade portuguesa," letter by the Foreign Minister to Portuguese Consul in Berne, 30 June 1917.

69. AHD PA12M100, "Israelitas de origem portuguesa, residents em Salonica que pretendem adquirir a nacionalidade portuguesa," letter by Portuguese Consul d'Oliveira to the Foreign Minister, 25 June 1917.

70. TNA FO 286/682, "Foreign Office: Consulate and Legation, Greece (formerly Ottoman Empire)," letter by British Consul Wratislav to Consul Granville, 26 February 1919.

71. AHD 3PA12M100, "Israelitas de origem portuguesa, residents em Salonica que pretendem adquirir a nacionalidade portuguesa," letter from Armando Tavares, Portuguese Consul in Paris to Foreign Minister, 13 June 1916 and 24 July 1916

72. For an articulation of this policy, see, for example, AMAE CPC, 1897–1918 [nouvelle série], vol. 971, "Ottomans en France," "Dossier général, 1917, aout–1918, janv.," Minister of Foreign Affairs to Minister of Interior, 18 August 1917.

73. AHD 3PA12M100, "Israelitas de origem portuguesa, residents em Salonica que pretendem adquirir a nacionalidade portuguesa," letter from the Foreign Minister to Armando Tavares, Portuguese Consul in Paris, 3 August 1916.

74. AHD 3PA12M100, "Israelitas de origem portuguesa, residents em Salonica que pretendem adquirir a nacionalidade portuguesa," letter from the Foreign Minister to the Portuguese Consul in Lausanne, 13 September 1917.

75. AHD 3PA12M100, "Israelitas de origem portuguesa, residents em Salonica que pretendem adquirir a nacionalidade portuguesa," letter from the Foreign Minister to the Portuguese Consul in Rio de Janeiro, 13 September 1917.

76. AHD 3PA12M100, "Israelitas de origem portuguesa, residents em Salonica que pretendem adquirir a nacionalidade portuguesa," letter by the Foreign Minister to Portuguese Consul in Salonica, 8 May 1918. This point is reiterated in correspondence preserved by the British

Foreign Office: TNA FO 286/682, letter by the Portuguese Foreign Minister to the Portuguese Consul in Salonica, 31 December 1917.

77. AHD 3PA12M100, "Israelitas de origem portuguesa, residents em Salonica que pretendem adquirir a nacionalidade portuguesa," letter by the Foreign Minister to Portuguese Consul in Salonica, 31 December 1917.

78. On the fire of 1917, see Naar, "Jewish Salonica,"106–22; Rena Molho, "Jewish Working-Class Neighborhoods Established in Salonika Following the 1890 and 1917 Fires," in *The Last Ottoman Century and Beyond: The Jews in Turkey and the Balkans, 1808–1945*, ed. Minna Rozen (Tel Aviv: Goldstein-Goren Diaspora Research Center, 2002).

79. Naar, "Jewish Salonica."

80. AHD 3PA12M100, "Israelitas de origem portuguesa, residents em Salonica que pretendem adquirir a nacionalidade portuguesa," Consul Antonio de Portugal de Faria, Visconde de Faria, Lausanne, to the Foreign Minister, 2 August 1917.

81. AHD 3PA12M100, "Israelitas de origem portuguesa, residents em Salonica que pretendem adquirir a nacionalidade portuguesa," letter by the Portuguese Consul in Rio de Janeiro [name unintelligible] to the Foreign Minister, 10 December 1917.

82. AHD 3PA12M100, "Israelitas de origem portuguesa, residents em Salonica que pretendem a nacionalidade portuguesa," see especially letters by the Foreign Minister to Portuguese Consul in Lausanne, 13 September 1917; to Portuguese Consul in Rio de Janeiro, 13 September 1917; to Portuguese Consul in Berne, 30 June 1917; to Portuguese Consul in Salonica, 31 December 1917; to Portuguese Consul in London, 31 December 1917.

83. Filipe Ribeiro de Menses, *Salazar: A Political Biography* (New York: Enigma Books, 2009–10).

84. AHD 3PA12 M312, "Inspeções em Levante, Inspector Roza de Oliveira," letter by Foreign Minister Brederode to Consul Missir, 10 April 1926.

85. AHD 3PA12 M312, "Inspeções em Levante, Inspector Roza de Oliveira," letter by J. D. Missir to Foreign Minister Brederode, 23 April 1926.

86. AHD 3PA12 M312, "Inspeções em Levante, Inspector Roza de Oliveira," letter by Foreign Minister Brederode to Consul Missir, 29 April 1926.

87. Milgram, *Portugal, Salazar, and the Jews*, 235.

88. De Oliveira determined that the Portuguese consul in Casablanca had protected fifty-five subjects, all but five of whom were Jewish; that the consul in Alexandria had protected fifteen Jewish (of a total of seventeen) subjects; and that the consul in Port Said had protected twenty-three individuals, all of whom were Jews.

89. Among these new Portuguese subjects were members of the da Costa and Andrade families, western Sephardic merchants long invested in Goa's diamond trade. AHD 3PA12 M312, "Inspeções em Levante, Inspector Roza de Oliveira," undated (~1936) list of registrations by the Portuguese Consulate in Port Said.

90. AHD 3PA12 M312, "Inspeções em Levante, Inspector Roza de Oliveira," letter by Roza de Oliveira to the Foreign Minister, 15 November 1936.

91. Ibid., and Roza de Oliveira to the Foreign Minister, 5 December 1936.

92. AHD 3PA12 M312, "Inspeções em Levante, Inspector Roza de Oliveira," letter by Roza de Oliveira to the Foreign Minister, 15 November 1936.

93. AHD 3PA12 M312, "Inspeções em Levante, Inspector Roza de Oliveira," report by Roza de Oliveira, "Supressao do consulado de Carreira em Athens," 16 February 1937.

94. AHD 3PA12 M312, "Inspeções em Levante, Inspector Roza de Oliveira," Roza de Oliveira to the Foreign Minister, 5 December 1936.

95. Stein, "Protected Persons?"

CHAPTER 2

1. AMAE CPC, "Turquie, Français en Turquie, Ottomans en France," dossier of Askenazi family.

2. The Jewish population of Greater Syria (which included the territory that would be called Lebanon in 1920), though difficult to pinpoint with precision, was approximately 28,500 at the outbreak of the war. The majority of this population (12,000) lived in Aleppo, 11,000 in Damascus, 5,000 in Beirut, and 500 in Sidon [Saida]. In Palestine, the prewar Jewish population was concentrated in Jerusalem and Jaffa, which had 53,800 and 15,000 Jews (respectively). Additional smaller Jewish communities were clustered around Jaffa, in Acre, and in Haifa. Michael Menachem Laskier, "Syria and Lebanon," in *The Jews of the Middle East and North Africa in Modern Times*, ed. Reeva Spector Simon, Michael Menachem Laskier, and Sara Reguer (New York: Columbia University Press, 2003), 325; Ruth Kark and Joseph B. Glass, "Eretz Israel/Palestine, 1890–1948," in *The Jews of the Middle East and North Africa in Modern Times*, ed. Simon, Laskier, and Reguer, 339. A far lower number of expelled Jews (500) cited by M. Talha Çiçek underestimates the Jewish aspect to this story, perhaps because of Çiçek's failure to recognize many of the foreign nationals as Jews. M. Talha Çiçek, *War and State Formation in Syria: Cemal Pasha's Governorate during World War I, 1914–1917* (New York: Routledge Press, 2014), 84. On the immigration of Jews to Palestine: Selim Deringil, "Jewish Immigration to the Ottoman Empire at the Time of the First Zionist Congresses: A Comment," in *The Last Ottoman Century and Beyond*, ed. Minna Rozen (Ramat Aviv: Tel Aviv University, 2002).

3. According to M. Talha Çiçek, Cemal Paşa obtained "absolute power over both civil and military officials" in Syria. Çiçek, *War and State Formation in Syria*, 2, chapter 2. The figure is from Hassan Kayali, *Arabs and Young Turks: Ottomanism, Arabism, and Islamism in the Ottoman Empire, 1908–1918* (Berkeley: University of California Press, 1997), 193. Among the many firsthand accounts of this period are Glenda Abramson, *Soldiers' Tales: Two Palestinian Jewish Soldiers in the Ottoman Army during the First World War* (London: Vallentine Mitchell, 2013); Abramson, "Haim Nahmias and the Labour Batallions: A Diary of Two Years in the First World War," *Jewish Culture and History* 14, no. 1 (2014); Salim Tamari, *Year of the Locust: A Soldier's Diary and the Erasure of Palestine's Ottoman Past* (Berkeley: University of California Press, 2011). On literary responses to wartime mobilization, see Najwa al-Qattan, "*Safarbarlik*: Ottoman Syria and the Great War," in *From the Syrian Land to the States of Syria and Lebanon*, ed. Thomas Philipp and Christoph Schumann (Beirut: Ergon Verlag Würzburg in Kommission, 2004).

4. Najwa al-Qattan, "When Mothers Ate Their Children: Wartime Memory and the Language of Food in Syria and Lebanon," *International Journal of Middle East Studies* 46, no. 4 (2014); Çiçek, *War and State Formation in Syria*, chapter 7; Donna Robinson Divine, "Palestine

in World War I," in *The Middle East and North Africa: Essays in Honor of J. C. Horowitz*, ed. Reeva Spector Simon (New York: Columbia University Press, 1990); Linda Schatkowski Schilcher, "The Famine of 1915–1918 in Greater Syria," in *Problems of the Modern Middle East in Historical Perspective: Essays in Honour of Albert Hourani*, ed. John P. Spagnolo and Albert Hourani (Reading: Ithaca Press, 1996); Melanie Schulze Tanielian, "Feeding the City: The Beirut Municipality and the Politics of Food during World War I," *International Journal of Middle East Studies* 46, no. 4 (2014); Elizabeth Thompson, *Colonial Citizens: Republican Rights, Paternal Privilege, and Gender in French Syria and Lebanon* (New York: Columbia University Press, 2000), especially chapter 1.

5. On the Ottoman entry into the war, and the authorities' nuanced use of the concept of jihad [*cihad*]: Mustafa Aksakal, "'Holy War Made in Germany'? Ottoman Origins of the 1914 Jihad," *War in History* 18, no. 184 (2011); Aksakal, *The Ottoman Road to War in 1914: The Ottoman Empire and the First World War* (Cambridge: Cambridge University Press, 2008). For a detailed account of the state of the capitulatory regime in the course of the conflict, see Jean-Albert, *Le régime des capitulations en Turquie pendant la guerre de 1914* (Alger: Imprimerie Jean Gaudet, 1923).

6. Especially Peter Gatrell, *A Whole Empire Walking: Refugees in Russia during World War I* (Bloomington: Indiana University Press, 1999); Gatrell, *The Making of the Modern Refugee* (Oxford: Oxford University Press, 2013); Eric Lohr, *Nationalizing the Russian Empire: The Campaign against Enemy Aliens during World War I* (Cambridge: Harvard University Press, 2003); Michael Marrus, *The Unwanted: European Refugees in the Twentieth Century* (New York: Oxford University Press, 1995). Other relevant scholarship will be cited below.

7. The number of victims of the Armenian genocide is disputed, with a range of 1 million to 1.5 million victims in most cases acknowledged. Akçam, *The Young Turks' Crime against Humanity*; Üngör, *The Making of Modern Turkey*, chapter 2; Kévorkian, *The Armenian Genocide*.

8. On the forced migration of Greek citizens from Izmir, see Aksakal, "'Holy War Made in Germany'?," 195. On the population transfers, see Özsu, "A Thoroughly Bad and Vicious Solution"; Özsu, *Formalizing Displacement*; Özsu, "Fabricating Fidelity."

9. These tendencies had long histories, but were especially important to the reign of sultan Abdülhamid II (1876–1909). Deringil, *The Well-Protected Domains*, especially chapter 2; Karpat, *The Politicization of Islam*. For the Jewish response to and involvement in these trends, see Cohen, "Between Civic and Islamic Ottomanism."

10. Cemal Paşa's reign of terror has long assumed a place of prominence for scholars of Arab nationalism, delineating—in James Gelvin's words—"a critical boundary in the history of the evolution of the 'Arab movement.'" Cemal Paşa's horrific rule has loomed particularly large in Middle Eastern historiography as the crucial catalyst to the Arab Revolt of 1916–18 (and, in turn, of 1936–39). James Gelvin, *Divided Loyalties: Nationalism and Mass Politics in Syria at the Close of Empire* (Berkeley: University of California Press, 1998), 76. For a revisionist view that includes a discussion of the more traditional historiography, see Kayali, *Arabs and Young Turks*. On the ways in which Cemal Paşa's reign encouraged a turn towards Ottomanism among Jews and Muslims in Palestine, see Campos, *Ottoman Brothers*; Abigail Jacobson, *From Empire to Empire: Jerusalem between Ottoman and British Rule* (Syracuse: Syracuse University Press, 2011); Jacobson, "Practices of Citizenship and Imperial Loyalty: The Ottomanization

Movement as a Case Study" [in Hebrew], in *Zionism and the Empires* (Jerusalem: Van Leer Academic Institute, forthcoming); Jacobson, "Negotiating Ottomanism in Times of War: Jerusalem during World War I through the Eyes of a Local Muslim Resident," *International Journal of Middle East Studies* 40, no. 1 (2008). On the importance of wartime violence in encouraging a turn to Zionist militancy see, among other sources, Anita Shapira, *Land and Power: The Zionist Resort to Force, 1881–1948* (Stanford: Stanford University Press, 1992), 85–98. The refugee camps in Alexandria, it should be noted, have come to be seen as a nearly mythic nursery of the Zionist movement, bringing together such influential pioneers as Vladimir Jabotinsky and Joseph Trumpeldor. For a purple recounting of the swearing in of young Jewish volunteers at the refugee camp at Gabbari, see John Henry Patterson, *With the Zionists in Gallipoli* (New York: George H. Doran Company), 48–55. Also vivid in this regard is David Yudelowits, "Goley Eretz Israel be-mitsrayim (be-yemei milhemet ha-'olam," *Mi-yamim rishonim* 1, no. 7–12 (1934–35). My warm thanks to Jeffrey Culang for alerting me to this source.

11. These questions build on Isabel Hull's efforts to think about the Great War as an event constructed and interpreted through international law; I bring to this conversation an interest in the legal wartime problems raised by refugees and (to a far lesser extent) genocide, themes that Hull herself neglects. I borrow this question from Michael Marrus; Marrus, *The Unwanted*, 13.

12. United States Department of State, *Papers Relating to the Foreign Relations of the United States, 1914* (Washington, D.C.: U.S. Government Printing Office, 1928), Leland B. Morris to American Ambassador in Turkey [Morgenthau], 8 August 1914.

13. Ibid., Ambassador Morgenthau to the Secretary of State, 13 August and 17 August 1914.

14. See Aksakal, *The Ottoman Road to War in 1914*.

15. For an English translation of the *irade*, see J. C. Hurewitz, ed. *The Middle East and North Africa in World Politics: A Documentary Record* (New Haven: Yale University Press, 1975), 2–4.

16. The legally pluralistic nature of the Jewish (as well as Christian) population in Palestine rendered it a thorn in the side of the Ottoman administration well before the rise of Zionism. Friedman, "System of Capitulations." On the Ottoman critique of the capitulatory regime see, among other sources already cited: Ahmad, "Ottoman Perceptions"; Ginio, "Jews and European Subjects"; "Perceiving French Presence in the Levant: French Subjects in the *Sicil* of 18th Century Ottoman Salonica," *Südost-Forschungen* 65/66 (2006/2007); Goffman, *The Ottoman Empire and Early Modern Europe*; İnalcık, "Imtíyāzāt—the Ottoman Empire."

17. Eduardo Manzano Moreno and Roberto Mazza, eds., *Jerusalem in World War I: The Palestinian Diary of a European Diplomat* (London: I. B. Tauris, 2011), 27.

18. See Abraham Elmaleh, *Eretz Israel ve-Suriya bemilhemet ha-'olam ha-rishona* (Jerusalem: Mizrah u-Ma'arav, 1927–28). See also Abigail Jacobson, "A City Living through Crisis: Jerusalem during World War I," *British Journal of Middle Eastern Studies* 36, no. 1 (2009); Jacobson, "Practices of Citizenship"; Jacobson, *From Empire to Empire*.

19. "Ha-Shavua'," *Ha-Po'el ha-Tsa'ir*, 27 November 1914, 2.

20. The Hebrew press of Jerusalem was for the most part unified in this position. However, when an article vilifying those Jews who refused to relinquish their foreign papers was published under the penname "Mevashen" in *Ha-Herut* in January 1915, it was roundly criticized as "Jewish anti-Semitism." "Ha-Mistolelim be-'amam," *Moria*, 6 January 1915; see also Yaakov Malcov, "Le-Mevashen ashiv," *Moria*, 7 January 1915. Perhaps no more vocal supporter of the

pro-Ottomanist position existed than Eliezer Ben Yehuda, who repeatedly celebrated the mandatory Ottomanization effort in his Hebrew-language journal *Ha-Or/Ha-Tsvi* over the course of 1914 and 1915.

21. A. Kretschmer, "Le-Verur histadrutenu hahukit," *Ha-Po'el ha-Tsa'ir*, 27 November 1914, 7–10. The notion of Ottomanism as a vehicle of Zionism is ably explored in Campos, *Ottoman Brothers*.

22. "Ha-Shavua'," *Ha-Po'el ha-Tsa'ir*, 11 January 1915.

23. United States Department of State, *Papers Relating to the Foreign Relations of the United States, 1914, Supplement, the World War* (Washington, D.C.: Government Printing Co., 1914), letter by American Ambassador Henry Morgenthau to the Secretary of the State, 10 September 1914.

24. Lucius Thayer, "The Capitulations of the Ottoman Empire and the Question of Their Abrogation as It Affects the United States," *American Journal of International Law* 17, no. 209 (1923): 228.

25. Jacobson, "A City Living through Crisis," 78.

26. On the establishment of European consuls in Jerusalem, see Friedman, "The System of Capitulations," 290n14.

27. Kayali, *Arabs and Young Turks*, 193.

28. A number of American dragomans serving in the empire were also arrested, tried, or deported during the war; se Sousa, *The Capitulatory Regime of Turkey*, 197–98.

29. TNA FO 383/100, "Turkey: Prisoners, Including: Deportation of Jews and Relief for Refugees, Including: British and Foreign Jews . . . ," including letter by British vice consulate Palma Maganea to the Foreign Office, 1 August 1915; and Hoffman Phillip [American chargé d'affaires, Istanbul] to Buckler [FO], 3 September 1915.

30. TNA FO 383/88, "Turkey: Prisoners, Including: Treatment of Ottoman Prisoners in the UK and Colonies," "Noureddin Ferouf Bey, member of staff of the late Turkish Embassy, still remaining in the building: enquiries regarding action to be taken in respect of him," including letter by M. L. Walter to Foreign Office, 25 May 1915 and reply of 26 May 1915.

31. Kechriotis demonstrates that there were 52,000 Greek citizens and Ottoman Greeks living in Izmir in 1890; most of these had lived in the city for decades. Kechriotis, "The Greeks of Izmir," 59–60. This process, and the Jewish response to it, is also discussed in Cohen, "Between Civic and Islamic Ottomanism," 244–45; Cohen, *Becoming Ottomans*, 80–86.

32. Aksakal, "'Holy War Made in Germany'?," 195.

33. AMAE CPC, vol. 946, "Protégés français israélites et musulmans, 1915, janv.–déc.," Salomon Padova, Abraham Amado, David Arditti, undated [~June 1915], "Journal de nos suffrances."

34. AIU France IC 5, letter by Jacob Moses Toledano to the Alliance israélite universelle, 11 March 1919.

35. For a discussion class break-down of those French Jews who were taken to a refugee camp in Alexandria and Corsica (respectively), for example, see: AMAE CPC, vol. 947, "Protégés français israélite et musulmans, 1916, janv.–1917, déc.," letter by French Consulate, Alexandria to Foreign Ministry, 14 February 1916, and AIU France IC 5, letter by Jacob Moses Toledano to the Alliance israélite universelle, 11 March 1919.

36. "Cruelties to Jews Deported from Jaffa: Report of Consul Garrels," *New York Times*, 3 June 1917. Mark Levene has suggested that British and American reports on the expulsions intentionally exaggerated their horror in order to show Ottoman brutality. Mark Levene, *War, Jews, and the New Europe: The Diplomacy of Lucien Wolf, 1914–1919* (Oxford: Littman Library of Jewish Civilization, 2009), 85. For the phrase "atrocity propaganda," see Y. Doğan Çetinkaya, "Atrocity Popaganda and the Nationalization of the Masses in the Ottoman Empire during the Balkan Wars (1912–1913)," *International Journal of Middle East Studies* 46, no. 4 (2014).

37. AIU France IC 5, letter by Jacob Moses Toledano to the AIU Central Committee, 11 March 1919.

38. Çiçek, *War and State Formation in Syria*, 83.

39. Ibid., 84. See also Y., "Le-Ragley ha-matsav," *Ha-Po'el ha-Tsa'ir*, 27 November 1914, 3–5.

40. Y., "Le-Ragley ha-matsav," *Ha-Po'el ha-Tsa'ir*, 27 November 1914, 3–5. On the suspected alliance between the clerks of Palestine and Syria and the sultanic leadership of the pre-1908 era, see Campos, *Ottoman Brothers*, 94–95.

41. TNA FO 383/100, "Turkey: Prisoners, Including: Deportation of Jews and Relief for Refugees, Including: British and Foreign Jews . . . ," telegram by U.S. Secretary of State to British FO, cited in memo of 15 December 1915.

42. AMAE CPC, vol. 946, letter by American Consular Agent Charles E. Allen [Edirne] to the French Foreign Ministry, 23 November 1915.

43. AHD 3PA12M312, "Diversos: Consulta do Consul G. em Paris sobre se deve renovar a inscrição consular de Leon Mitrami, Maurice Yacoel e Edgard Kasari e proceder a inscrição de Mair de Botton e seu filho Alfredo Archer de Botton como cidadãos portugeses." Despite the name of this archival file it contains a wealth of material on d'Avilla; see especially letter by Isaac d'Avilla to the Spanish Embassy in Istanbul, 14 January 1918; letter by Isaac d'Avilla to the Portuguese Consul in Jerusalem, 16 May 1935, with appendix from the Portuguese Consul in Alexandria, 11 March 1912.

44. Among them were a hundred foreign nationals, including eighty Jews, who were settled in Izmir. AMAE CPC, vol. 946, letter by Vital Circurel to M. Raphael Arditti, 24 June 1915.

45. Felix Moritz Warburg, *Reports Received by the Joint Distribution Committee of Funds for Jewish War Sufferers*, ed. Joint Distribution Committee (New York, 1916), 141–42.

46. For example, see JDC (NY), 1914–18, Subcollection 3, Record Group 3–5; CZA J27, J28/1–3; AIU France IC5; Yudelowits, "Goley Erets Israel be-mitsrayim," 1, no. 7, December 1934, 183.

47. "Refugies israélites de palestine en Egypt," *L'Univers israélite* 72, no. 1 (1917); Warburg, "Reports Received," 141.

48. For the number 8,000, see Yudelowits, "Goley Erets Israel be-mitsrayim," 2, no. 1, June 1935, 35.

49. AMAE CPC, vol. 946, unsigned telegram to the French Foreign Minister from Alexandria, 4 January 1915.

50. TNA FO 383/100, "Turkey: Prisoners, Including: Deportation of Jews and Relief for Refugees, Including: British and Foreign Jews . . . ," letter to the Foreign Office by Henry McMahon [British high commissioner in Egypt] (Alexandria), 7 August 1915.

51. With the expelled parties journeyed other non-Jewish "enemy aliens," including Italian, British, and French subjects and consular agents, and Jewish subjects of neutral regimes—Greece, Romania, Spain, and the United States—vulnerable to the ravages of war. On the fate of those roughly 750 French Jews from the Syria and Palestine who were settled in a camp in Ajaccio, Crete, see AIU France IC5 and "Israélites de Palestine, refugies en Corse," *L'Univers israélite* 71, no. 24 (1916); "Autour de la guerre: les refugies de Syrie," *L'Univers israélite* 71, no. 20 (1916); "Cruelties to Jews Deported from Jaffa."

52. On the philanthropy that supported refugees in Alexandria, see Refugees Administration Ministry of the Interior, "Charity Reports. Jewish Refugee Camps. 1915 to 1918" (Alexandria, 1918). On those French protégés settled in Corsica, see Florence Berceot, "Une escale dans la tempête. Des Juifs palestiniens en Corse (1915–1920)," *Archives juives* 1, no. 38 (2005).

53. AMAE CPC, vol. 946, unsigned letter to Foreign Ministry, 10 September 1915.

54. AHD 3PA12M312, "Diversos: Consulta do Consul G. em Paris sobre se deve renovar a inscrição consular de Leon Mitrami, Maurice Yacoel e Edgard Kasari e proceder a inscrição de Mair de Botton e seu filho Alfredo Archer de Botton como cidadãos portugeses." Letter by Isaac d'Avilla to the Portuguese Consul in Jerusalem, 16 May 1935, with appendix from the Portuguese Consul in Alexandria, 11 March 1912 [*sic*, though by d'Avilla's own testimony, likely 1915].

55. Letter by Henry Morgenthau, ambassador in Turkey, to the U.S. Secretary of State, 11 May 1915, as cited in United States Department of State, *Papers Relating to the Foreign Relations of the United States, 1914, Supplement, the World War*, 974.

56. Yudelowits, "Goley Erets Israel be-mitsrayim," 1, no. 8, January 1935, 210.

57. Ibid., 269.

58. TNA FO 383/100, "Turkey: Prisoners, Including: Deportation of Jews and Relief for Refugees, Including: British and Foreign Jews . . . ," draft of letter by Under Secretary of State for Foreign Affairs to Leopold de Rothschild, 3 September 1915.

59. On the reciprocal registration of Allied subjects, see TNA FO 383/100, "Turkey: Prisoners, Including: Deportation of Jews and Relief for Refugees, Including: British and Foreign Jews . . . ," telegrams by British Consul in Athens [Elliot] and Henry McMahon to the British Foreign Office, 29 August 1915 and 31 August 1915 (respectively).

60. TNA FO 383/100, "Turkey: Prisoners, Including: Deportation of Jews and Relief for Refugees, Including: British and Foreign Jews . . . ," telegram by Henry McMahon to the British Foreign Office, 31 August 1915.

61. The suspects in question included David Ben Gurion and Yitzhak Ben Zvi. Yudelowits, "Goley Erets Israel be-mitsrayim," 1, no. 9, February 1935, 22.

62. AIU France IC 5, letter by I. Barouch to the AIU president, 9 January 1916.

63. AMAE CPC, "Turquie, Français en Turquie, Ottomans en France," dossier of Amélie Nahon.

64. Yudelowits, "Goley Erets Israel be-mitsrayim," 1, no. 7, December 1935, 183.

65. TNA FO 383/91, "Turkey, Prisoners. . . . ," telegram and letter from Frances Elliot, British consul general, Athens, to the Foreign Office, 3 and 11 September 1915, and letters by British vice consul E. C. Donaldson Rawlins, Canea, to Foreign Office, 1 and 6 September 1915.

66. TNA FO 383/91, "Turkey, Prisoners . . . ," letter from British legation in Athens to Foreign Office, 11 September 1915.

67. TNA FO 383/91, "Turkey, Prisoners . . . ," draft of letter from FO to British consul, Canea, 15 September 1915.

68. TNA FO 383/100, "Turkey: Prisoners, Including: Deportation of Jews and Relief for Refugees, Including: British and Foreign Jews . . . ," letter by Downing Street to FO, 6 November 1914.

69. AMAE CPC, vol. 946, "Note pour le minister, 19 January 1915."

70. For the numerical accounting, see AMAE CPC, vol. 946, Reffye [Alexandria] to the Minister of Foreign Affairs, 3 February 1915. Within the same file, one can find the assurances of the Tunisians regarding the would-be repatriates, and more on the history of the Tunisian refugee population in and of itself: telegram from Tunis to the FM, 31 January 1915.

71. AMAE CPC, "Turquie, Français en Turquie, Ottomans en France," dossiers of Moïse/ Maurice Sidi (these dossiers span two folders within the general collection, including those of "PIT-RIV" and "RIZ-SWA"). Rendering Sidi's journey all the more noteworthy is the fact that, while in transit in Alexandria, he met François Georges-Picot, the French diplomat who had the unfortunate honor of having his named forever linked to the document that divided the Ottoman provinces of the Middle East into British, French, and Russian hands.

72. AMAE CPC, "Turquie, Français en Turquie, Ottomans en France," dossier of Salomon Lévy.

73. AMAE CPC, vol. 946, "Note pour le minister, 19 January 1915"; AMAE, vol. 970, "Ottomans en France," "Dossier général, 1917, mars–juil," Ministry of Foreign Affairs to Ministry of the Interior, 5 July 1917.

74. The "New Christians" of Bayonne were protected by a series of sixteenth-century letters of patent issued by the French king guaranteeing their residency rights. Malino, *The Sephardic Jews of Bordeaux.*

75. AMAE CPC, "Ottomans en France," dossier of David Levy, letter by Minister of Foreign Affairs to the French Consul, Rio de Janeiro, 11 Oct. 1916. I am thankful to Aron Rodrigue for confirming the existence of this trend—evidence of which one can find in various archives and memoiristic accounts.

76. This is evocative of the many inventive ways in which émigré Sephardim in diasporic settings sought to identify themselves in order to obtain legal advantage. Mays, "Transplanting Cosmopolitans," chapter 4.

77. The Foreign Office could marshal an accounting of this population only imprecisely: it estimated that, inclusive of Istanbul and the Dardanelles alone, it was 166 in 1914. TNA FO 383/91, "Turkey, Prisoners . . . ," letter by Under Secretary of State, Foreign Office to Board of Deputies of British Jews, 15 March 1915.

78. TNA FO 881/9245, "Correspondence re National Status and Registration in the Ottoman Dominions of Persons of British Descent 1888–1905," including "Nationality of the Descendants of British Subjects (beyond the Second Generation) Born Abroad," C. B. Robertson to the Foreign Office, 18 June 1902; Consul General Cumberbatch to Marquess of Lansdowne (Foreign Office), 11 August 1902.

79. TNA FO 383/91, "Turkey, Prisoners . . . ," letter by the editor, *Jewish Chronicle,* to the Under Secretary of State for Foreign Affairs, 26 February 1915.

80. Telegram by the French Foreign Ministry to the American Ambassador, 1 August 1915. TNA FO 383/91, "Turkey, Prisoners. . . ." See, for example, Board of Deputies Relief of the Jewish Poor to Under Secretary of State, Foreign Office, 5 March 1915.

81. AMAE CPC, vol. 947, letter by Consulate of France, Alexandria, to the Foreign Minister, 25 March 1916.

82. "Les Algeriennes, Tunisiennes et Marocaines," *Le Jeune-Turc* (1915). See also François Arnoulet, "Les Tunisiens et la première guerre mondiale (1914–1918)," *Revue de l'Occident musulman et de la Méditerranée* 38, no. 38 (1984): 56–57.

83. AMAE CPC, vol. 946, letter by American Ambassador Morgenthau to French Foreign Ministry, 18 February 1915, and to Sublime Porte, 16 April 1915, and replies by Sublime Porte to French Foreign Ministry (via the American Embassy in Istanbul), 25 May 1915 and 5 December 1915; and AMAE CPC, vol. 947, letters by British Embassy, Paris, to French Foreign Minister, 15 January 1916.

84. As Mustafa Aksakal has described, in the course of the war the Ottoman authorities drew upon the notion of jihad—which already had a "quotidian place in the Ottoman cultural register" instrumentally—as a tool of alliance, to include non-Muslims in the Ottoman fold, and to marginalize Muslim and Christian opponents. Aksakal, " 'Holy War Made in Germany'?"

85. AMAE CPC, vol. 947, telegram from Viceroy of India to British "Foreign Department," 24 January 1916.

86. Deringil, *The Well-Protected Domains*; Karpat, *The Politicization of Islam*. For the Jewish response to and involvement in these trends, see Cohen, "Between Civic and Islamic Ottomanism."

87. AMAE CPC, vol. 947, letter by Ambassador Morgenthau to French Foreign Ministry, 4 January 1916.

88. TNA FO 383/100, "Turkey: Prisoners, Including: Deportation of Jews and Relief for Refugees, Including: British and Foreign Jews . . . ," British Vice Consul Francis Elliot [Canea] to the Foreign Office, 23 September 1915. The men in question were Antebi Sebbeday, Nerdehay Ohana, Rahamin Ohana, and Nessmi Setton.

89. Borrowing from Peter Gatrell, we might point to this is an instance in which it is useful to "guard against an understandable tendency to treat refugees entirely as helpless casualties of war"—understanding them instead as individuals who were active in influencing and improving their own fate. Gatrell, *A Whole Empire Walking*, 11–12.

90. AIU France IC5, letter from the Franco-Syrian Jewish Committee [Jacob Moses Toledano, Moïse Abbo, Simon Soussan, Raphaël Dohan], Ajaccio, to the Alliance israélite universelle, 17 September 1918. A similar set of queries was penned to the AIU, in Hebrew, by Jacob Moses Toledano on 13 August 1918.

91. Richard S. Fogarty, "Between Subjects and Citizens: Algerians, Islam, and French National Identity during the Great War," in *Race and Nation: Ethnic Systems in the Modern World*, ed. Paul Spickard (New York: Routledge, 2005); Fogarty, *Race and War in France: Colonial Subjects in the French Army, 1914–1918* (Baltimore: Johns Hopkins University Press, 2008).

92. Berceot, "Une escale dans la tempête. Des Juifs palestiniens en Corse (1915–1920)"; ibid.

93. AIU France IC5, letter by Jacob Moses Toledano to the Alliance israélite universelle, 11 March 1919.

94. AIU France IC5, letter by Aïcha Coublu to the Alliance israélite universelle, 13 July 1920.

95. Ministry of the Interior, "Charity Reports."

96. Ibid., 7.

97. Yudelowits, "Goley Erets Israel be-mitsrayim," 2, no. 1, June 1935, 35.

98. Isaac d'Avilla petitioned the Portuguese Foreign Ministry as late as 1927, but apparently received no recompense. AHD 3PA12M312, "Diversos: Consulta do Consul G. em Paris sobre se deve renovar a inscrição consular de Leon Mitrami, Maurice Yacoel e Edgard Kasari e proceder a inscrição de Mair de Botton e seu filho Alfredo Archer de Botton como cidadãos portugeses," letter by Isaac d'Avilla to the Spanish Consulate in Jerusalem, 30 August 1927.

CHAPTER 3

1. University of Washington Special Collections, Jack Azose papers, 1978, accession no. 2795-001, transcript of tape-recorded interview conducted by F. Roberts in February 1978 [hereafter, UWSC Azose interview], 1–7.

2. On the role of passports, protégé status, and the carrying of papers in the modern Mediterranean context, see Hanley, "Foreignness and Localness in Alexandria"; Hanley, "When Did Egyptians Stop Being Ottomans?"; Hanley, "Papers for Going, Papers for Staying"; Lewis, *Divided Rule*, especially chapter 3; Marglin, "In the Courts of the Nations." For the broader contours of this theme, see Donald N. Baker, "The Surveillance of Subversion in Interwar France," *French Historical Studies* 10, no. 3 (1979); Clifford Rosenberg, *Policing Paris: The Origins of Modern Immigration Control between the Wars* (Ithaca: Cornell University Press, 2006); Torpey, *The Invention of the Passport*.

3. Certificate issued to Fritz Ephraim Reisner by the chief rabbi of Turkey, Istanbul, 27 September 1911, reissued 13 March 1939. The earlier document bears a stamp of the German consulate of Istanbul, the latter a stamp of the French consulate in the same city. Documents courtesy Monique Reisner.

4. Aron Rodrigue and Esther Benbassa, *Sephardi Jewry: A History of the Judeo-Spanish Community, 14th–20th Centuries* (Berkeley: University of California Press), chapter 3, 90.

5. Stein, "Protected Persons?" On the earlier history of French protection of Jews in Salonica, see Ginio, "Jews and European Subjects"; Göçek, *East Encounters West*; Rozen, "Contest and Rivalry"; Schwarzfuchs, "The Salonica 'Scale.'"

6. Rosenberg, *Policing Paris*, chapter 1; Weil, *How to Be French*, chapter 3.

7. One thinks, in a comparative vein, of the idiosyncratic legal nomenclature and privileges granted Algerians living outside of Algeria, residents of the M'zab, in southern Algeria, certain protected subjects of the Tunisian Bey, and residents of Saharan lands claimed by Morocco (among many other groups). Noureddine Amara, "Etre algérien en situation impériale, fin XIX siécle–début XXéme siécle: l'usage de la catégorie 'nationalité algérienne' par les consulats français dans leur relation avec les algériens fixes au Maroc et dans l'empire Ottoman," *European Review of History—Revue européenne d'histoire* 19, no. 1 (2012); Benjamin Claude Brower, *A Desert Named Peace: The Violence of France's Empire in the Algerian Sahara, 1844–1902* (New York:

Columbia University Press, 2009); Lewis, *Divided Rule*; Shepard, *The Invention of Decolonization*; Stein, *Saharan Jews and the Fate of French Algeria*. The colonial logic behind certain of these policies is explored in Patricia M. E. Lorcin, *Imperial Identities: Stereotyping, Prejudice, and Race in Colonial Algeria* (London: I. B. Tauris, 1995).

8. AMAE CPC, Français en Turquie-Ottomans en France, "Ottomans en France," dossier of Youda Leon Nissim.

9. AMAE CPC, 1897–1918 [nouvelle série], vol. 970, "Ottomans en France," "Dossier général, 1917, mars–juil," letter by the Minister of Foreign Affairs to the Minister of Interior, 22 May 1917.

10. A number of sources identify the total number of Ottomans living in France at this time at 12,000. When, in the early years of the war, the prefecture of police in Paris sought to identify on all the Ottoman subjects living in that city in 1914, it assembled 7,000 dossiers. AMAE CPC, vol. 970, letter by the Minister of Foreign Affairs to the Minister of Interior, 22 May 1917. On Ottoman-born Jews' voluntary conscription, see Sylvain Halff, "The Participation of the Jews of France in the Great War," *The American Jewish Yearbook* 21 (1919–20).

11. Maud S. Mandel, *In the Aftermath of Genocide: Armenians and Jews in Twentieth-Century France* (Durham: Duke University Press, 2003), 11.

12. Sam Lévy, "Les Israélites Sefardis en France," *L'Univers israélite*, 26 February 1926. An English translation of this article by Erin Corber appears in Cohen and Stein, *Sephardi Lives*, 359–61.

13. The French laws of 7 April 1915 and 18 June 1917 enabled the denaturalization of naturalized citizens of enemy origin. Weil, *How to Be French*, 60–62, 187. On enemy alien camps in France, see Jean-Claude Farcy, *Les camps de concentration français de la première guerre mondiale (1914–1920)* (Paris: Anthropos-Economica, 1995).

14. For an articulation of this policy, see AMAE CPC, 1897–1918 [nouvelle série], vol. 971, "Ottomans en France," "Dossier général, 1917, août–1918, janv.," Minister of Foreign Affairs to Minister of Interior, 18 August 1917.

15. UWSC Azose interview, 5–6.

16. UWSC Azose interview, 6.

17. This policy was made public on 7 November 1914, when it was published in various journals. AMAE CPC, vol. 970, "Avis concernant les sujets ottomans resident en France, approuvé par le Conseil des Ministres le 7 Novembre 1914 et publié dans la presse." It took a bit longer for the ministry to communicate its new policy to its representatives overseas; see, for example: AMAE CPC, 1897–1918 [nouvelle série], vol. 968, "Ottomans en France," "Dossier général, 1916, fév–août," confidential dispatch by Minister of Foreign Affairs to France's diplomatic agents and consular representatives, 1 March 1916.

18. "Le statut des Juifs orientaux en France," *L'Univers israélite* 23 (1922); "Les Israélites du Levant protégés francais," *Paix et droit*, 1 February 1922.

19. On the history of the AIU and its ties to the Third Republic: Aron Rodrigue, *French Jews, Turkish Jews: The Alliance Israelite Universelle and the Politics of Jewish Schooling in Turkey 1860–1925* (Bloomington: Indiana University Press, 1992), 155–57.

20. On the successful lobbying efforts of the AIU in November of 1914; AIU Série France FR IV 16, "Notice lue devant le groupe des deputes de Paris par M. Alfred Levy, le 28 November

[1914]"; AMAE CPC, vol. 970, letter by Minister of Foreign Affairs to Minister of Interior, 22 May 1917, appendix, "Alliance israélite universelle"; AMAE CPC, 1897–1918 [nouvelle série], vol. 960, "Alliance israélite universelle."

21. AMAE CPC, vol. 970, Minister of Foreign Affairs to Minister of Interior, 22 May 1917.

22. AMAE CPC, vol. 970, Minister of Foreign Affairs to M. Laurent, Police Prefect, 22 May 1917.

23. For an erudite description of the notion of *laïcité* as it has been shaped in France relative to Muslim subjects in the contemporary period, see Joan Wallach Scott, *The Politics of the Veil* (Princeton: Princeton University Press, 2007).

24. Evidence of this surfaces most vividly in the British archives. In 1916, the British consul in Johannesburg wrote his superiors in the British Foreign Office notifying them that fifteen Jewish men (and, one assumes, unidentified numbers of wives and children) from Rhodes living in South Africa were under the protection of the Italian consul in Pretoria. This information was transmitted to London in order to exempt the Jews in question from being deemed "enemy aliens" by Britain. TNA FO 383/88, "Turkey: Prisoners, Including: Treatment of Ottoman Prisoners in the UK and Colonies," letter by Ped. Medici, Italian Consul in Johannesburg, to the Governor-General's Office, Pretoria, 5 January 1915. Associated correspondence in this file documents the transmission of this letter to British Foreign Office. Aron Rodrigue's ongoing work on Rhodes' Jewish community promises to deepen and reframe this complex context.

25. AMAE CPC, vol. 968, Minister of Foreign Affairs to Police Prefect M. Laurent, 24 November 1916.

26. Founded in 1909 in a cafe in the eleventh arrondissement of Paris by Nissim Rozanes [Rosanes], a native of Istanbul who had come to France as a small-scale trader and made a fortune in the gem trade, the Association cultuelle orientale was formed to support the Judeo-Spanish immigrant community of Paris. Due in large part to Rozanes' generosity, it could boast some 2,000 members by the outbreak of the First World War, at which point it also claimed its own address and employed (with the financial assistance of the grand rabbi of Istanbul) an "orator." Rozanes had earlier come under the suspicion of the Minister of Foreign Affairs due to his extended visits to Germany (and to the apparently suspicious fact that the outbreak of the war had plunged him into a three-week-long depression, during which he never left his apartment). Subsequent police surveillance found him trustworthy, however, fit to partner with the Quai d'Orsay in its management of its would-be special protégés. AMAE CPC, vol. 970, letter by Minister of Foreign Affairs to Minister of the Interior, 22 May 1917, appendix, "Association cultuelle orientale en Paris," and vol. 965, "Ottomans en France," "Dossier général, 1914, oct–nov," letter by Minister of Foreign Affairs to the Minister of Interior, 14 November 1914.

27. Lewis, *Divided Rule*, especially chapter 3. For a general discussion of the shaping of French policies towards "Muslims" at this time, see Henry Laurens, "La politique musulmane de la France: caractères généraux," *Monde arab Maghreb Machrek*, no. 152 (1996); Jalila Sbaï, "La République et la Mosquée: genèse et institution(s) de l'islam en France," in *Le choc colonial et l'islam: les politiques religieuses des puissances coloniales en terres d'islam* (Paris: La Découverte, 2006); Shepard, *The Invention of Decolonization*.

28. AIU Série France FR IV 16, "Notice lue devant le groupe des deputes de Paris par M. Alfred Levy, le 28 November [1914]."

29. In 1915, for example, the police identified twelve Ottoman-born Jews as enemy aliens and sent them to an internment camp in Blanzy. This despite the fact that the Jews in question possessed the requisite papers identifying them as "honorable." This group of Jews was shortly freed by order of the Minister of Foreign Affairs. AMAE CPC, "Ottomans en France," dossier of Joseph Levy.

30. Criticism of the government's treatment of Ottoman subjects flared up in the popular press at various points, sparking impassioned responses by the Minister of Foreign Affairs. See, for example, AMAE CPC vol. 970, Minister of Foreign Affairs to Minister of Interior, 5 July 1917.

31. AMAE CPC vol. 970, Minister of Foreign Affairs to Minister of the Interior, 4 January 1918.

32. AIU Série France FR IV D, Secretary of AIU to Minister of Foreign Affairs, 23 July 1916. In Great Britain, the Home Office was struggling with the same concerns of classification: Had Salonican Jews transferred their loyalties to Greece when their city became Greek? Did they carry this fealty with them to émigré settings, regardless of what passport (if any) they held? See, for example, the extensive correspondence on this subject in TNA FO 383/88, "Turkey: Prisoners, Including: Treatment of Ottoman Prisoners in the UK and Colonies" and "Treatment of Salonika Jews," among other files.

33. See n15, above.

34. Naar, "Jewish Salonica," 22.

35. As cited in Edgar Morin, "Vidal and His People," *Journal of Mediterranean Studies* 4, no. 2 (1994).

36. Weil, *How to Be French*, 64, see also chapter 8. In 1927, the Senate and Chamber of Deputies adopted a code that allowed Frenchwomen who had married foreigners to "reintegrate" to their French nationality, and granted them the choice of retaining their nationality upon marriage to a foreigner. Nonetheless, the complexity of such marriages, and the built-in ambiguities associated with the 1927 nationality code, lingered on. Lewis, *The Boundaries of the Republic*, chapter 4; Camiscioli, "Intermarriage, Independent Nationality, and the Individual Rights of French Women."

37. AMAE CPC, "Ottomans en France," dossier of Mathilde Arditi Levy.

38. AMAE CPC, "Ottomans en France," dossier of Albert Nassi.

39. Tabili, "Outsiders in the Land of Their Birth," 807–08. Similar arguments arise in Gullace, *The Blood of Our Sons*. For a comparative context, see Kerber, *No Constitutional Right to Be Ladies*.

40. Algerian men were granted French nationality by the Senatus Consulte of 1865, but were denied French citizenship (and all associated rights) because that they fell under "local civil status law." This signaled that most Algerian Muslims and a portion of southern Algerian Jews were to be regulated by Koranic or Mosaic laws, eligible for citizenship only if they forsook their right to be adjudicated by local civil law or local law courts, which few Muslims or Jews were willing to do. The legal position of the Third Republic was upheld by the 1889 Nationality Code, which consolidated the barrier to legal assimilation. Historians have interpreted these developments variously. Patrick Weil has argued that the principle of *jus soli* regained an important place within French nationality law after 1889, while Todd Shepard has launched an effective

critique, arguing that Weil's interpretation denies the nationality of Algerian Muslims, leaving "in place a normative and coherent conception of French nationality as race-blind and egalitarian . . . while defining the case of Algerian 'Muslims' as an aberration." Shepard, *The Invention of Decolonization*, 33; Weil, *How to Be French*.

41. AMAE CPC, "Ottomans en France," dossier of David Levy, letter by Police Prefect to Minister of Foreign Affairs, 30 June 1917.

42. AMAE CPC vol. 970, Minister of Foreign Affairs to Prefect of Police M. Laurent, 26 March 1917.

43. AMAE CPC, "Ottomans en France," dossiers of Youda Leon Nissim, Moise Nichli, Elia Levy, and Raphael Lévy. This is evocative of the creative ways in which Sephardi émigrés in Mexico inventively described themselves to obtain perceived legal advantage. Mays, "Transplanting Cosmopolitans," 39–41, chapter 4.

44. These claims stood in stark counterpoint to contemporaneous expressions of Ottomanism that had become a regular feature of Sephardic political culture since the late nineteenth century. See Campos, *Ottoman Brothers*; Cohen, *Becoming Ottomans*. Cohen also explores Sephardic Jews' sense of fealty to Spain, which reached a crescendo in this period.

45. UWSC Azose interview, 1.

46. According to the census of 1911, there were estimated to be 3,981 persons "born in Turkey" living in England and Wales. Cited in Ben-Ur, "Identity Imperative." For discussion of the numbers of Ottoman subjects dwelling (and interned) in the United Kingdom more generally: TNA FO 383/88, "Turkey: Prisoners, including: Treatment of Ottoman prisoners in the UK and colonies," especially letter by Home Office to Foreign Office, 8 July 1917. Though there has been extensive exploration of Anglo-Jewish history, the particular history of Britain's Mediterranean and Middle Eastern Jews remains relatively unexplored. In addition to those sources cited elsewhere in this and the subsequent chapter, see especially: ibid.; Stein, "Protected Persons?"

47. Exploration of the treatment and experience of enemy aliens in wartime Britain has been extensive; far less attention has been paid to the experience and treatment of friendly aliens. C. C. Aronsfeld, "Jewish Enemy Aliens in England during the First World War," *Jewish Social Studies* 18, no. 4 (1956): 275–83; J. C. Bird, *Control of Enemy Alien Civilians in Great Britain, 1914–1918* (London: Routledge Revivals, 1986); David Cesarani and Tony Kushner, eds., *The Internment of Aliens in Twentieth Century Britain* (London: F. Cass, 1993); Norman Davies, "The Poles of Great Britain, 1814–1919," *Slavonic and East European Review* 50 (1972); "The Destruction of the German Communities in Britain during the First World War," in *Germans in Britain, 1500 to the Present* (London: 1996); Richard Dove, ed., *"Totally Un-English?": Britain's Internment of "Enemy Aliens" in Two World Wars*, vol. 7, The Yearbook of the Research Centre for German and Austrian Exile Studies (Amsterdam: Editions Rodopi BV, 2005); Fahrmeir, *Citizens and Aliens*; David Gainer, *The Alien Invasion: The Origins of the Aliens Act of 1905* (Oxford: Oxford University Press, 1971); Paniko Panayi, *The Enemy in Our Midst: Germans in Britain during World War One* (New York: St. Martin's Press, 1991).

48. Britain's Foreign Office kept tabs on French policies through its consuls overseas. For example, in March 1915 the British consul in Cairo wrote a series of dispatches to the Foreign

Office detailing "the treatment in the allied countries of Ottoman subjects belonging to a community well known to be opposed to the Turkish regime." TNA FO 383/88, "Turkey: Prisoners, Including: Treatment of Ottoman Prisoners in the UK and Colonies ," letter by Sir E. Grey Bart to the Foreign Office, 8 March 1915.

49. CZA Z4/41236, Z4/40169, Z4/41198, Z4/41083, Z4/41082. To the great consternation of the Zionist Organisation, some seekers of the designation "friendly alien" circumvented that agency altogether, seeking affirmation of their legal status from the Commissioner of Oaths, which had little expertise in the intricacies of Sephardic history or Mediterranean geography. CZA Z4/41083, letter by J. Leon, Zionist Organisation, Manchester, to Harry Sacher, Zionist Organisation, London, 16 July 1918.

50. CZA Z4/40169, letter by Ronald Graham, Foreign Office, to Zionist Organisation, 28 June 1918. Examples of the wartime registration of Ottoman-born Jews living in Manchester have been preserved in the archive of the Police Museum, Manchester, as "Alien Registers."

51. For the original, see Almeric FitzRoy, "Aliens Restriction," *Law Times: The Law and the Lawyer* 138 (1915). Though scant attention has been paid to this measure, some coverage of it— and the Exemption Order it spawned—may be found in Joan George, *Merchants in Exile: The Armenians in Manchester, England, 1835–1935* (London: Taderon Press, 2002), 151.

52. Basil Jeuda, *World War One and the Manchester Sephardim* (Manchester: Shaare Hayim Synagogue, 2014), 64–66.

53. CZA Z4/40169, letter by Rabbi Moses Gaster to Zionist Organisation, 1 August 1918.

54. Jeuda, *World War One and the Manchester Sephardim*, 54.

55. Most of petitions in this vein were penned by Charles Emanuel, solicitor for the board, and Lucien Wolf, member of the board's cojoint committee and one of Anglo-Jewry's most tireless activists. The quotation is drawn from LMA ACC/3121/C/11/12/047, "Board of Deputies of British Jews; Committees: Foreign Appeals Committee Minutes," letter by Charles Emanuel to the Home Office, 20 January 1915.

56. On the theme of Jewish patriotism to empire, see Campos, *Ottoman Brothers*; Cohen, "Between Civil and Islamic Ottomanism"; Cohen, *Becoming Ottomans*; Cohen, "Oriental by Design: Ottoman Jews, Imperial Style, and the Performance of Heritage," *American Historical Review* 119, no. 2 (2015).

57. LMA ACC/3121/C/11/12/047, letter by Lucien Wolf to Home Office, 7 May 1917.

58. No single order in council effected a change in this regard; the earliest reference I have seen to the expansion of wartime protection of Ottoman-born Jews dwelling in the United Kingdom appears in a 3 July 1915 telegraph from the Governor General of the Union of South Africa to the Secretary of State for the Colonies [TNA FO 383/88], "Turkey: Prisoners, Including: Treatment of Ottoman Prisoners in the UK and Colonies," acknowledging a telegram from the latter office that dictated "that all Christian and Jewish subjects of the Turkish Empire have been exempted from internment but otherwise Turkish subjects are to be dealt with in the same manner as German and Austrian civilians." The convolution of the archival trail tells a story in itself, mirroring the legally convoluted treatment of Ottoman-born Jews.

59. TNA FO 383/88 "Turkey: Prisoners, Including: Treatment of Ottoman Prisoners in the UK and Colonies," "Treatment of Salonika Jews," and "Turkey: Prisoners, Including:

Treatment of Ottoman Prisoners in the UK and Colonies"; HO 45/10760/269116, "WAR: Detention of Enemy Aliens as Prisoners of War (1914–1915)."

60. Other methods of demonstrating loyalty were also exercised. Moise Anticoni volunteered for National Service during the war, whether out of patriotism or self-protection. This act subsequently strengthened Anticoni's appeal for British nationality, which he acquired in 1923. TNA HO 144/3289, "Nationality and Naturalisation: Moise Anticoni."

61. See, for example, the range reflected in CZA A4/41082.

62. Manchester Jewish Museum Archive, MANJM: 2005, "Photograph of 1917 Iraq Jewish Merchants Petition," 26 March 1917, 120/9.6. It is striking that one of the four points of the petition was focused on the commercial utility of the Baghdadi Jewish émigré community. It reads, "Your petitioners are informed that according to official returns the exports of Lancashire to Persia and Baghdad amount to between 2 and 3 million pounds and they believe that the bulk of these exports by themselves and the other members of their race and religion who have already become naturalized subjects, or have been born in this country."

63. TNA FO 383/88, "Treatment of Salonika Jews," letter by Lucien Wolf to Lancelot Oliphant, Foreign Office, 19 July 1915.

64. TNA FO 383/88, "Treatment of Salonika Jews," especially Foreign Office to Lucien Wolf, 16 October 1915; TNA HO 144/7336, "Nationality and Naturalisation: Vidal [Vital] Coenca."

65. In addition to the archival sources already cited, see Jeuda, *World War One and the Manchester Sephardim*. The number of Ottoman Jews interned during the war is uncertain; it is estimated that some 10 percent of Ottoman subjects were placed in British enemy alien camps in the course of the war. Eugene C. Black, *The Social Politics of Anglo-Jewry, 1880–1920* (Oxford: Basil Blackwell, 1988), 363.

66. TNA HO 144/3420, "Nationality and Naturalisation: Jacob Ascher Salem." This episode is also cited in Ben-Ur, "Identity Imperative." I am also thankful to Esme Michael for her reflections on the history of Jacques Ascher Salem, her maternal uncle, in a series of emails including, most recently, of 28 March 2015.

67. Among other examples, there is the case of Moses Shasha, TNA HO 144/7206, "Nationality and Naturalisation: Moses Shasha."

68. Jeuda, *World War One and the Manchester Sephardim*, 72–74 and 77–82. This category of interned merchant included the brothers Joseph and Khedouri Shasha, Raphael Habib, Meir Somekh, and Sion Michel.

69. Greater Manchester Police Museum, Manchester, "Register of Aliens," serial nos. 399–807, book 1 box X/1 serial nos. 633–636, c. 7 November 1914 (and with subsequent additions).

70. The order in council was issued on 18 June 1917, and mandated that the earlier order exempting those "shown by satisfaction to be by race a Greek, Armenian, or Syrian, or a member of any other community well known as opposed to the Turkish regime, and to be a Christian" would be amended to read "shown by satisfaction to be a) by race a Greek, Armenian, or Syrian, or a member of any other community well known as opposed to the Turkish regime, and to be a Christian; or b) by race a Jew or an Arab, and to be a native of Baghdad or any other place in Mesopotamia." For further discussion of this order, and the British Board of Jewish Deputies' reaction to it, see Jeuda, *World War One and the Manchester Sephardim*, 90–92.

71. AMAE CPC vol. 968, unsigned letter by Association cultuelle orientale to the Jewish community of New York [City, aka the Kehillah], 4 April 1916.

72. Michel Abitbol, *Les deux terres promises: les juifs de France et le sionisme, 1897–1945* (Paris: Olivier Orban, 1989), 70; Rodrigue, *French Jews, Turkish Jews*, 156.

73. AMAE CPC vol. 970, Minister of Foreign Affairs to Minister of Interior, 5 July 1917.

74. AMAE CPC, "Ottomans en France," dossier of Raphael Lévy, letter by Lévy to the Minister of Foreign Affairs, 13 July 1916.

75. Cohen, *Becoming Ottomans*, chapter 2.

76. Watenpaugh, "The League of Nations' Rescue of Armenian Genocide Survivors and the Making of Modern Humanitarianism," 1320. See also Samuel Moyn, *The Last Utopia: Human Rights in History* (Cambridge, MA: Harvard University Press, 2010).

77. On the shaping of French wartime ambitions in the Middle East, see, among other sources: Christopher M. Andrew and A. S. Kanya-Forstner, *France Overseas: The Great War and the Climax of French Imperial Expansion* (London: Thames and Hudson, 1981); Edward Peter Fitzgerald, "France's Middle Eastern Ambitions, the Sykes-Picot Negotiations, and the Oil Fields of Mosul, 1915–1918," *Journal of Modern History* 66, no. 4 (1884); Jukka Nevakivi, *Britain, France, and the Arab Middle East, 1914–1920* (London: Athlone, 1969); Jan Karl Tanenbaum, *France and the Arab Middle East, 1914–1920* (Philadelphia: American Philosophical Society, 1978).

78. AMAE CPC vol. 970, Minister of Foreign Affairs to Minister of Interior, 5 July 1917.

79. There is evidence that this legal nomenclature may have continued to carry weight outside the boundaries of France: in 1920 and 1921, the French consul in London reaffirmed, Selemia Elnecavé and Dario [David] Albagli as "Israélite[s] du Levant" by nationality. In both cases, the British Home Office appears to have accepted the legal designations without comment. TNA HO 144/10288, "Nationality and Naturalisation: Elnecavé, Selemia"; TNA HO 144/7337, "Nationality and Naturalisation: Albagli, Dario."

80. UWSC Azose interview; "Passport deliveré à un étranger de nationalité Israélite du Levant [Jacques Azouz (Azose)], 1 March 1920." Warm thanks to Hazzan Isaac (Ike) Azose and the Sephardic Studies Digital Library at the University of Washington, Seattle (where it is filed as ST00705), for sharing a copy of the passport with me, and to Maureen Jackson for facilitating an earlier introduction to Hazzan Azose.

81. Captain Alfred Dreyfus, a military officer of Alsatian Jewish descent was famously accused of passing state documents to the German embassy in Paris, convicted in 1894 (upon the suppression by military authorities of evidence of his innocence), and sent to the French penal colony on Devil's Island to serve a life sentence. Dreyfus' arrest stoked the flames of anti-Semitism in France and Algeria—flames that continued to burn even after the captain was exonerated and reinstated into the French military in 1906. On the play *Dreyfus* and its staging in Seattle, see Marc D. Angel, "The Sephardic Theater of Seattle," *American Jewish Archives* 25, no. 2 (1973); Olga Borovaya, *Modern Ladino Culture: Press, Belles Lettres, and Theater in the Late Ottoman Empire* (Bloomington: Indiana University Press, 2012). For the play itself, see Jacques Loria, *Dreyfus* trans. Olga Borovaya, the Sephardi Studies Project, Stanford University, accessed 22 April 2014: http://www.stanford.edu/dept/jewishstudies/programs/sephardi/borovaya_texts.html.

CHAPTER 4

1. "Buddhist Memorial Service for the Late Mr. S. A. Hardoon," *Israel's Messenger*, 1 August 1931; "Death Hardoon," *North China Daily News*, 20 June 1931; Samson Raphael Hirsch, "S. A. Hardoon," *International Jewish News*, 2 July 1931; "Mixed Rituals Mark Funeral," *Los Angeles Times*, 19 July 1931; "China's Richest Foreigner Dies: Controlled Shanghai Broadway," *New York Times*, 20 June 1932; "Effigy of Dead Man Was Host at Three-Day Funeral Banquet," *New York Times*, 23 August 1931; "Silas Aaron Hardoon," *Der Forverts*, 8 June 1932. For a critical reading of the funeral through the lens of Hardoon's "own eclectic life-style," see Chiara Betta, "Silas Aaron Hardoon and Cross-Cultural Adaptation in Shanghai," in *The Jews of China*, ed. Jonathan Goldstein and Frank Joseph Shulman (Armonk, NY: M. E. Sharpe, 1999).

2. Chiara Betta, "Silas Aaron Hardoon (1815–1931): Marginality and Adaptation in Shanghai" (Ph.D. dissertation, University of London, 1997); Betta, "From Orientals to Imagined Britons: Baghdadi Jews in Shanghai," *Modern Asian Studies* 37, no. 4 (2003); Ruth Fredman Cernea, *Almost Englishmen: Baghdadi Jews in British Burma* (Lanham: Lexington Books, 2006); Stanley Jackson, *The Sassoons* (London: Heinemann, 1968); Maisie J. Meyer, *From the Rivers of Babylon to the Whangpoo: A Century of Sephardi Jewish Life in Shanghai* (Lanham, MD: University Press of America, 2003); Ezekiel N. Musleah, *On the Banks of the Ganga: The Sojourn of Jews in Calcutta* (North Quincy, MA: Christopher Pub. House, 1975); Caroline Plüss, "Sephardic Jews in Hong Kong: Constructing Communal Identities," *Sino-Judaica: Occasional Papers of the Sino-Judaic Institute* 4 (2003); Marcia R. Ristaino, "Reflections on the Sephardi Trade Diaspora in South, Southeast, and East Asia," *Sino-Judaica: Occasional Papers of the Sino-Judaic Institute* 4 (2003); Joan G. Roland, *The Jewish Communities of India: Identity in a Colonial Era* (New Brunswick, NJ: Transaction, 1998); Jael Sillman, "Crossing Borders, Maintaining Boundaries: The Life and Times of Farha, a Woman of the Baghdadi Jewish Diaspora," *Journal of Indo-Judaic Studies*, no. 1 (1998); Thomas A. Timberg, "Baghdadi Jews in Indian Port Cities," in *Jews in India*, ed. Thomas Timberg (New Delhi: Vikas, 1986).

3. Founded by the Baghdadi-born David Sassoon in the 1830s, this family firm came to have a monopoly on the lucrative trade of legal opium between Britain and China and maintained outposts selling this and other goods across South, Southeast, and East Asia, including Bombay, Calcutta, Shanghai, Canton, Hong Kong, Yokohama, Nagasaki, Rangoon, and Singapore. Many of the young Jewish men who emigrated to these regions from Ottoman Mesopotamia in the nineteenth and the early twentieth centuries did so to staff the firm's commercial tributaries. Although dated, the best sources on the history of the Sassoon family remain Jackson, *The Sassoons*; Cecil Roth, *The Sassoon Dynasty* (London: R. Hale Limited, 1941). Future scrutiny of the as yet uncatalogued papers of the Sassoon family, recently donated to the Jewish National and University Library in Jerusalem and currently being curated by Professor Yaron Ben-Naeh, promises to yield fascinating insights on this towering institution of the Indian Ocean, British Empire, and Jewish world.

4. TNA FO 917/3107.

5. On the longer history of extraterritoriality in Shanghai, see Eileen P. Scully, *Bargaining with the State from Afar: American Citizenship in Treaty Port China, 1844–1942* (New York: Columbia University Press, 2000).

6. These questions build on the scholarship of Julia Clancy-Smith and Mary Dewhurst Lewis, especially Clancy-Smith, "Women, Gender, and Migration"; *Mediterraneans*; Lewis, "Geographies of Power: The Tunisian Civic Order, Jurisdictional Politics, and Imperial Rivalry in the Mediterranean, 1881–1935," *Journal of Modern History* 80 (2008); Lewis, *Divided Rule*. Also relevant is the work of Will Hanley, including Hanley, "Foreignness and Localness in Alexandria"; Hanley, "When Did Egyptians Stop Being Ottomans?"

7. Priya Satia, "Developing Iraq: Britain, India and the Redemption of Empire and Technology in the First World War," *Past & Present* 197 (2007): 255.

8. For one manifestation of this trend, see the petition by Iraqi Jews seeking British citizenship that was submitted to the Foreign Office in the wake of the First World War: Norman Stillman, *The Jews in Arab Lands in Modern Times* (Philadelphia: Jewish Publication Society, 1991), 256–59.

9. Among the works on Shanghai that have informed this study are Nara Dillon and Jean Chun Oi, *At the Crossroads of Empires: Middlemen, Social Networks, and State-Building in Republican Shanghai* (Stanford: Stanford University Press, 2008); Jos Gamble, *Shanghai in Transition: Changing Perspectives and Social Contours of a Chinese Metropolis* (London: RoutledgeCurzon, 2003); Bryna Goodman, *Native Place, City, and Nation: Regional Networks and Identities in Shanghai, 1853–1937* (Berkeley: University of California Press, 1995); Ristaino, "Reflections on the Sephardi Trade Diaspora"; Wen-Hsin Yeh, *Shanghai Splendor: Economic Sentiments and the Making of Modern China, 1843–1949* (Berkeley: University of California Press, 2007); Meng Yue, *Shanghai and the Edges of Empire* (Minneapolis: University of Minnesota Press, 2006); Robert Bickers, *Britain in China: Community, Culture and Colonialism, 1900–1949* (Manchester: Manchester University Press, 1999); Marie-Claire Bergère, *Shanghai: China's Gateway to Modernity* (Stanford: Stanford University Press, 2009). The most crucial sources on the history of the Baghdadi Jewish community of Shanghai, and on Silas Aaron Hardoon in particular, are by Maisie Meyer and Chiara Betta, to whose superb work I am greatly indebted.

10. For further meditation on the rather more contemporary self-representation of the Baghdadi Jewish diaspora, see Lital Levy, "Self and the City: Literary Representations of Jewish Baghdad," *Prooftexts* 26, no. 16 (2006); Levy, "Historicizing the Concept of Arab Jews in the Mashriq," *Jewish Quarterly Review* 98, no. 4 (Fall 2008); Nancy E. Berg, *Exile from Exile: Israeli Writers from Iraq* (New York: SUNY Press, 1996).

11. This hints at how very deep the excavation of Jews' relationship to colonialism can take us, for here we see an instance in which a diasporic community that geographically spanned multiple modern empires saw a certain reason, even glamour, in adopting a moniker spawned by the expansion of European power into the medieval Mediterranean—in reaction, no less, to an encounter with a second modern Jewish diaspora transitioning from one imperial terrain to another. On the encounter between Baghdadi and Ashkenazi Jews in Shanghai, and the shifting terminology employed by the latter community, see Maisie Meyer, "The Sephardi Jewish Community of Shanghai and the Question of Identity," in *From Kaifeng—to Shanghai: Jews in China*, ed. Roman Malek (Nettetal: Steyler, 2000); Meyer, *From the Rivers of Babylon to the Whangpoo*.

12. Useful as a transitional marker in this regard is the Sassoon family. David Sassoon is reputed to have commanded a fair knowledge of Hebrew, Arabic, Persian, Turkish, and

Hindustani as well as Judeo-Arabic, but his sons—who maintained the family business after his death in 1864—and their families appear to have transitioned to English around the time of their father's death. As mentioned above, the Sassoon family papers hold the key to the linguistic habits of this diasporic unit, and to so much else about this population that is as yet not precisely known.

13. Meyer, *From the Rivers of Babylon to the Whangpoo*, especially chapter 12. A similar argument is evinced in Cernea, *Almost Englishmen*. More can be gleaned about the nuances of the court system in place in Shanghai at this time, and the advantages that Baghdadi Jews and other émigré populations garnered from the manifold legal systems in place in the city, from Robert T. Bryant, "Territoriality and the Mixed Court in China," *Virginia Law Review* 13, no. 1 (1926); Manley O. Hudson, "Rendition of the International Mixed Court at Shanghai," *American Journal of International Law* 21, no. 3 (1927); Wester W. Willoughby, *Foreign Rights and Interests in China* (Baltimore: Johns Hopkins Press, 1920). For comparative purposes, Brown, "The Precarious Life and Slow Death of the Mixed Courts of Egypt," has been useful.

14. Meyer, *From the Rivers of Babylon to the Whangpoo*, 21; Betta, "From Orientals to Imagined Britons."

15. Reference to this practice was cited often in the correspondence between the Consul General, Shanghai, and the Foreign Office. See, for example, TNA FO 372/5, Consul General Pelham Warren, Shanghai, to Secretary of State for the Colonies Henry George Grey, 2 June 1906.

16. The most oft-cited authorities of the period included Norman Bentwich and his mentor John Westlake, whose 1905 book was viewed as the definitive work on this theme. According to Westlake, British protection, as distinct from British subjecthood, did not tie a person who resided in "an Eastern country" to Britain's "civil society" or to the personal laws that hold sway there. In his view, then, the protected British subject forever retained the personal law that had applied to him before he obtained protection—i.e., the personal law of his country of birth. Norman Bentwich, *The Mandates System* (London: Longman, 1930); John Westlake, *A Treatise on Private International Law, with Particular Reference to Its Practice in England* (London: Sweet & Maxwell, 1905). Also frequently invoked is William Edward Hall, *A Treatise on the Foreign Powers and Jurisdiction of the British Crown* (Oxford: Clarendon, 1894). On the evolution of these laws, and the positivist legal tradition of which Westlake was a part, see Antony Anghie, "Finding the Peripheries: Sovereignty and Colonialism in Nineteenth-Century International Law," *Harvard International Law Journal* 40 (1999); Randell Hansen, *Citizenship and Immigration in Post-War Britain: The Institutional Origins of a Multicultural Nation* (Oxford: Oxford University Press, 2000). Relevant to this study, in particular, is Norman Bentwich, "The Recognition of Jewish Law in Private International Jurisprudence," *Journal of the Society of Comparative Legislation* 304 (1914). On the shaping of the mandate system, see Pedersen, *The Guardians*.

17. This practice seems to have been exercised with particular frequency in port cities such as Tripoli, Alexandria, Cairo, Aleppo, Smyrna, and Istanbul, which were dense with merchants who could enjoy the protection of Ottoman capitulations and whose business was, from the perspective of the Foreign Office, "the mainstay of British commerce in the East." The quotation is drawn from TNA FO 881/9245, "Correspondence Relative to the National Status

and Registration in the Ottoman Dominions of Persons of British Descent, 1888–1905," including letters by T. H. S., June 17, 1895, 4; and Sir N. O'Connor (Istanbul) to the Marquess of Lansdowne, 12 January 1903, 19–22.

18. Baghdadi Jews in India were not uniformly successful in these endeavors; rather, there, as in China, the likelihood that any given request for naturalization would be approved depended on the luck of timing and a certain chemistry between the desires of state representatives and the applicant's credentials. Roland, *The Jewish Communities of India.*

19. TNA FO 671/464, undated and unsigned notes of the Foreign Office (likely from February 1930). For more on the Ezra family, see Betta, "From Orientals to Imagined Britons," 1005.

20. TNA FO 372/5, handwritten memo by F. A. Campbell [senior officer in Far Eastern Affairs in the Foreign Office], 1906.

21. Despatch 3 Treaty, 4 October 1906. On anti-alienism and the 1905 decree, see David Feldman, "The Importance of Being English: Jewish Immigration and the Decay of Liberal England," in *Metropolis London: Histories and Representations since 1800,* ed. David Feldman and Gareth Stedman Jones (London: Routledge Press, 1989); Feldman, *Englishmen and Jews: Social Relations and Political Culture, 1840–1914* (New Haven: Yale University Press, 1994); Gainer, *The Alien Invasion*; John Garrard, *The English and Immigration, 1880–1910* (London: Oxford University Press, 1971); Laura Tabili, *"We Ask for British Justice": Workers and Racial Difference in Late Imperial Britain* (Ithaca: Cornell University Press, 1994); Tabili, "Outsiders in the Land of Their Birth"; Tabili, *Global Migrants, Local Culture: Natives and Newcomers in Provincial England, 1841–1939* (New York: Palgrave Macmillan, 2011). The scandal that rocked the American consuls led to the creation of the U.S. District Court for China, an institution without precedent in American history. I have found no archival evidence that the British consuls were reined in in response to this event, but the coincidence of timing is striking. See Scully, *Bargaining with the State from Afar,* 6.

22. TNA FO 372/99, Consul General Pelham Warren, Shanghai, to Sir Edward Grey Bart, 18 March 1908.

23. This is reminiscent of the bureaucratization of naturalization applications within Britain itself. As Laura Tabili has described, in the early years of the century investigations of would-be Britons by the Home Office had become exhaustive, and "membership in the British nation became negotiated among the national state, the individual seeking British nationality, local native-born Britons, and the police representing the local government." Tabili, "Outsiders in the Land of Their Birth," 800.

24. Anxiety spread, too, among those who had roots in other regional entrepôts. Such was the case with Solomon Haig Sassoon, who wrote the Foreign Office in search of registration papers in 1931. Sassoon's family migrated in the late nineteenth century from Baghdad to India to Singapore to Java, whence Sassoon's own appeals emanated. TNA CO 273/571/8.

25. TNA FO 671/464. While it is true that the British Foreign Office denied many men's applications for naturalization papers, it is striking, though not surprising, that few instances of leniency toward women (including women of means) surface in the archival record. To offer but a few examples among many: Flora Kate Hayim and her mother-in-law, the widow Hannah Hayim; Agnes Nissim; and the Solomon siblings (including Flora, Rachel, Juliet, and Jacob) all sought to use their protected person status to acquire naturalization papers in the 1920s. All

had their requests denied; TNA FO 671/465. On the other hand, Sophie Hardoon, the sister of Silas Aaron Hardoon, succeeded in the same venture in the same decade; TNA FO 671/462.

26. TNA FO 372/5, memo [possibly by F. A. Campbell], 1906.

27. TNA FO 372/5, D. Silman Somekh to British Consul General, Shanghai, 29 January 1906.

28. TNA FO 372/5, Secretary of State for Foreign Affairs to Consul General, Shanghai, 2 June 1906.

29. TNA FO 372/423, Simon Abraham Levy to British Consulate General, Shanghai, 1 May 1907.

30. TNA FO 671/465, Nissim Jeremiah to British Consul General, Shanghai, 22 November 1923. On related issues of identity as it pertained to the British settlement community in Shanghai, see Robert Bickers, "Shanghailanders: The Formation and Identity of the British Settler Community in Shanghai 1843–1937," *Past and Present*, no. 159 (1998).

31. BL, Asia, Pacific, and Africa Collections, IOR/L/PS/11/154/3819/1919, President of the Jewish Law Committee et al. to Edwin S. Montagu, Secretary of State for India (London office), 28 May 1919. This was not the first petition this group advanced; a year earlier, they had outlined their concerns and requests to the civil commissioner in Baghdad. It is in this earlier missive that they voiced distrust of the creation of an Arabic-speaking Sunni leadership in Iraq. This epistolary request was followed by a delegation's visit to the high commissioner, Sir Percy Cox. Nissim Rejwan, *The Jews of Iraq: 3,000 Years of History and Culture* (New York: Westwide Press, 1985), 211–12. Whether these letter writers knew that Montagu was Jewish and whether this knowledge, if it existed, influenced their decision to approach this official is unclear. Their request was denied.

32. On the complex legal status of residents of mandate Palestine, see Assaf Likhovski, *Law and Identity in Mandate Palestine* (Chapel Hill: University of North Carolina Press, 2006); Shira Robinson, *Citizen Strangers: Palestinians and the Birth of Israel's Liberal Settler State* (Stanford: Stanford University Press, 2013); Shamir, *The Colonies of Law*. Norman Bentwich also addressed this issue in the period under discussion in, among other sources, Bentwich, "Palestine Nationality and the Mandate"; Bentwich, "The Legal System of Palestine under the Mandate."

33. On the latter decision, see TNA FO 228/3213, coded telegram of 29 January 1918. On the former, see TNA FO 671/464, unsigned and undated note, possibly by J. F. Brenan, Consul General, Shanghai, from roughly 12 February 1930. The British state's treatment of Baghdadi Jews in China reverberated, in this instance, with its history of colonial rule in India, where, as Elizabeth Kolsky has demonstrated, state-generated respect for "the rule of law" bumped up against local exigencies, in particular the resistance of the local nonofficial European population. Elizabeth Kolsky, "Codification and the Rule of Colonial Difference: Criminal Procedure in British India," *Law and History Review* 23, no. 3 (2005).

34. This treaty aimed to resolve various unclarities that emerged with the adoption of the (Lausanne) Treaty of Peace–enabled Laws of Nationality, which attempted to resolve the nationality of inhabitants of territories detached from Turkey. Norman Bentwich, "Nationality in Mandated Territories Detached from Turkey," *British Yearbook of International Law* 97 (1926). On the wave of British naturalizations of Ottoman-born Jews that were approved in the late

1920s (and the fascinating legal calisthenics these approvals demanded on the part of the state), Ben-Ur, "Identity Imperative."

35. Bentwich maintained that polities of different natures (and with different juridical and political histories) must pursue this goal by following discrete paths of legal reform. Mandatory regimes such as Palestine, Syria, and Iraq, he argued, must appoint foreign judges to supervise and train a judiciary of the country; countries with capitulatory systems still in place, such as Turkey and Persia, must repudiate them entirely, "leaving matters of personal status to be dealt with by a foreign court." Lastly, in places such as Egypt and Tangier, where local courts have no authority in criminal cases concerning foreigners, "an introduction of an international element into the legislature" could transform "foreign privilege into international co-operation." Bentwich, "The End of the Capitulatory System."

36. Martin Bunton, "'Progressive Civilizations and Deep-Rooted Traditions': Land Laws, Development, and British Rule in Palestine in the 1920s," in *Colonialism and the Modern World: Selected Studies*, ed. Gregory Blue, Martin Bunton, and Ralph Croizier (Armonk: M. E. Sharpe, Inc., 2002); Bunton, "Demarcating the British Colonial State: Land Settlement in the Palestinian Jiftlik Villages of Sajad and Qazaza," in *New Perspectives on Property and Land in the Middle East*, ed. Martin Bunton and Roger Owen (Cambridge: Cambridgue University Press, 2008). Bentwich, legal theorist, legal secretary to the British military administration in Palestine (1918–29), attorney general of Palestine (1922–29), Weizmann Chair of International Law and Peace at Hebrew University (ca. 1932), director of the League of Nations High Commission for Refugees from Germany (1933–35), author of popular history (including a number of works on Jewish history) and a series of memoirs, is himself entirely worthy of further study. My impression of his oeuvre comes from his extensive published works and from selected papers held by the Central Zionist Archives (Norman Bentwich, A255) and the London Metropolitan Archive's collection of the papers of the Board of Deputies of British Jews (Professor Norman Bentwich: correspondence, ACC/3121/E/02/029). Also relevant are materials held by St. Antony's College, Oxford University (Bentwich, Norman de Mattos [1882–1971], GB165-0025), and the papers of Bentwich's wife, Helen, who was active in British Labour politics and has written penetratingly about her time with her husband in Mandate Palestine (Papers of Helen Bentwich, the Women's Library, London Metropolitan University).

37. Here, as in other instances, Jews of Middle Eastern or Mediterranean origin could pose a conceptual threat to Zionist theoreticians that paralleled and informed those posed by Palestinians. This is to but touch upon a complex conceptual terrain that others have explored in more detail, particularly as concerns the more contemporary period. See, in particular, Amnon Raz-Krakotzkin, "The Zionist Return to the West and the Mizrahi Jewish Perspective," in *Orientalism and the Jews*, ed. Ivan Kalman and Derek Penslar (Brandeis: Brandeis University Press, 2005); Yehouda Shenhav, *The Arab Jew: A Postcolonial Reading of Nationalism, Religion, and Ethnicity* (Stanford: Stanford University Press, 2006).

38. TNA FO 372/99. On Elias's service conducting circumcisions and ritual slaughter for Shanghai's Baghdadi Jewish community, Meyer, *From the Rivers of Babylon to the Whangpoo*, 88.

39. Although Hardoon was registered as a British protected person as early as 1896, he was formally accepted as a British subject by a "special act of grace" of the Foreign Office only

in 1925. The 1907 "treaty" referred to above was dated 5 March; I quote here from a subsequent discussion of the case: TNA FO 671/462, handwritten note of March 1930. This "treaty" and the history that undergirded it are also reviewed in TNA FO 369/2190 and FO 372/423; "The Hardoon Will Case Heard in British Supreme Court," *Israel's Messenger*, 1 July 1932.

40. TNA FO 369/2190, Byron Brenan, British Consul General, Shanghai, to Sir Miles Lampson, 26 October 1931.

41. The history of the Hardoons' legal relationship with the Crown was explored in detail in subsequent coverage of the trial and will be discussed in more detail below. See also the synopsis of this history referenced by the Foreign Office in 1928, when it reconsidered Sophie Aaron Hardoon's status; TNA FO 671/462. This history is also recapped in Meyer, *From the Rivers of Babylon to the Whangpoo*, appendix, "The Hardoon Will Case." As Meyer explains, a similar set of circumstances was in effect when the consul general approved Edward Ezra's requests for nationality in 1917. As we have seen, this did not extend to his son Cecil, perhaps because by the time Cecil applied for registration, the Crown had already gathered £400,000 in duties on Edward's estate.

42. TNA FO 369/2304, Consul General J. W. O. Davidson, Shanghai, to Foreign Office, 12 June 1933.

43. Bentwich, "The End of the Capitulatory System," 100.

44. TNA FO 369/2243. Heading the list of signatures was Ezra Abdullah Hardun, who had resided in Shanghai for eight years. Ezra was an itinerant merchant who, by his own account, maintained occasional contact with the deceased, on at least one occasion receiving charity from him.

45. According to Iraqi law, the plaintiffs argued, a will in favor of one heir is not valid without the consent of the others; additionally, that Liza Hardoon was a Chinese citizen rendered her unable by law to inherit an Iraqi estate. On the first day of the trial, the judge presiding over the proceedings, Grant Jones, compelled Ezra Hardoon and his coplaintiffs to be joined by another ostensible contender for Silas Aaron Hardoon's estate: Isaac Jacob Silas Hardoon, a resident of Bombay. Horace B. Samuel, representing Isaac Silas Jacob Hardoon, and Hiram Shaw Wilkinson, representing the Baghdadi Hardoons, were forcibly joined as cocounsels. The two attorneys viewed the case differently and, though both representing the plaintiffs, attempted to pursue different legal strategies, a dynamic that added to the cacophony of the trial. On 1 October 1931, *Israel's Messenger*, the monthly journal of Shanghai's Jewish community, published a copy of a telegram received from Isaac Silas Jacob Hardoon announcing his interest in joining the Hardoon will case. See also "Hardoon Will Contested in the British Supreme Court," *Israel's Messenger*, 1 October 1931.

46. On the face of it, this argument contradicted the tenets of the 1870 Nationality Act, which did allow British subjects to divest themselves of British nationality. To support their claim, the plaintiffs cited an 1888 case, *Abdul ul-Nessiah v. Farra*, which determined that an Ottoman Christian registered with the British consulate in Cairo could not obtain a domicile of choice in the British community in Egypt. A British protected person, they extrapolated, could not acquire a domicile of choice in an extraterritorial community. See the summary of the Hardoon case submitted on 4 January 1933, by Eric Beckett, Chief Legal Officer for the British Foreign Office, TNA FO 369/2304; "The Hardoon Will Case Heard in British Supreme Court";

Norman Bentwich, "Domicile in the International Settlement of Shanghai," *Law Journal* 124 (1932).

47. TNA FO 369/2443, Iraqi Ministry for Foreign Affairs, Baghdad, 24 September 1931, to the Secretariat, The Residency, Baghdad. A copy of this letter was shared with the British consulate in Shanghai, whose representatives, in turn, submitted a duplicate to the Foreign Office in London. Other telegrams from the Iraqi authorities testified to their zeal; see, for example, TNA FO 369/2304, Iraqi Ministry of Foreign Affairs to British Foreign Office, 15 August 1931; TNA FO 369/2190, which includes a series of telegrams sent in November 1931 to the British Foreign Office by the high commissioner of Iraq. That the Iraqi government was "intent" on the case was an estimation offered by the British Chancery in Baghdad, writing from that city's British embassy, 7 December 1933; TNA FO 369/2304.

48. Orit Bashkin, *The Other Iraq: Pluralism and Culture in Hashemite Iraq* (Stanford: Stanford University Press, 2009); Bashkin, *New Babylonians: A History of Jews in Modern Iraq* (Stanford: Stanford University Press, 2012); Reeva Spector Simon and Eleanor H. Tejirian, eds., *The Creation of Iraq, 1914–1921* (New York: Columbia University Press, 2004); Reeva Spector Simon, *Iraq between the Two World Wars: The Creation and Implementation of a Nationalist Ideology* (New York: Columbia University Press, 1986).

49. Bashkin, *New Babylonians*; Joel Beinin, "Jews as Native Iraqis: An Introduction," in *The Last Jews in Baghdad: Remembering a Lost Homeland*, ed. Nissim Rejwan (Austin: University of Texas Press, 2010); Reeva Spector Simon, "Iraq," in *The Jews of the Middle East and North Africa in Modern Times*, ed. Reeva Spector Simon, Michael Menachem Laskier, and Sara Reguer (New York: Columbia University Press, 2003). Scholarship on the dissolution of the notion of the Iraqi Jew—especially as it was understood by non-Jewish Iraqis and Jews of other backgrounds, in Israel particularly—has been ideologically riven, with one camp emphasizing the diversity of Jewish political expression in Iraq (and, significantly, the prominence of Jews in Iraq's communist movement) and the role of Israel and Zionist leaders in aggressively (and sometimes violently) fissuring relations between Jews and non-Jews beginning in the 1940s, and the other camp dubiously emphasizing an unbroken history of Jewish unbelonging in the country (as elsewhere in the Arab Middle East) and Iraqi Jews' slow but steady march toward Zionism and *aliyah*. Useful in its framing of this historiographic debate (and representing the former school) is Joel Beinin, *The Dispersion of Egyptian Jewry: Culture, Politics, and the Formation of a Modern Diaspora* (Berkeley: University of California Press, 1998). On the theoretical questions surrounding representations of the Iraqi Jewish past, see Levy, "Self and the City"; Ella Shohat, "Rupture and Return: Zionist Discourse and the Study of Arab Jews," *Social Text* 21, no. 2 (2003).

50. TNA FO 369/2304, Sir Miles Lampson, British Consulate, Peking, to Sir John Pratt, Eastern Department, Colonial Office, July 1932. Lampson reasserted this point elsewhere, for example, TNA FO 369/2190, comments by Sir Miles Lampson, British Consulate, Peking, 8 January 1931.

51. On Hardoon's father's history, see TNA FO 374/423, Consul General Pelham Warren, Shanghai, to Foreign Office, 12 January 1907.

52. The China Order in Council, which would prove crucial to the case, in Article 3 defined a British protected person as "a person who by virtue of the Foreign Jurisdiction Act of 1890,

or otherwise enjoys His Majesty's protection in China." The phrase "or otherwise" became crucial to the defense, who argued that it mattered little whether Hardoon's protected status came about through error, or, indeed, whether he was also viewed by the Iraqi state as a citizen. The very elasticity of this phrase ("or otherwise"), they maintained, allowed the British state the right to view as a citizen any individual to whom protection had been extended.

53. This according to Article 7 of the Iraqi Nationality Law, which offered Ottoman subjects born in Iraq but not habitually residing there the right to claim Iraqi nationality by filing the requisite paperwork between 23 August 1921 and 6 August 1924. The émigré Jewish community in Shanghai had been informed of this requirement by the Iraqi Passport Department.

54. TNA FO 369/2243, Sir Miles Lampson, British Consulate, Shanghai, to Foreign Office, 5 April 1932. Here the defense was responding to the plaintiffs' argument that a British protected person could not acquire a domicile of choice in an extraterritorial community; in their defense, they cited the precedent raised in 1919 in *Casdagli v. Casdagli*.

55. Moshe Myers, "Hardoon's Will and Marriage—Mr. R. D. Abraham Criticized," *Israel's Messenger*, 1 October 1931; "Hardoon Will Case Enters Another Important Stage," *Israel's Messenger*, 1 January 1932.

56. "Hardoon Will Case Enters Another Important Stage"; "The Late Mr. S. A. Hardoon's Estate," *Israel's Messenger*, 1 February 1932. The quotation referring to the "presumption of marriage" is taken from a summary of Judge Grain's judgment contained in the minutes of Eric Beckett, Chief Legal Advisor to the Foreign Office, TNA FO 369/2304, 4 January 1933.

57. TNA FO 369/2190, Consul General Brenan, Shanghai, to Sir Miles Lampson, 26 October 1931. One can find parallels to this trial elsewhere, as in the Parsi Panchayat case, one of the most discussed lawsuits in the Parsi diaspora of the twentieth century. This case evaluated whether a French woman who had married into a Parsi family in a Zoroastrian ceremony was permitted access to Parsi fire temples and charitable aid. Mitra Sharafi, "Judging Conversion to Zoroastrianism: Behind the Scenes of the Parsi Panchayat Case (1908)," in *Parsis in India and the Diaspora*, ed. John R. Hinnells and Alan Williams (London: Routledge University Press, 2007).

58. "The Hardoon Will Case Heard."

59. TNA FO 369/2304. This according to J. W. O. Davidson, British Acting Consul General, Shanghai, who in June 1933 met with representatives of the organization to assess their views.

60. Bentwich, "Domicile in the International Settlement of Shanghai." Bentwich thus confirmed the views of Eric Beckett, chief legal officer for the British Foreign Office, who articulated his reactions to the Hardoon trial in official correspondence with the Foreign Office and in an article published in the *Law Quarterly Review* shortly before Bentwich's own commentary appeared. TNA FO 369/2304; W. Eric Beckett, "Recognition of Polygamous Marriages under English Law," *Law Quarterly Review* 48 (1932). Arguably, Bentwich's position also echoed the Austrian Jewish Marxist legal theorist Karl Renner's notion of "personality principle"; Ephraim Nimni, *National Cultural Autonomy and Its Critics* (New York: Routledge Press, 2004).

61. Jordanna Bailkin, *The Afterlife of Empire* (Berkeley: University of California Press, 2014), especially chapter 4.

62. It was the litigious Hardoons who appear to have coaxed from the Iraqi minister of foreign affairs this overly definitive proclamation about the reach of shari'a. This was in their personal interest, as the application of shari'a to the Hardoon estate would have privileged

male next of kin, including cousins in Iraq. TNA FO 369/2443, correspondence between the Hardoons' representatives in Shanghai and the Ministry for Foreign Affairs and between Ezra Hardoon and the Ministry of Foreign Affairs of June and July 1932. Apparently the Hardoons succeeded in extracting such an affidavit from the ministry; a telegram to this effect by the British high commissioner for Iraq was thereafter cited in a letter by His Majesty's Consul General, Shanghai, to Judge Grain. Ibid., 20 July 1932.

63. "The Hardoon Will Case: Sir Peter Grain Rules Will Is Good and Valid: Judgment for Defendant," *North-China Daily News*, 12 July 1932; "Shanghai Law Reports: H. M. Supreme Court, Hardoon Will Case," *North China Herald*, 20 July 1932.

64. In support of this position, Grain cited various legal precedents, including that raised by the case *Ibrahims v. The King* (1914), in which a natural-born subject of Afghanistan who was enrolled as a private in the British forces in India was convicted of murder after killing an officer in his regiment. The Privy Council confirmed the findings of a lower court: that Ibrahims, as a British protected person, ought to be viewed as a British subject when it came to matters of the court. Judge Grain's argument was not airtight. Certain British Orders in Council did indeed establish British protected persons and British citizens to be indivisible under the law, including the landmark Zanzibar Order of 1897, the China, Japan, and Korea Order of 1884 and 1904, the Ottoman Order of 1910, the Abyssinia Order of 1913, the Siam Order of 1914, and the Muscat Order of 1915. These orders all referred to the Foreign Jurisdiction Act of 1890 for legal precedent, as did the defense in the Hardoon trial. However, the China Order of 1925, the Morocco Order of 1929, and the Egypt Order of 1930, all of which drew upon the British Nationality and Status of Aliens Act of 1914 as their legal basis, maintained discrete definitions of British subjects and protected persons. A more thorough review of the legal issues at stake here was offered by Judge P. Grant Jones in a subsequent trial over the Hardoon estate convened in the wake of Liza's death in 1937, on which more later. "H. M. Supreme Court—Another Hardoon Will Case," *China Daily Herald*, 3 December 1936; "H. M. Supreme Court Hardoon Will Case," *North China Herald*, 24 February 1937. See also the summary of the Hardoon case submitted on 4 January 1933, by Eric Beckett, Chief Legal Officer for the British Foreign Office, TNA FO 369/2304.

65. TNA FO 369/2304, letter to Foreign Office from Chancery, British Embassy, Baghdad, 7 December 1933.

66. TNA FO 91/3107, letter to Foreign Office, [name obscured], mailed from Hadad, India, 31 December 1936.

67. "Shanghai Law Reports, H. M. Supreme Court Hardoon Will Case," *North China Herald*, 24 February 1937. Two versions of Liza Hardoon's will can be found in the National Archives of the United Kingdom, dated 1931 and 1937: TNA FO 917/3970 and FO 917/3970. On the ways in which the news media constructed public opinion of, and indeed influenced, judicial decision making in Shanghai at this time, see Sei Jeong Chin, "Politics of Trial, the News Media, and Social Networks in Nationalist China: The New Life Weekly Case, 1935," in *At the Crossroads of Empires: Middlemen, Social Networks, and State-Building in Republican Shanghai*, ed. Nara Dillon and Jean C. Oi (Stanford: Stanford University Press, 2007).

68. "Shanghai Law Reports: H. M. Supreme Court, Hardoon Will Case."

69. Nor would this judgment forestall the Hardoon family's encounters with the law: in 1941, the family was in court once again. This time, the British Supreme Court in Shanghai and the

Shanghai District Court were called upon to probe the legality of Liza Hardoon's will, as she had disinherited one of her sons four years before her death. The claimants included a group of ten ostensible cousins in Baghdad and Liza Hardoon's son David George Hardoon. David George was the principal beneficiary of his mother's first will but was all but cut out of her second, which left the bulk of the family estate to his brother Reuben Victor and five of her nephews (who went by the surname Loo) whom she had also adopted. The Baghdadi cousins sought the representation of a Japanese lawyer prominent in Shanghai, Mr. O. Okamoto, while David George sought recognition of the original will in the British Supreme Court in Shanghai. These overlapping legal proceedings were interrupted by the Japanese occupation of the International Settlement in the course of the war. The case was settled in the Shanghai District Court in October of 1945. TNA FO 917/3970; "Hardoons in Baghdad Seek Claim Rise," *Shanghai Times*, 15 May 1942. For a personal account of the trial conducted in the Shanghai District Court, see Frank Ching, *Ancestors: 900 Years in the Life of a Chinese Family* (New York: Morrow, 1988).

70. TNA FO 372/6638, handwritten and unsigned comments of 16 December 1948. Prompting these meditations were requests by Reuben Victor Hardoon and David George Hardoon, adopted sons of Silas Aaron, that they be registered as British protected persons.

71. Ibid., Minutes, 21 December 1948.

CONCLUSION

1. Corry Guttstadt, *Turkey, the Jews, and the Holocaust* (Cambridge: Cambridge University Press, 2013), 99.

2. In the summer of 1908, opponents of the Ottoman sultan Abdülhamid II orchestrated a bloodless coup that forced the sultan to reinstate the 1876 Constitution and reintroduce a parliamentary government. Although Abdülhamid II retained the sultanate, the Committee of Union and Progress (CUP), popularly known as the Young Turks, became the de facto leadership of the empire. This transition of authority left some disgruntled, leading, in 1909, to a countercoup by soldiers loyal to the sultan and Muslims who felt the new regime favored non-Muslims. These forces briefly seized the capital by force, instilling great fear in the Jewish community of the empire. For more on Jewish responses to this event, see "A Coup in the Capital: The Ottoman Chief Rabbi Watches in Fear," translated by Miriam Kochan, in Cohen and Stein, *Sephardi Lives*, 140–41. My thanks to Jackie Slutzky for helping me reconstruct this family history.

3. Cohen, "Oriental by Design." Devi Mays has pointed out that some Jews did leave the empire to avoid conscription, regardless of the general trend. See Mays, "Transplanting Cosmopolitans," 126–29.

4. Avni, *Spain, the Jews, and Franco*, 148. For a general history of Greek Jews and the Holocaust, see Steven B. Bowman, *The Agony of Greek Jews, 1940–1945* (Stanford: Stanford University Press, 2009); Michael Molho and Yehuda Nehama, *Sho'at Yehude Yavan: 1941–1944* (Jerusalem: Yad Vashem, 1965); Fleming, *Greece: A Jewish History*, chapters 7–8; Mark Mazower, *Inside Hitler's Greece: The Experience of Occupation, 1941–44* (New Haven: Yale University Press, 1995); Recanati, *Zikhron Saloniki*. On those Spanish nationals allowed to remain in Greece see, in addition to Avni's book, Haim Avni, "Spanish Nationals in Greece and Their Fate during the Holocaust," *Yad Vashem Studies* 8 (1970). Among the arresting primary accounts

of the Holocaust in Greece that have been translated into English is Steven B. Bowman, *The Holocaust in Salonika: Eyewitness Accounts* (New York: Sephardic House, 2002). See also an extraordinary new search engine dedicated to Greek Jewish survivors' testimonies: "Database of Greek Jewish Holocaust Survivors' Testimonies," http://gjst.ha.uth.gr/en/. For a survey of the Sephardi experience of the war, see Benbassa and Rodrigue, *Sephardi Jewry*, chapter 5.

5. On German policies of repatriation, see Leni Yahil, *The Holocaust: The Fate of European Jewry, 1932–1945*, trans. Ina Friedman and Haya Galai (Oxford: Oxford University Press, 1990), 415–16.

6. Avni, *Spain, the Jews, and Franco*.

7. Even with Radigales' intervention, the survival of the Spanish Jews in Bergen-Belsen was by no means guaranteed. In the spring of 1944, while Spain continued to waffle on whether the Salonican "Spaniards" from Athens deserved to be repatriated from Bergen-Belsen, German officials boarded the interned foreign nationals onto trains directed eastward—presumably to Auschwitz, where the annihilation of Hungarian Jewry was proceeding at an intensified pace. Through an incredible accident of timing, the train was apprehended by American troops, who liberated the prisoners. After the war, Spain settled these survivors in Spanish Morocco, whence many emigrated to Palestine. Michael Molho and Yehuda Nehama, *Sho'at yehude Yavan: 1941–1944* (Jerusalem: Yad Vashem, 1965), 221; Avni, *Spain, the Jews, and Franco*, 158.

8. Yad Vashem, "Sebastián de Romero Radigales of Spain to Be Recognized as Righteous among the Nations," http://www.yadvashem.org/yv/en/pressroom/pressreleases/pr_details.asp?cid=890.

9. D. Gershon Lewental, "Nehama, Joseph," in *Encyclopedia of Jews in the Islamic World*, ed. Norman Stillman (Leiden: BrillOnline Reference Works, 2010).

10. See, for example, the correspondence in the various folders catalogued as AHD MISC 2PA50M40, "Repatriação de judeus portuguêses residentes no Reich a territórios ocupados, incluindo a França."

11. These instructions reached the Portuguese authorities in December 1943. Milgram, *Portugal, Salazar, and the Jews*, 254.

12. Paperwork concerning the Benvenistes' story appears in AHD 2PA50M40, "Judeus Listas incrições da França (1)," including letters by International Committee of the Red Cross to the Portuguese Mission, Geneva, 10 February 1944; Portuguese Legation, Timis de Sus [Romania], to Foreign Minister, 6 May 1944, with handwritten comments by Foreign Minister Eduardo Vieira Leitão in margins. In addition to these original sources, I am indebted to the discussion of the Benvenistes and larger context for Portugal's disinterest in this family in Milgram, *Portugal, Salazar, and the Jews*, 255–56.

13. Spanish consulates had (at least in the course of the twentieth century) served as proxies for Portugal when/if that country lacked representatives in a given Mediterranean locale. Why Portuguese officials based in Athens (such as Consul Eduardo de Carvalho, or Chargé d'affaires Almeida Pile) did not complete this task is unclear. It is also possible that the Spanish certifying authorities were acting on their own.

14. AJA, Manuscript Collection no. 361, "World Jewish Congress Records, 1918–1982," box D50 folder 15, "Deportees, Greece, Portuguese Jews arrested in Athens, Mar–Apr 1944." Those deported included members of the Ardetti, Barzilay/Barzilaiy, Benveniste, Benyacar, Dosti,

Levy, Nahum, Ronsso, Salmona, and Cdren [*sic*] families. My thanks to Aron Rodrigue for sharing this astonishing document.

15. Renée Poznanski, *Jews in France during World War II*, trans. Nathan Bracher (Waltham, MA: Brandeis University Press, 2001), 386.

16. On Merci, see "Lucillo Merci (1899–1984)," WEFOR, http://www.gariwo.net/wefor /persona.php?idPersona=25&idGiardino=6. A copy of Merci's Italian-language diary is available on that site; an English-language translation, with an introduction by Menahem Shelach, has been published as Joseph Rochlitz (compiler), "Excerpts from the Salonika Diary of Lucillo Merci (February–August 1943)," *Yad Vashem Studies* 18 (1987). On the migration of Salonican Jews to Athens in the years leading up to the war, see Michele Sarfatti, *The Jews in Mussolini's Italy: From Equality to Persecution*, trans. John Tedeschi and Anne C. Tedeschi (Madison: University of Wisconsin Press, 2006), 25.

17. Susan Zuccotti, *The Italians and the Holocaust: Persecution, Rescue, and Survival* (New York: Basic Books, 1987), 9–10. A beautiful visual rendition of this horrific episode focuses on the experience of the one Ashkenazi couple lodged at the Behars' Hotel Meina: Andrea Ventura and Mimmo Franzinelli, "The Hotel Meina," *New York Times*, January 27 2013.

18. This directive proved an informal way for Turkey to free itself of legal obligations towards vast numbers of non-Muslims who lived outside the borders of the Turkish Republic. Guttstadt, *Turkey, the Jews, and the Holocaust*, 54–55, 95; Benbassa and Rodrigue, *Sephardi Jewry*, 180.

19. Among many cases one could point to are TNA HO 144/7336, "Nationality and Naturalisation: Coenca, Vidal"; TNA HO 144/11685, "Nationality and Naturalisation: Sassoon, José Vital"; TNA HO 144/12369, "Nationality and Naturalisation: Gracial, Michel."

20. Approximately two-thirds of the Jews deported from Vichy France were immigrants or recently naturalized citizens retroactively stripped of their status as Frenchmen and Frenchwomen. Among them were some 1,750 holders of Spanish papers whom the Spanish Foreign Ministry disqualified from repatriation. For the general picture, see Michael Robert Marrus and Robert Paxton, *Vichy France and the Jews* (New York: Basic Books, 1981), especially chapter 6. On Spain's disinclination to help its subjects in France, see Avni, *Spain, the Jews, and Franco*. On Nehama's history, see Lewental, "Nehama, Joseph."

21. On Turkey's disinterest in the repatriation of Turkish nationals in the course of the war, see Guttstadt, *Turkey, the Jews, and the Holocaust*, 142–51. See also Marc Baer, "Turk and Jew in Berlin: The First Turkish Migration to Berlin and the Shoah," *Comparative Studies in Society and History* 55, no. 2 (2013).

22. Letter by Yaco Soulam, writing from Drancy, to Rebecca Soulam (née Bensasson), Paris, ca. 1941–42. Courtesy of Laurent and Florence Soulam; an English translation of this letter, translated by Julia Phillips Cohen, appears in Cohen and Stein, *Sephardi Lives*, 265–66.

23. "The 86th Annual Report of the Anglo-Jewish Association" (London: Office of the Anglo-Jewish Association, 1957–58), 17.

24. AJA, Manuscript Collection no. 361, "World Jewish Congress Records, 1918–1982," box C266 folder 2, "Greece, Claims and Spanish Jews, 1962–1964." The letter in question was dated 7 October 1962, sent from Salonica, and signed by Jacques Revah and Sabetay Saltiel; subsequent appeals were sent from Tel Aviv on 15 October 1915 and signed by Joseph Ousiel

[Ouziel], Chairman, Association of Immigrants from Greece. Ouziel also served as president of the Union of Greek Jews in Israel.

25. AJA, Manuscript Collection no. 361, "World Jewish Congress Records, 1918–1982," box C266 folder 2, "Greece, Claims and Spanish Jews, 1962–1964," Dr. E. Katzenstein to Union de los subditos Espanoles [*sic*] de Grecia por sus reclamaciones ante Alemania," 12 December 1963.

26. I borrow the phrase from Brown, "The Precarious Life and Slow Death of the Mixed Courts of Egypt."

27. Beinin, *The Dispersion of Egyptian Jewry*, 38.

28. For a splendid set of histories of the complex legal tapestry in Egypt, including discussion of many cases involving Jews, see Hanley, "Foreignness and Localness in Alexandria"; Hanley, "When Did Egyptians Stop Being Ottomans?"; Hanley, "Papers for Going, Papers for Staying." Communal courts continued to be granted authority by the state until 1955; therefore Jewish courts, too, would have weighed legal questions concerning Jewish residents of Egypt.

29. Beinin, *The Dispersion of Egyptian Jewry*, 87. For an exploration of Jews' role in the commercial fabric of Cairo in the decades preceding these events, see Nancy Reynolds, *A City Consumed: Urban Commerce, the Cairo Fire, and the Politics of Decolonization in Egypt* (Stanford: Stanford University Press, 2012).

30. André Aciman, *Out of Egypt: A Memoir* (New York: Macmillan, 1994), 3–5. For a marvelous exploration of literary tropes of cosmopolitan Egypt, see Deborah Starr, *Remembering Cosmopolitan Egypt: Literature, Culture, and Empire* (New York: Routledge, 2009).

31. I refer here to the works that have been published in English as Patrick Modiano, *Suspended Sentences: Three Novellas* (New Haven: Yale University Press, 2014).

32. The hostile reaction to this trend on the part of some Muslim Turkish commentators is detailed in Ceylan Yeginsu, "Sephardic Jews Feel Bigotry's Sting in Turkey and a Pull Back to Spain," *New York Times*, 26 May 2015. On an earlier episode that resonates with the contemporary growth in anti-Jewish resentment in Turkey, see Bali, *Cumhuriyet yıllarında Türkiye Yahudileri*, 77–84.

BIBLIOGRAPHY

ARCHIVAL COLLECTIONS CONSULTED

Archivio Storico Diplomatico del Ministero degli Affari Esteri, Rome
Archives de l'Alliance israélite universelle, Paris
Archives de la Préfecture de police, Paris
Archives du ministère des Affaires étrangères, Paris—La Courneuve
Bibliothèque de l'Alliance israélite universelle, Paris
British Library, London
Central Archive for the History of the Jewish People, Jerusalem
Central Zionist Archive, Jerusalem
Greater Manchester Police Museum and Archive, Manchester
Instituto Diplomático, Ministério dos Negócios Estrangeiros, Arquivo-histórico diplomático, Lisboa
International Committee of the Red Cross Archives, Geneva
The Jacob Rader Marcus Center of the American Jewish Archives, Cincinnati
Joint Distribution Committee, Jerusalem
Joint Distribution Committee, New York
League of Nations Archives, Geneva
London Metropolitan Archives, London
Manchester Jewish Museum Archives, Manchester
The National Archives of the United Kingdom, Kew
Österreichisches Staatsarchiv, Vienna
University of Washington Libraries Special Collections, Seattle
YIVO Institute for Jewish Research, New York

PUBLISHED SOURCES CONSULTED

"The 86th Annual Report of the Anglo-Jewish Association." London: Office of the Anglo-Jewish Association, 1957–58.

Abitbol, Michel. *Les deux terres promises: les juifs de France et le sionisme, 1897–1945*. Paris: Olivier Orban, 1989.

Abramson, Glenda. "Haim Nahmias and the Labour Batallions: A Diary of Two Years in the First World War." *Jewish Culture and History* 14, no. 1 (2014): 18–32.

———. *Soldiers' Tales: Two Palestinian Jewish Soldiers in the Ottoman Army during the First World War*. London: Vallentine Mitchell, 2013.

Aciman, André. *Out of Egypt: A Memoir*. New York: Macmillan, 1994.

Ahmad, Feroz. "Ottoman Perceptions of the Capitulations 1800–1914." *Journal of Islamic Studies* 11, no. 1 (2000).

Akçam, Taner. *The Young Turks' Crime against Humanity: The Armenian Genocide and Ethnic Cleansing in the Ottoman Empire*. Princeton: Princeton University Press, 2012.

Aksakal, Mustafa. "'Holy War Made in Germany'? Ottoman Origins of the 1914 Jihad." *War in History* 18, no. 184 (2011): 184–99.

———. *The Ottoman Road to War in 1914: The Ottoman Empire and the First World War*. Cambridge: Cambridge University Press, 2008.

al-Qattan, Najwa. "*Safarbarlik*: Ottoman Syria and the Great War." In *From the Syrian Land to the States of Syria and Lebanon*, edited by Thomas Philipp and Christoph Schumann, 163–74. Beirut: Ergon Verlag Würzburg in Kommission, 2004.

———. "When Mothers Ate Their Children: Wartime Memory and the Language of Food in Syria and Lebanon." *International Journal of Middle East Studies* 46, no. 4 (2014): 719–36.

Alpert, Michael. "Dr. Angel Pulido and Philo-Sephardism in Spain." *Jewish Historical Studies* 40 (2005): 105–19.

Amara, Noureddine. "Etre algérien en situation impériale, fin XIX siécle–début XXéme siécle: l'usage de la catégorie 'nationalité algérienne' par les consulats français dans leur relation avec les Algériens fixes au Maroc et dans l'empire Ottoman." *European Review of History—Revue européenne d'histoire* 19, no. 1 (2012): 59–74.

Andrew, Christopher M., and A. S. Kanya-Forstner. *France Overseas: The Great War and the Climax of French Imperial Expansion*. London: Thames and Hudson, 1981.

Angel, Marc D. "The Sephardic Theater of Seattle." *American Jewish Archives* 25, no. 2 (1973): 156–61.

Angell, J. B. "The Turkish Capitulations." *American Historical Review* 6, no. 2 (1901): 33–37.

Anghie, Antony. "Finding the Peripheries: Sovereignty and Colonialism in Nineteenth-Century International Law." *Harvard International Law Journal* 40 (Winter 1999): 31–80.

Arnoulet, François. "Les Tunisiens et la première guerre mondiale (1914–1918)." *Revue de l'Occident musulman et de la Méditerranée* 38, no. 38 (1984): 47–61.

Aronsfeld, C. C. "Jewish Enemy Aliens in England during the First World War." *Jewish Social Studies* 18, no. 4 (1956): 275–83.

Artunç, Cihan. "The Price of Legal Institutions: The Protégé System and Beratlı Merchants in the Eighteenth-Century Ottoman Empire." *Journal of Economic History* 75/3 (September 2015): 720–48.

Asuero, Pablo Martín. *El consulado de España en Estambul y la protección de los sefardíes entre 1804 y 1930*. Istanbul: Editorial ISIS, 2011.

———. "The Spanish Consulate in Istanbul and the Protection of the Sephardim (1804–1903)." *Quaderns de la Mediterrània* 8 (2007): 320–26.

Avni, Haim. *Spain, the Jews, and Franco*. Philadelphia: Jewish Publication Society of America, 1982.

———. "Spanish Nationals in Greece and Their Fate during the Holocaust." *Yad Vashem Studies* 8 (1970): 46–66.

Baer, Marc. "Turk and Jew in Berlin: The First Turkish Migration to Berlin and the Shoah." *Comparative Studies in Society and History* 55, no. 2 (April 2013): 350–55.

Baganha, Maria Joannis, and Constança Urbano de Sousa. "The Portuguese Nationality Law." In *Acquisition and Loss of Nationality*, edited by Rainer Bauböck, Eva Ersbøll, Kees Groenendijk, and Herald Waldrauch, 435–76. Amsterdam: Amsterdam University Press, 2006.

Bailkin, Jordanna. *The Afterlife of Empire*. Berkeley: University of California Press, 2014.

Baker, Donald N. "The Surveillance of Subversion in Interwar France." *French Historical Studies* 10, no. 3 (Spring 1979): 486–516.

"The Balkan Wars and the Jews." *American Jewish Yearbook* 15 (1913–14): 188–206.

Bali, Rıfat. *Cumhuriyet yıllarında Türkiye Yahudileri: Bir Türkleştirme Serüveni (1923–1945)*. Istanbul: İletişim, 1999.

Bashkin, Orit. *New Babylonians: A History of Jews in Modern Iraq*. Stanford: Stanford University Press, 2012.

———. *The Other Iraq: Pluralism and Culture in Hashemite Iraq*. Stanford: Stanford University Press, 2009.

Bauman, Zygmunt. "Allosemitism: Premodern, Modern, Postmodern." In *Modernity, Culture and the "Jew,"* edited by Bryan Cheyette and Laura Marcus, 143–56. Stanford: Stanford University Press, 1998.

Beckett, W. Eric. "Recognition of Polygamous Marriages under English Law." *Law Quarterly Review* 48 (1932): 341–73.

Beckwith, Stacy N., ed. *Charting Memory: Recalling Medieval Spain*. New York: Garland Publishing, Inc., 2000.

Beinin, Joel. *The Dispersion of Egyptian Jewry: Culture, Politics, and the Formation of a Modern Diaspora*. Berkeley: University of California Press, 1998.

———. "Jews as Native Iraqis: An Introduction." In *The Last Jews in Baghdad: Remembering a Lost Homeland*, edited by Nissim Rejwan, xii-xxii. Austin: University of Texas Press, 2010.

Ben-Ur, Aviva. "Identity Imperative: Ottoman Jews in Wartime and Interwar Britain." *Immigrants & Minorities: Historical Studies in Ethnicity, Migration, and Diaspora* 33.2 (2014):165–95.

———. *Sephardic Jews in America: A Diasporic History*. New York: New York University Press, 2009.

Ben-Zvi, Yitzhak. "Ha-tnua ha-sotsialistit be-Saloniki." In *Saloniki, 'irva-em be-Yisra'el*. Tel Aviv: Makhon le-heker Yahadut Saloniki, 1967.

Benaroya, Avraam. "A Note on the Socialist Federation of Saloniki." *Jewish Social Studies* 11, no. 1 (1949): 69–72.

Benbassa, Esther. "Presse d'Istanbul et de Salonique au service du sionisme (1908–1914): les motifs d'une allégeance." *Revue historique* 560 (October–December 1986): 337–65.

Benbassa, Esther, and Aron Rodrigue. *Sephardi Jewry: A History of the Judeo-Spanish Community, 14th–20th Centuries.* Berkeley: University of California Press, 2000.

Benton, Lauren. *Law and Colonial Cultures: Legal Regimes in World History, 1400–1900.* Cambridge: Cambridge University Press, 2002.

Bentwich, Norman. "Domicile in the International Settlement of Shanghai." *Law Journal* 124 (17 December 1932): 33–34.

———. "The End of the Capitulatory System." *British Yearbook of International Law* 89 (1933): 89–100.

———. "The Legal System of Palestine under the Mandate." *Middle East Journal* 2, no. 1 (1948): 33–46.

———. *The Mandates System.* London: Longman, 1930.

———. "Nationality in Mandated Territories Detached from Turkey." *British Yearbook of International Law* 97 (1926): 97–109.

———. "Palestine Nationality and the Mandate." *Journal of Comparative Legislation and International Law* 21, no. 4 (1939): 230–32.

———. "The Recognition of Jewish Law in Private International Jurisprudence." *Journal of the Society of Comparative Legislation* 304 (1914): 304–13.

Berceot, Florence. "Une escale dans la tempête. Des Juifs palestiniens en Corse (1915–1920)." *Archives juives* 1, no. 38 (2005): 144.

Berg, Nancy E. *Exile from Exile: Israeli Writers from Iraq.* New York: SUNY Press, 1996.

Bergère, Marie-Claire. *Shanghai: China's Gateway to Modernity.* Stanford: Stanford University Press, 2009.

Betta, Chiara. "From Orientals to Imagined Britons: Baghdadi Jews in Shanghai." *Modern Asian Studies* 37, no. 4 (2003): 999–1023.

———. "Silas Aaron Hardoon (1815–1931): Marginality and Adaptation in Shanghai." Ph. D. dissertation, University of London, 1997.

———. "Silas Aaron Hardoon and Cross-Cultural Adaptation in Shanghai." In *The Jews of China*, edited by Jonathan Goldstein and Frank Joseph Shulman, 216–29. Armonk, NY: M. E. Sharpe, 1999.

Bickers, Robert. *Britain in China: Community, Culture and Colonialism, 1900–1949.* Manchester: Manchester University Press, 1999.

———. "Shanghailanders: The Formation and Identity of the British Settler Community in Shanghai 1843–1937." *Past and Present*, no. 159 (May 1998): 161–211.

Bird, J. C. *Control of Enemy Alien Civilians in Great Britain, 1914–1918.* London: Routledge Revivals, 1986.

Birnbaum, Pierre. *Jewish Destinies: Citizenship, State, and Community in Modern France.* Translated by Arthur Goldhammer. New York: Hill and Wang, 1995.

Birnbaum, Pierre, and Ira Katznelson. *Paths of Emancipation: Jews, States, and Citizenship.* Princeton: Princeton University Press, 1995.

Black, Eugene C. *The Social Politics of Anglo-Jewry, 1880–1920.* Oxford: Basil Blackwell, 1988.

Bodian, Miriam. *Dying in the Law of Moses: Crypto-Jewish Martyrdom in the Iberian World.* Bloomington: Indiana University Press, 2007.

———. *Hebrews of the Portuguese Nation: Conversos and Community in Early Modern Amsterdam.* Bloomington: Indiana University Press, 1997.

Borovaya, Olga. *Modern Ladino Culture: Press, Belles Lettres, and Theater in the Late Ottoman Empire.* Bloomington: Indiana University Press, 2012.

Bowman, Steven B. *The Agony of Greek Jews, 1940–1945.* Stanford: Stanford University Press, 2009.

———. *The Holocaust in Salonika: Eyewitness Accounts.* New York: Sephardic House, 2002.

Braude, Benjamin. "The Rise and Fall of Salonica Woolens, 1500–1650: Technology Transfer and Western Competition." *Mediterranean Historical Review* 6, no. 2 (1991): 216–36.

Brower, Benjamin Claude. *A Desert Named Peace: The Violence of France's Empire in the Algerian Sahara, 1844–1902.* New York: Columbia University Press, 2009.

Brown, Nathan J. "The Precarious Life and Slow Death of the Mixed Courts of Egypt." *International Journal of Middle East Studies* 25, no. 1 (1993): 33–36.

Brown, P. M. *Foreigners in Turkey: Their Juridical Status.* Princeton: Princeton University Press, 1914.

Brubaker, Rogers. "Unmixing of Peoples." In *After Empire: Multiethnic Societies and Nation-Building, the Soviet Union and the Russian, Ottoman, and Habsburg Empires,* edited by Karen Barkey and Mark Von Hagen, 155–81. Boulder, CO: Westview Press, 1997.

Brummett, Palmira. *Image and Imperialism in the Ottoman Revolutionary Press, 1908–1911.* Albany: Syracuse University Press, 2000.

Bryant, Robert T. "Territoriality and the Mixed Court in China." *Virginia Law Review* 13, no. 1 (1926): 27–36.

Bunis, David N. "Modernization and the Language Question among Judezmo-Speaking Sephardim of the Ottoman Empire." In *Sephardi and Middle Eastern Jewries: History and Culture in the Modern Era,* edited by Harvey E. Goldbert, 225–39. Bloomington: Indiana University Press, 1996.

Bunton, Martin. "Demarcating the British Colonial State: Land Settlement in the Palestinian Jiftlik Villages of Sajad and Qazaza." In *New Perspectives on Property and Land in the Middle East,* edited by Martin Bunton and Roger Owen, 121–58. Cambridge: Cambridgue University Press, 2008.

———. "'Progressive Civilizations and Deep-Rooted Traditions': Land Laws, Development, and British Rule in Palestine in the 1920s." In *Colonialism and the Modern World: Selected Studies,* edited by Gregory Blue, Martin Bunton, and Ralph Croizier, 121–60. Armonk: M. E. Sharpe, Inc., 2002.

Burdelez, Ivana. "Jewish Consuls in the Service of the Republic of Dubrovnik." In *Diplomacy of the Republic of Dubrovnik,* edited by Svjetlan Berkovic, 357–42. Zagreb: Ministry of Foreign Affairs of the Republic of Croatia, Diplomatic Academy, 1998.

Burke, Timothy. *Lifebuoy Men, Lux Women: Commodification, Consumption, and Cleanliness in Modern Zimbabwe.* Durham: Duke University Press, 1996.

Camiscioli, Elisa. "Intermarriage, Independent Nationality, and the Individual Rights of

French Women: The Law of 10 August 1927." *French Politics, Culture, and Society* 17, no. 3–4 (Summer/Fall 1999): 52–74.

Campos, Michelle. *Ottoman Brothers: Muslims, Christians, and Jews in Early Twentieth-Century Palestine*. Stanford: Stanford University Press, 2010.

Caplan, Jane, and John C. Torpey, eds. *Documenting Individual Identity: The Development of State Practices in the Modern World*. Princeton: Princeton University Press, 2001.

Carnegie Foundation. *International Commission to Enquire into the Causes and Conduct of the Balkan Wars*. Paris: Carnegie Foundation, 1914.

Cernea, Ruth Fredman. *Almost Englishmen: Baghdadi Jews in British Burma*. Lanham: Lexington Books, 2006.

Cesarani, David, and Tony Kushner, eds. *The Internment of Aliens in Twentieth Century Britain*. London: F. Cass, 1993.

Çetinkaya, Y. Doğan. "Atrocity Popaganda and the Nationalization of the Masses in the Ottoman Empire during the Balkan Wars (1912–1913)." *International Journal of Middle East Studies* 46, no. 4 (2014): 759–78.

Childs, Timothy Winston. *Italo-Turkish Diplomacy and the War over Libya: 1911–1912*. Leiden: Brill, 1997.

Chin, Sei Jeong. "Politics of Trial, the News Media, and Social Networks in Nationalist China: The New Life Weekly Case, 1935." In *At the Crossroads of Empires: Middlemen, Social Networks, and State-Building in Republican Shanghai*, edited by Nara Dillon and Jean C. Oi, 131–54. Stanford: Stanford University Press, 2007.

Ching, Frank. *Ancestors: 900 Years in the Life of a Chinese Family*. New York: Marrow, 1988.

Chronakis, Paris Papamichos. "The Jewish, Greek, Muslim and Donme Merchants of Salonica, 1882–1919: Class and Ethnic Transformations in the Course of Hellenization" (in Greek). Ph.D. dissertation, University of Crete, 2011.

Çiçek, M. Talha. *War and State Formation in Syria: Cemal Pasha's Governorate during World War I, 1914–1917*. New York: Routledge Press, 2014.

Clancy-Smith, Julia. *Mediterraneans: North Africa and Europe in an Age of Migration, c. 1800–1900*. Berkeley: University of California Press, 2011.

———. "Women, Gender, and Migration along a Mediterranean Frontier: Pre-Colonial Tunisia, c. 1815–1870." *Gender and History* 17, no. 1 (2005): 62–92.

Cohen, Julia Phillips. *Becoming Ottomans: Sephardi Jews and Imperial Citizenship in the Modern Era*. Oxford: Oxford University Press, 2014.

———. "Between Civic and Islamic Ottomanism: Jewish Imperial Citizenship in the Hamidian Era." *International Journal of Middle East Studies* 44 (2012): 237–55.

———. "Oriental by Design: Ottoman Jews, Imperial Style, and the Performance of Heritage." *American Historical Review* 119, no. 2 (2015): 364–98.

Cohen, Julia Phillips, and Sarah Abrevaya Stein, eds. *Sephardi Lives: A Documentary History, 1700–1950*. Stanford: Stanford University Press, 2014.

———. "Sephardi Scholarly Worlds: Towards a Novel Geography of Modern Jewish History." *Jewish Quarterly Review* 100, no. 3 (2010): 349–84.

Colley, Linda. "Going Native, Telling Tales: Captivity, Collaborations, and Empire." *Past and Present* 168 (2000): 170–93.

Collins, Lydia. *The Sephardim of Manchester: Pedigrees and Pioneers.* Manchester: Shaare Hayim, the Sephardi Congregation of South Manchester, 2006.

Danon, Dina. "Abraham Danon, la vie d'un *maskil* Ottoman, 1857–1925." In *Itinéraires séphirades*, edited by Esther Benbassa, 181–92. Paris: Presses de l'Université Paris-Sorbonne, 2010.

Davies, Norman. "The Destruction of the German Communities in Britain during the First World War." In *Germans in Britain, 1500 to the Present*, 116–22. London, 1996.

———. "The Poles of Great Britain, 1814–1919." *Slavonic and East European Review* 50 (1972): 63–89.

Davison, Roderic H. "The French Dragomanate in Mid-Nineteenth Century Istanbul." In *Istanbul et les langues orientales*, edited by Frédéric Hitzel, 271–80. Montreal: L'Harmattan Inc., 1997.

———. "Ottoman Diplomacy at the Congress of Paris (1856) and the Question of Reforms." In *VII. Türk Tarih Kongresi, Ankara 25–29 Eylül 1970, bildiriler*, 580–86. Ankara: TTK Basımevi, 1973.

Deringil, Selim. *Conversion and Apostasy in the Late Ottoman Empire.* Cambridge: Cambridge University Press, 2012.

———. "Jewish Immigration to the Ottoman Empire at the Time of the First Zionist Congresses: A Comment." In *The Last Ottoman Century and Beyond*, edited by Minna Rozen, 141–49. Ramat Aviv: Tel Aviv University, 2002.

———. "Some Aspects of Muslim Immigration into the Ottoman Empire in the Late 19th Century." *Al-Abhath* 38 (1990): 37–41.

———. *The Well-Protected Domains: Ideology and the Legitimization of Power in the Ottoman Empire, 1876–1909.* London: I. B. Tauris, 1998.

Díaz-Más, Paloma. *Sephardim: The Jews from Spain.* Chicago: University of Chicago Press, 1992.

Dillon, Nara, and Jean Chun Oi. *At the Crossroads of Empires: Middlemen, Social Networks, and State-Building in Republican Shanghai.* Stanford: Stanford University Press, 2008.

Divine, Donna Robinson. "Palestine in World War I." In *The Middle East and North Africa: Essays in Honor of J. C. Horowitz*, edited by Reeva Specter Simon, 71–94. New York: Columbia University Press, 1990.

Donati, Sabina. *A Political History of National Citizenship and Identity in Italy, 1861–1950.* Stanford: Stanford University Press, 2013.

Dove, Richard, ed. *"Totally Un-English?": Britain's Internment of "Enemy Aliens" in Two World Wars.* Vol. 7, The Yearbook of the Research Centre for German and Austrian Exile Studies. Amsterdam: Editions Rodopi BV, 2005.

Dubin, Lois C. *The Port Jews of Habsburg Trieste: Absolutist Politics and Enlightenment Culture.* Stanford: Stanford University Press, 1999.

Dumont, Paul. "A Jewish, Socialist, and Ottoman Organization: The Workers' Federation of Salonica." In *Socialism and Nationalism in the Ottoman Empire, 1876–1923*, edited by Mete Tunçay and Erick J. Zürcher, 49–75. New York: British Academic Press, 1994.

Dundar, Fuat. "Empire of Taxonomy: Ethnic and Religious Identities in the Ottoman Surveys and Census." *Middle Eastern Studies* (2015): 136–58.

Eldem, Edhem. "French Trade and Commercial Policy in the Levant in the Eighteenth Century." *Oriente moderno* 18, no. 79 (1999): 27–47.

Elliot, Matthew. "Dress Codes in the Ottoman Empire: The Case of the Franks." In *Ottoman Customs: From Textile to Identity*, edited by Suraiya Faroqhi and Christoph K. Neumann, 103–23. Istanbul: Eren, 2004.

Elmaleh, Abraham. *Erets Israel ve-Suriya be-milhemet ha-'olam ha-rishona*, volumes 1 and 2. Jerusalem: Mizrah u-Ma'arav, 1927–28.

Fahmy, Ziad. "Jurisdictional Borderlands: Extraterritoriality and 'Legal Chameleons' in Precolonial Alexandria, 1840–1870." *Comparative Studies in Society and History* 55, no. 2 (2013): 305–29.

Fahrmeir, Andreas. *Citizens and Aliens: Foreigners and the Law in Britain and the German States, 1789–1870*. New York: Berghahn Books, 2000.

Farcy, Jean-Claude. *Les camps de concentration français de la première guerre mondiale (1914–1920)*. Paris: Anthropos-Economica, 1995.

Favell, Adrian. *Philosophies of Integration: Immigration and the Idea of Citizenship in France and Britain*. New York: Palgrave, 1988.

Feldman, David. *Englishmen and Jews: Social Relations and Political Culture, 1840–1914*. New Haven: Yale University Press, 1994.

———. "The Importance of Being English: Jewish Immigration and the Decay of Liberal England." In *Metropolis London: Histories and Representations since 1800*, edited by David Feldman and Gareth Stedman Jones, 56–84. London: Routledge Press, 1989.

Fisher, Michael H. "Excluding and Including 'Natives of India': Early-Nineteenth-Century British-Indian Race Relations in Britain." *Comparative Studies of South Asia, Africa, and the Middle East* 27, no. 2 (2007): 303–14.

Fitzgerald, Edward Peter. "France's Middle Eastern Ambitions, the Sykes-Picot Negotiations, and the Oil Fields of Mosul, 1915–1918." *Journal of Modern History* 66, no. 4 (1884): 697–725.

FitzRoy, Almeric. "Aliens Restriction." *Law Times: The Law and the Lawyer* 138 (1915): 258.

Fleming, K. E. *Greece: A Jewish History*. Princeton: Princeton University Press, 2008.

Fogarty, Richard S. "Between Subjects and Citizens: Algerians, Islam, and French National Identity during the Great War." In *Race and Nation: Ethnic Systems in the Modern World*, edited by Paul Spickard, 171–95. New York: Routledge, 2005.

———. *Race and War in France: Colonial Subjects in the French Army, 1914–1918*. Baltimore: Johns Hopkins University Press, 2008.

Franco, Manuela. "Uma influencia portuguesa no Levante? A diplomacia ao serviço da propaganda do prestígio da República." *Política Internacional*, no. 26 (2002).

Frankel, Jonathan. *The Damascus Affair: "Ritual Murder," Politics, and the Jews in 1840*. Cambridge: Cambridge University Press, 1997.

Friedman, Isaiah. "The System of Capitulations and Its Effect on Turco-Jewish Relations in Palestine, 1856–1897." In *Palestine in the Late Ottoman Period: Political, Social, and Economic Transformations*, edited by David Kushner, 280–93. Jerusalem: Yad Izhak Ben-Zvi; Leiden: Brill, 1986.

Friedman, Michal. "Recovering Jewish Spain: Politics, Historiography and Institutionalization of the Jewish Past in Spain (1845–1935)." Ph.D. dissertation, Columbia University, 2012.

Gainer, David. *The Alien Invasion: The Origins of the Aliens Act of 1905.* Oxford: Oxford University Press, 1971.

Galante, Avram. *Histoire des juifs de Turquie.* 9 vols. Istanbul: ISIS, 1985–86.

Gamble, Jos. *Shanghai in Transition: Changing Perspectives and Social Contours of a Chinese Metropolis.* London: RoutledgeCurzon, 2003.

Gampel, Benjamin R., ed. *Crisis and Creativity in the Sephardic World, 1391–1648.* New York: Columbia University Press, 1997.

Garrard, John. *The English and Immigration, 1880–1910.* London: Oxford University Press, 1971.

Gatrell, Peter. *The Making of the Modern Refugee.* Oxford: Oxford University Press, 2013.

———. *A Whole Empire Walking: Refugees in Russia during World War I.* Bloomington: Indiana University Press, 1999.

Gelber, N. M. "An Attempt to Internationalize Salonika, 1912–1913." *Jewish Social Studies* 17, no. 2 (April 1955): 105–20.

Gelvin, James. *Divided Loyalties: Nationalism and Mass Politics in Syria at the Close of Empire.* Berkeley: University of California Press, 1998.

George, Joan. *Merchants in Exile: The Armenians in Manchester, England, 1835–1935.* London: Taderon Press, 2002.

Gerber, Haim. *Crossing Borders: Jews and Muslims in Ottoman Law, Economy, and Society.* Istanbul: ISIS, 2008.

Ginio, Alisa Meyuhas. "Reencuentro y despedida: Dr. Ángel Pulido Fernández y la diáspora sefardí." In *España e Israel. Veinte años después,* edited by Raanan Rein, 57–66. Sevilla: Fundación Tres Culturas del Mediterráneo, 2007.

———. "The Sephardic Diaspora Revisited: Dr. Ángel Pulido Fernández (1852–1932) and His Campaign." In *Identities in an Era of Globalization and Multiculturalism: Latin America and the Jewish World,* edited by Judit Bosker Liwerant et al., 287–96. Leiden: Brill, 2008.

Ginio, Eyal. "Jews and European Subjects in Eighteenth-Century Salonica: The Ottoman Perspective." *Jewish History* 28/3–4 (2014): 289–312.

———. "Mobilizing the Ottoman Nation during the Balkan Wars (1912–1913)—Awakening from the Ottoman Dream." *War in History* 12 (2005): 156–77.

———. "'Ottoman Jews! Run to Save Our Homeland!'—Ottoman Jews in the Balkan Wars" [in Hebrew]. *Pe'amim* 105–6, no. 23 (2005/2006): 5–28.

———. "Perceiving French Presence in the Levant: French Subjects in the *Sicil* of 18th Century Ottoman Salonica." *Südost-Forschungen* 65/66 (2006/2007): 137–64.

———. *The Social and Cultural History of Ottoman Society during the Balkan Wars (1912–1913).* Forthcoming.

Göçek, Fatma Müge. *East Encounters West: France and the Ottoman Empire in the Eighteenth Century.* Oxford: Oxford University Press, 1987.

Goffman, Daniel. *Britons in the Ottoman Empire, 1642–1660.* Seattle: University of Washington Press, 1998.

———. *Izmir and the Levantine World, 1550–1650*. Seattle: University of Washington Press, 1990.

———. *The Ottoman Empire and Early Modern Europe*. Cambridge: Cambridge University Press, 2002.

Goode, Joshua. *Impurity of Blood: Defining Race in Spain, 1870–1930*. Baton Rouge: Lousiana State University Press, 2009.

Goodman, Bryna. *Native Place, City, and Nation: Regional Networks and Identities in Shanghai, 1853–1937*. Berkeley: University of California Press, 1995.

Griffiths, John. "What Is Legal Pluralism." *Journal of Legal Pluralism* 24 (1986): 1–55.

Groot, Alexander H. de. "Dragomans' Careers: The Change of Status in Some Families Connected with the British and Dutch Embasses at Istanbul 1785–1829." In *Friends and Rivals in the East: Studies in Anglo-Dutch Relations in the Levant from the Seventeenth to the Early Nineteenth Century*, edited by Alastair Hamilton, Alexander H. de Groot, and Maurits H. van den Boogert, 223–46. Leiden: Brill, 2000.

———. "The Historical Development of the Capitulatory Regime in the Ottoman Middle East from the Fifteenth to the Nineteenth Century." *Oriente moderno* 23, no. 3 (2003): 575–604.

Gullace, Nicoletta F. *The Blood of Our Sons: Men, Women, and the Renegotiation of British Citizenship during the Great War*. New York: Palgrave Macmillan, 2003.

Guttstadt, Corry. *Turkey, the Jews, and the Holocaust*. Cambridge: Cambridge University Press, 2013.

Hall, Catherine. *Civilising Subjects: Colony and Metropole in the English Imagination*. Chicago: University of Chicago Press, 2002.

Hall, Richard C. *The Balkan Wars 1912–1913: Prelude to the First World War*. London: Routledge, 2000.

Hall, William Edward. *A Treatise on the Foreign Powers and Jurisdiction of the British Crown*. Oxford: Clarendon, 1894.

Hanley, Will. "Foreignness and Localness in Alexandria, 1880–1914." Ph.D. dissertation, Princeton University, 2007.

———. "Papers for Going, Papers for Staying: Identification and Subject Formation in the Eastern Mediterranean." In *A Global Middle East: Mobility, Materiality, and Culture in the Modern Age, 1880–1940*, edited by Liat Kozma, Avner Wishnitzer, and Cyrus Schayegh. London: I. B. Tauris, 2014.

———. "When Did Egyptians Stop Being Ottomans? An Imperial Citizenship Case Study." In *Multilevel Citizenship*, edited by Willem Mass, 89–109. Philadelphia: University of Pennsylvania Press, 2013.

Hansen, Randell. *Citizenship and Immigration in Post-War Britain: The Institutional Origins of a Multicultural Nation*. Oxford: Oxford University Press, 2000.

Hirschon, Renée. *Crossing the Aegean: An Appraisal of the 1923 Compulsory Population Exchange between Greece and Turkey* New York: Berghahn Books, 2003.

Hudson, Manley O. "Rendition of the International Mixed Court at Shanghai." *American Journal of International Law* 21, no. 3 (July 1927): 451–71.

Hull, Isabel V. *A Scrap of Paper: Making and Breaking International Law during the Great World War*. Ithaca: Cornell University Press, 2014.

Hunt, Nancy Rose. *A Colonial Lexicon: Of Birth Ritual, Medicalization, and Mobility in the Congo*. Durham: Duke University Press, 1999.

Hurewitz, J. C., ed. *The Middle East and North Africa in World Politics: A Documentary Record*. New Haven: Yale University Press, 1975.

Hyman, Paula. *Gender and Assimilation in Modern Jewish History*. Seattle: University of Washington Press, 1995.

İnlalcık, Halil. "Imtíyāzāt—the Ottoman Empire." In *The Encyclopedia of Islam*, 1179–89. Leiden: Brill, 1960–2000.

İnalcık, Halil, and Donald Quataert. *An Economic and Social History of the Ottoman Empire*. 2 vols. Vol. 1. Cambridge: Cambridge University Press, 1997.

"Israélites de Palestine, Refugies en Corse." *L'univers Israélite* 71, no. 24 (February 1916).

Issawi, Charles. *The Economic History of Turkey, 1800–1914*. Chicago: University of Chicago Press, 1980.

———. "The Transformation of the Economic Position of Millets in the Nineteenth Century." In *Christians and Jews in the Ottoman Empire: The Functioning of a Plural Society*, edited by Benjamin Braude and Bernard Lewis. New York: Holmes & Meier Publishers, 1982.

Jackson, Stanley. *The Sassoons*. London: Heinemann, 1968.

Jacobson, Abigail. "A City Living through Crisis: Jerusalem during World War I." *British Journal of Middle Eastern Studies* 36, no. 1 (2009): 73–92.

———. *From Empire to Empire: Jerusalem between Ottoman and British Rule*. Syracuse: Syracuse University Press, 2011.

———. "Negotiating Ottomanism in Times of War: Jerusalem during World War I through the Eyes of a Local Muslim Resident." *International Journal of Middle East Studies* 40, no. 1 (2008): 69–88.

———. "Practices of Citizenship and Imperial Loyalty: The Ottomanization Movement as a Case Study" [in Hebrew]. In *Zionism and the Empires*. Jerusalem: Van Leer Academic Institute, forthcoming.

Jasanoff, Maya. "Cosmopolitan: A Tale of Identity from Ottoman Alexandria." *Common Knowledge* 11, no. 3 (2005): 393–409.

Jeuda, Basil. *World War One and the Manchester Sephardim*. Manchester: Shaare Hayim Synagogue, 2014.

Kark, Ruth, and Joseph B. Glass. "Eretz Israel/Palestine, 1890–1948." In *The Jews of the Middle East and North Africa in Modern Times*, edited by Reeva Spector Simon, Michael Menachem Laskier, and Sara Reguer, 335–47. New York: Columbia University Press, 2003.

Karpat, Kemal H. "Jewish Population Movements in the Ottoman Empire, 1862–1914." In *The Jews of the Ottoman Empire*, edited by Avigdor Levy, 399–421. Princeton: Darwin Press, Inc., 1994.

———. "The Ottoman Emigration to America, 1860–1914." *International Journal of Middle East Studies* 17 (May 1985): 175–209.

———. *Ottoman Population, 1830–1914*. Madison: University of Wisconsin Press, 1985.

———. *The Politicization of Islam*. New York: Oxford University Press, 2001.

Kasaba, Reşat. *The Ottoman Empire and the World Economy: The Nineteenth Century*. Albany: State University of New York Press, 1988.

Kayali, Hassan. *Arabs and Young Turks: Ottomanism, Arabism, and Islamism in the Ottoman Empire, 1908–1918*. Berkeley: University of California Press, 1997.

Kayaoğlu, Turan. *Legal Imperialism: Sovereignty and Extraterritoriality in Japan, the Ottoman Empire, and China*. Cambridge: Cambridge University Press, 2010.

Kechriotis, Vangelis Constantinos. "The Greeks of Izmir at the End of the Empire: A Non-Muslim Ottoman Community between Autonomy and Patriotism." Ph.D. dissertation, University of Leiden, 2005.

Kerber, Linda. *No Constitutional Right to Be Ladies: Women and the Obligations of Citizenship*. New York: Hill and Wang, 1999.

Kerem, Yitzchak. "The Influence of Anti-Semitism on the Jewish Immigration Pattern from Greece to the Ottoman Empire in the Nineteenth Century." In *Decision Making and Change in the Ottoman Empire*, edited by Cesar E. Farah, 305–14. Kirksville, MO: Thomas Jefferson University Press, 1993.

Kévorkian, Raymond H. *The Armenian Genocide: A Complete History*. New York: I. B. Tauris, 2011.

Kolsky, Elizabeth. "Codification and the Rule of Colonial Difference: Criminal Procedure in British India." *Law and History Review* 23, no. 3 (2005):631–83.

Lahiri, Shompa. "Contested Relations: The East India Company and Lascars in London." In *The Worlds of the East India Company*, edited by H. V. Bowen, Margarette Lincoln, and Nigel Rigby, 169–81. Woodbridge: D. S. Brewer, 2002.

———. "Patterns of Resistance: Indian Seamen in Imperial Britain." In *Language, Labour, and Migration*, edited by Anne J. Kershen, 155–78. Aldershot, UK: Ashgate, 2000.

Laskier, Michael Menachem. "Syria and Lebanon." In *The Jews of the Middle East and North Africa in Modern Times*, edited by Reeva Spector Simon, Michael Menachem Laskier, and Sara Reguer, 316–35. New York: Columbia University Press, 2003.

Laurens, Henry. "La politique musulmane de la France: caractères généraux." *Monde arab Maghreb Machrek*, no. 152 (April–June 1996): 3–14.

League of Nations. *Report of the Special Body of Experts on Traffic in Women and Children*. Geneva: Publications of the League of Nations, 1927.

Lehmann, Matthias. "A Livornese 'Port Jew' and the Sephardim of the Ottoman Empire." *Jewish Social Studies* 11, no. 2 (Winter 2005): 51–76.

Lemoine, Martine. "El Doctor Pulido y los 'Españoles sin patria.'" *El Olivo* 9 (1970): 92–95.

Levene, Mark. " 'Ni Grec, ni Bulgare, ni Turc'—Salonika Jewry and the Balkan Wars, 1912–1913." *Simon Dubnow Institute Yearbook* 2 (2003): 65–98.

———. *War, Jews, and the New Europe: The Diplomacy of Lucien Wolf, 1914–1919*. Oxford: Littman Library of Jewish Civilization, 2009.

Levy, Avigdor. "The Siege of Edirne (1912–1913) as Seen by a Jewish Witness: Social, Political, and Cultural Perspectives." In *Jews, Turks, Ottomans: A Shared History, Fifteenth through the Twentieth Century*, edited by Avigdor Levy, 153–94. Syracuse: Syracuse University Press, 2002.

Lévy, Lionel. *La nation juive portugaise: Livourne, Amsterdam, Tunis, 1591–1951.* Paris: Harmattan, 1999.

Levy, Lital. "Historicizing the Concept of Arab Jews in the Mashriq." *Jewish Quarterly Review* 98, no. 4 (Fall 2008): 452–69.

———. "Self and the City: Literary Representations of Jewish Baghdad." *Prooftexts* 26, no. 16 (2006): 163–211.

Lewental, D. Gershon. "Nehama, Joseph." In *Encyclopedia of Jews in the Islamic World*, edited by Norman Stillman. Leiden: Brill Online Reference Works, 2010.

Lewis, Mary Dewhurst. *The Boundaries of the Republic: Migrant Rights and the Limits of Universalism in France, 1918–1940.* Stanford: Stanford University Press, 2007.

———. *Divided Rule: Sovereignty and Empire in French Tunisia, 1881–1938.* Berkeley: University of California Press, 2013.

———. "Geographies of Power: The Tunisian Civic Order, Jurisdictional Politics, and Imperial Rivalry in the Mediterranean, 1881–1935." *Journal of Modern History* 80 (December 2008): 791–830.

Likhovski, Assaf. *Law and Identity in Mandate Palestine.* Chapel Hill: University of North Carolina Press, 2006.

Lohr, Eric. *Nationalizing the Russian Empire: The Campaign against Enemy Aliens during World War I.* Cambridge: Harvard University Press, 2003.

———. *Russian Citizenship: From Empire to Soviet Union.* Cambridge: Harvard University Press, 2012.

Lorcin, Patricia M. E. *Imperial Identities: Stereotyping, Prejudice, and Race in Colonial Algeria.* London: I. B. Tauris, 1995.

"Lucillo Merci (1899–1984)." WEFOR, http://www.gariwo.net/wefor/persona.php?idPersona =25&idGiardino=6.

Maier, Charles S. "Consigning the Twentieth Century to History: Alternative Narratives for the Modern Era." *American Historical Review* 105, no. 3 (2000): 807–31.

Malino, Frances. *The Sephardic Jews of Bordeaux: Assimilation and Emancipation in France.* Tuscaloosa: University of Alabama Press, 2003.

Mandel, Maud S. *In the Aftermath of Genocide: Armenians and Jews in Twentieth-Century France.* Durham: Duke University Press, 2003.

Marglin, Jessica. "The Extraterritorial Mediterranean." Presented at Middle East Studies Conference. Washington, D.C., 2014.

———. "In the Courts of the Nations: Jews, Muslims, and Legal Pluralism in Nineteenth-Century Morocco." Ph.D. dissertation, Princeton University, 2012.

———. "The Two Lives of Mas'ud Amoyal: Pseudo-Algerians in Morocco, 1830–1912." *International Journal of Middle East Studies* 44, no. 4 (2012): 651–70.

Marrus, Michael. *The Unwanted: European Refugees in the Twentieth Century.* New York: Oxford University Press, 1995.

Marrus, Michael Robert, and Robert Paxton. *Vichy France and the Jews.* New York: Basic Books, 1981.

Martín, José Antonio Lisbona. *Retorno a Sefarad: La política de España hacia sus judíos en el siglo XX.* Barcelona: Riopiedras, 1993.

Masters, Bruce. "The Sultan's Entrepreneurs: The Avrupa Tuccaris and the Hayriye Tuccaris in Syria." *International Journal of Middle East Studies* 24, no. 4 (1992): 579–97.

Mays, Devi. "Transplanting Cosmopolitans: The Migrations of Sephardic Jews to Mexico, 1900–1934." Ph.D dissertation, Indiana University, 2013.

Mazard, Jean-Albert. *Le régime des capitulations en Turquie pendant la guerre de 1914.* Alger: Imprimerie Jean Gaudet, 1923.

Mazower, Mark. *Governing the World: The History of an Idea, 1815 to the Present.* New York: Penguin Books, 2013.

———. *Inside Hitler's Greece: The Experience of Occupation, 1941–44.* New Haven: Yale University Press, 1995.

———. *Salonica, City of Ghosts: Christians, Muslims, and Jews 1430–1950.* New York: Vintage, 2006.

McCarthy, Justin. *The Population of Palestine: Population History and Statistics of the Late Ottoman Period and the Mandate.* New York: Columbia University Press, 1990.

Medina, Joao, and Joel Barromi. "The Jewish Colonization Project in Angola." *Studies in Zionism* 12, no. 1 (1991): 1–16.

Mendelsohn, Ezra. *On Modern Jewish Politics.* Oxford: Oxford University Press, 1993.

Menses, Filipe Ribeiro de. *Salazar: A Political Biography.* New York: Enigma Books, 2009–10.

Meron, Orly C. *Jewish Entrepreneurship in Salonica, 1912–1940.* Brighton, UK: Sussex Academic Publishing, 2011.

———. "Sub Ethnicity and Elites: Jewish Italian Professionals and Entrepreneurs in Salonica (1881–1912)." *Zakhor: Rivista di storia degli ebrei d'Italia* 8 (2005): 177–220.

Merry, Sally Engle. "Legal Pluralism." *Law and Society Review* 22, no. 5 (1988): 869–96.

Meyer, Maisie J. *From the Rivers of Babylon to the Whangpoo: A Century of Sephardi Jewish Life in Shanghai.* Lanham, MD: University Press of America, 2003.

———. "The Sephardi Jewish Community of Shanghai and the Question of Identity." In *From Kaifeng—to Shanghai: Jews in China,* edited by Roman Malek, 345–73. Nettetal: Steyler, 2000.

Milgram, Avraham. *Portugal, Salazar, and the Jews.* Translated by Naftali Greenwood. Jerusalem: Yad Vashem, 2011.

Ministry of the Interior, Refugees Administration. "Charity Reports. Jewish Refugee Camps. 1915 to 1918." Alexandria, 1918.

Moatti, Claude, and Wolfgang Kaiser, eds. *Gens de passage en Méditerranée de l'antiquité à l'époque moderne: procédures de contrôle et d'identification.* Paris: Maisonneuve & Larose, 2007.

Modiano, Patrick. *Suspended Sentences: Three Novellas.* New Haven: Yale University Press, 2014.

Molho, Michael, and Yehuda Nehama. *Sho'at yehude Yavan: 1941–1944.* Jerusalem: Yad Vashem, 1965.

Molho, Rena. "The Jewish Community of Salonika and Its Incorporation into the Greek State, 1912–19." *Middle Eastern Studies* 24, no. 4 (1988): 391–403.

———. "Jewish Working-Class Neighborhoods Established in Salonika Following the 1890 and 1917 Fires." In *The Last Ottoman Century and Beyond: The Jews in Turkey and the*

Balkans, 1808–1945, edited by Minna Rozen, 173–94. Tel Aviv: Goldstein-Goren Diaspora Research Center, 2002.

———. *Salonica and Istanbul: Social, Political, and Cultural Aspects of Jewish Life.* Istanbul: ISIS, 2005.

Morcillo, Matilde Rosillo. "La comunidad sefardita de Salónica: cuestión del reconocimiento de la nacionalidad española. Desde el final de las guerras balcánicas hasta la segunda guerra mundial." *Sefárdica* 17 (2008): 47–56.

Moreno, Eduardo Manzano, and Roberto Mazza, eds. *Jerusalem in World War I: The Palestinian Diary of a European Diplomat.* London: I. B. Tauris, 2011.

Morin, Edgar. "Vidal and His People." *Journal of Mediterranean Studies* 4, no. 2 (1994): 332–34.

Moyn, Samuel. *The Last Utopia: Human Rights in History.* Cambridge, MA: Harvard University Press, 2010.

Musleah, Ezekiel N. *On the Banks of the Ganga: The Sojourn of Jews in Calcutta.* North Quincy, MA: Christopher Pub. House, 1975.

Mutlu, Servet. "Late Ottoman Population and Its Ethnic Distribution." *Turkish Journal of Population Studies* 25 (2003): 3–38.

Myers, Norma. "The Black Poor of London: Initiatives of Eastern Seamen in the Eighteenth and Ninteenth Centuries." In *Ethnic Labour and British Imperial Trade: A History of Ethnic Seafarers in the UK*, edited by Diane Frost, 7–21. London: F. Cass, 1995.

Naar, Devin. "From the 'Jerusalem of the Balkans' to the Goldene Medina." *American Jewish History* 93, no. 4 (December 2007): 435–73.

———. "Jewish Salonica and the Making of the 'Jerusalem of the Balkans,' 1890–1943." Ph.D. dissertation, Stanford University, 2011.

———. *Jewish Salonica: Between the Ottoman Empire and the Greek Nation-State.* Forthcoming.

Nathans, Benjamin. *Beyond the Pale: The Jewish Encounter with Late Imperial Russia.* Berkeley: University of California Press, 2002.

Nevakivi, Jukka. *Britain, France, and the Arab Middle East, 1914–1920.* London: Athlone, 1969.

Nimni, Ephraim. *National Cultural Autonomy and Its Critics.* New York: Routledge Press, 2004.

Noiriel, Gérard, ed. *L'identification: Genèse d'un travail d'état.* Paris: Berlin, 2007.

Özsu, Umut. "Fabricating Fidelity: Nation-Building and the Greek-Turkish Population Exchange." *Leiden Journal of International Law* 24 (2011): 823–47.

———. *Formalizing Displacement: International Law and Population Transfers.* Oxford: Oxford University Press, 2015.

———. "Ottoman Empire." In *The Oxford Handbook of the History of International Law*, edited by Bardo Fassbender, Anne Peters, Simone Peter, and Daniel Högger, 429–48. Oxford: Oxford University Press, 2012.

———. "The Ottoman Empire, the Origins of Extraterritoriality, and International Legal Theory." In *The Oxford Handbook of the Theory of International Law*, edited by Florian Hoffmann and Anne Oreford, 429–48. Oxford: Oxford University Press, 2015.

———. "'A Thoroughly Bad and Vicious Solution': Humanitarianism, the World Court, and the Modern Origins of Population Transfer." *London Review of International Law* 1 (2013): 99–127.

Pamuk, Şevket. *The Ottoman Empire and European Capitalism.* Cambridge: University of Cambridge Press, 1987.

Panayi, Paniko. *The Enemy in Our Midst: Germans in Britain during World War One.* New York: St. Martin's Press, 1991.

Patterson, John Henry. *With the Zionists in Gallipoli.* New York: George H. Doran Company, 1916.

Pedersen, Susan. "Back to the League of Nations." *American Historical Review* 112, no. 4 (2007): 1091–117.

———. *The Guardians: The League of Nations and the Crisis of Europe.* Oxford: Oxford University Press, 2015.

———. "The Meaning of the Mandates System: An Argument." *Geschichte und Gesellschaft* 32, no. 4 (2006): 560–82.

Philliou, Christine. "Mischief in the Old Regime: Provincial Dragomans and Social Change at the Turn of the 20th Century." *New Perspectives on Turkey* 25 (2001): 103–21.

Plüss, Caroline. "Sephardic Jews in Hong Kong: Constructing Communal Identities." *Sino-Judaica: Occasional Papers of the Sino-Judaic Institute* 4 (2003): 57–80.

Poznanski, Renée. *Jews in France during World War II.* Translated by Nathan Bracher. Waltham, MA: Brandeis University Press, 2001.

Pulido, Ángel Fernández. *Españoles sin patria y la raza sefardí.* Madrid: Estab. Tip. de E. Teodoro, 1905.

Quataert, Donald. "The Age of Reforms, 1812–1914." In *An Economic and Social History of the Ottoman Empire*, edited by Halil İnalcık and Donald Quataert, 759–934. Cambridge: Cambridge University Press, 1994.

Raissiguier, Catherine. *Reinventing the Republic: Gender, Migration, and Citizenship in France.* Stanford: Stanford University Press, 2010.

Raz-Krakotzkin, Amnon. "The Zionist Return to the West and the Mizrahi Jewish Perspective." In *Orientalism and the Jews*, edited by Ivan Kalman and Derek Penslar. Brandeis: Brandeis University Press, 2005.

Recanati, David, ed. *Zikhron Saloniki: gedulatah ve-hurbanah shel Yerushalayim de-Balkan*, ha-'Orekh. Tel Aviv: ha-Va'ad le-hotsaat sefer Kehilat Saloniki, 1972.

———. "La maccabi-epoca heroica del sionismo en Salonique." In *Zikhron Saloniki: gedulatah ve-hurbanah shel Yerushalayim de-Balkan*, edited by David Recanati, 38–40. Tel Aviv: Ha-Va'ad le-hotsaat sefer kehilat Saloniki, 1971.

Rejwan, Nissim. *The Jews of Iraq: 3,000 Years of History and Culture.* New York: Westwide Press, 1985.

Renton, Alexander Wood. "The Revolt against the Capitulatory System." *Journal of Comparative Legislation and International Law* 15, no. 4 (1993): 212–31.

Rey, Francis. *La protection diplomatique et consulaire dans les échelles du Levant et de Barbarie.* Paris: L. Larose, 1899.

Reynolds, Nancy. *A City Consumed: Urban Commerce, the Cairo Fire, and the Politics of Decolonization in Egypt.* Stanford: Stanford University Press, 2012.

Risal, P. *La ville convoitée, Salonique.* Paris: Perrin et cie, 1918.

Ristaino, Marcia R. "Reflections on the Sephardi Trade Diaspora in South, Southeast, and East Asia." *Sino-Judaica: Occasional Papers of the Sino-Judaic Institute* 4 (2003): 105–25.

Robinson, Shira. *Citizen Strangers: Palestinians and the Birth of Israel's Liberal Settler State.* Stanford: Stanford University Press, 2013.

Rochlitz, Joseph (compiler). "Excerpts from the Salonika Diary of Lucillo Merci (February–August 1943)." *Yad Vashem Studies* 18 (1987): 306–8.

Rodrigue, Aron. *French Jews, Turkish Jews: The Alliance Israelite Universelle and the Politics of Jewish Schooling in Turkey 1860–1925.* Bloomington: Indiana University Press, 1992.

———. "From *Millet* to Minority: Turkish Jewry." In *Paths of Emancipation: Jews, States, and Citizenship*, edited by Pierre Birnbaum and Ira Katznelson, 238–61. Princeton: Princeton University Press, 1995.

———. *Jews and Muslims: Images of Sephardi and Eastern Jewries in Modern Times.* Seattle: University of Washington Press, 2003.

Rodrigue, Aron, and Esther Benbassa. *The Jews of the Balkans, the Judeo-Spanish Community, 15th–20th Centuries.* Oxford/Cambridge: Blackwell, 1993.

Rodrigue, Aron, and Sarah Abrevaya Stein. *A Jewish Voice from Ottoman Salonica: The Ladino Memoir of Sa'adi Besalel a-Levi.* Stanford: Stanford University Press, 2012.

Roland, Joan G. *The Jewish Communities of India: Identity in a Colonial Era.* New Brunswick, NJ: Transaction, 1998.

Rosenberg, Clifford. *Policing Paris: The Origins of Modern Immigration Control between the Wars.* Ithaca: Cornell University Press, 2006.

Roth, Cecil. *The Sassoon Dynasty.* London: R. Hale Limited, 1941.

Rothman, E. Natalie. *Brokering Empire: Trans-Imperial Subjects between Venice and Istanbul.* Ithaca: Cornell University Press, 2011.

———. "Intepreting Dragomans: Boundaries and Crossings in the Early Modern Mediterranean." *Comparative Studies in Society and History* 51, no. 4 (2009): 771–800.

Rozen, Minna. "Contest and Rivalry in Mediterranean Maritime Commerce in the First Half of the Eighteenth Century: The Jews of Salonika and the European Presence." *Revue des etudes juives* 147 (1988): 309–52.

———. "Les Marchands juifs livournais à Tunis et le commerce avec Marseille à la fin du XVIIe siècle." *Michael* 9 (1985): 87–129.

Saada, Emmanuelle. *Empire's Children: Race, Filiation, and Citizenship in the French Colonies.* Chicago: University of Chicago Press, 2012.

Saban, Giacomo. "À propos de la communauté juive italienne de Constantinople." *Revue des études juives* 158, no. 1–2 (January–June 1999): 89–106.

———. "I trattati di pace della primar guerra mondiale, il problema della cittadinanza e le leggi razziali fasciste." *Mondo contemporaneo*, no. 3 (2012): 149–59.

Sarfatti, Michele. *The Jews in Mussolini's Italy: From Equality to Persecution.* Translated by John Tedeschi and Anne C. Tedeschi. Madison: University of Wisconsin Press, 2006.

Satia, Priya. "Developing Iraq: Britain, India and the Redemption of Empire and Technology in the First World War." *Past & Present* 197 (2007): 211–55.

Sbaï, Jalila. "La République et la Mosquée: genèse et institution(s) de l'islam en France." In *Le choc colonial et l'islam: les politiques religieuses des puissances coloniales en terres d'islam*, 223–36. Paris: La Découverte, 2006.

Schilcher, Linda Schatkowski. "The Famine of 1915–1918 in Greater Syria." In *Problems of the Modern Middle East in Historical Perspective: Essays in Honour of Albert Hourani*, edited by John P. Spagnolo and Albert Hourani, 237–38. Reading: Ithaca Press, 1996.

Schreier, Joshua. *Arabs of the Jewish Faith: The Civilizing Mission in Colonial Algeria*. Piscataway: Rutgers University Press, 2010.

———. "From Mediterranean Merchant to French Civilizer: Jacob Lasry and the Economy of Conquest in Early Colonial Algeria." *International Journal of Middle East Studies* 44, no. 4 (2012): 631–49.

Schroeter, Daniel J. *The Sultan's Jew: Morocco and the Sephardi World*. Stanford: Stanford University Press, 2002.

Schwarzfuchs, Simon. "The Salonica 'Scale'—the Struggle between the French and the Jewish Merchants" [in Hebrew]. *Sefunot* 15 (1981): 79–80.

Scott, James C., John Tehranian, and Jeremy Mathias. "The Production of Legal Identities Proper to States: The Case of the Permanent Family Surname." *Comparative Studies in Society and History* 44, no. 1 (2002): 4–44.

Scott, Joan Wallach. *The Politics of the Veil*. Princeton: Princeton University Press, 2007.

Scully, Eileen P. *Bargaining with the State from Afar: American Citizenship in Treaty Port China, 1844–1942*. New York: Columbia University Press, 2000.

Serbestoğlu, Ibrahim. *Osmanli Kimdir? Osmanli Devleti'nde tabiiyet sorunu*. Istanbul: Yeditepe Yayınevi, 2014.

Shamir, Ronen. *The Colonies of Law: Colonialism, Zionism, and Law in Early Mandate Palestine*. Cambridge: Cambridge University Press, 2000.

Shapira, Anita. *Land and Power: The Zionist Resort to Force, 1881–1948*. Stanford: Stanford University Press, 1992.

Sharafi, Mitra. "Judging Conversion to Zoroastrianism: Behind the Scenes of the Parsi Panchayat Case (1908)." In *Parsis in India and the Diaspora*, edited by John R. Hinnells and Alan Williams, 159–80. London: Routledge University Press, 2007.

Shaw, Stanford. "The Ottoman Census System and Population, 1831–1914." *International Journal of Middle East Studies* 9 (1978): 325–38.

Shenhav, Yehouda. *The Arab Jew: A Postcolonial Reading of Nationalism, Religion, and Ethnicity*. Stanford: Stanford University Press, 2006.

Shepard, Todd. *The Invention of Decolonization: The Algerian War and the Remaking of France*. Ithaca: Cornell University Press, 2006.

Shields, Sarah D. *Fezzes in the River: Identity Politics and European Diplomacy in the Middle East on the Eve of World War II*. Oxford: Oxford University Press, 2011.

Shohat, Ella. "Rupture and Return: Zionist Discourse and the Study of Arab Jews." *Social Text* 21, no. 2 (2003): 49–74.

Sillman, Jael. "Crossing Borders, Maintaining Boundaries: The Life and Times of Farha, a Woman of the Baghdadi Jewish Diaspora." *Journal of Indo-Judaic Studies*, no. 1 (April 1998): 57–79.

Simon, Reeva Spector. *Iraq between the Two World Wars: The Creation and Implementation of a Nationalist Ideology*. New York: Columbia University Press, 1986.

———. "Iraq." In *The Jews of the Middle East and North Africa in Modern Times*, edited by

Reeva Spector Simon, Michael Menachem Laskier, and Sara Reguer, 347–66. New York: Columbia University Press, 2003.

——, and Eleanor H. Tejirian, eds. *The Creation of Iraq, 1914–1921*. New York: Columbia University Press, 2004.

Sousa, Nasim. *The Capitulatory Regime of Turkey: Its History, Origin and Nature*. Baltimore: Johns Hopkins University Press, 1933.

Starr, Deborah. *Remembering Cosmopolitan Egypt: Literature, Culture, and Empire*. New York: Routledge, 2009.

Starr, Joshua. "The Socialist Federation of Saloniki." *Jewish Social Studies* 7 (1945): 323–36.

Stein, Sarah Abrevaya. "Protected Persons? The Baghdadi Jewish Diaspora, the British State, and the Creation of the Jewish Colonial." *American Historical Review* 116, no. 1 (February 2011): 80–108.

——. *Saharan Jews and the Fate of French Algeria*. Chicago: University of Chicago Press, 2014.

Stillman, Norman. *The Jews in Arab Lands in Modern Times*. Philadelphia: Jewish Publication Society, 1991.

Svoronos, Nikos. *Le commerce de Salonique au XVIIIe siècle*. Paris: Presses universitaires de France, 1956.

Tabili, Laura. *Global Migrants, Local Culture: Natives and Newcomers in Provincial England, 1841–1939*. New York: Palgrave Macmillan, 2011.

——. "Outsiders in the Land of Their Birth: Exogamy, Citizenship, and Identity in War and Peace." *Journal of British History* 44 (October 2005): 796–815.

——. *"We Ask for British Justice": Workers and Racial Difference in Late Imperial Britain*. Ithaca: Cornell University Press, 1994.

Tamari, Salim. *Year of the Locust: A Soldier's Diary and the Erasure of Palestine's Ottoman Past*. Berkeley: University of California Press, 2011.

Tanenbaum, Jan Karl. *France and the Arab Middle East, 1914–1920*. Philadelphia: American Philosophical Society, 1978.

Tanielian, Melanie Schulze. "Feeding the City: The Beirut Municipality and the Politics of Food during World War I." *International Journal of Middle East Studies* 46, no. 4 (2014): 737–58.

Thayer, Lucius. "The Capitulations of the Ottoman Empire and the Question of Their Abrogation as It Affects the United States." *American Journal of International Law* 17, no. 209 (1923): 207–33.

Thompson, Elizabeth. *Colonial Citizens: Republican Rights, Paternal Privilege, and Gender in French Syria and Lebanon*. New York: Columbia University Press, 2000.

Timberg, Thomas A. "Baghdadi Jews in Indian Port Cities." In *Jews in India*, edited by Thomas Timberg, 273–84. New Delhi: Vikas, 1986.

Torpey, John. *The Invention of the Passport: Surveillance, Citizenship, and the State*. Cambridge: Cambridge University Press, 2000.

Trivellato, Francesca. *The Familiarity of Strangers: The Sephardic Diaspora, Livorno, and Cross-Cultural Trade in the Early Modern Period*. New Haven: Yale University Press, 2009.

Üngör, Uğur Ümit. *The Making of Modern Turkey: Nation and State in Eastern Anatolia, 1913–1950*. Oxford: Oxford University Press, 2011.

United States Department of State. *Capitulations of the Ottoman Empire. Report of Edward A. Van Dyck, Consular Clerk of the United States at Cairo, Upon the Capitulations of the Ottoman Empire since the Year 1150*. Washington, DC: Government Printing Office, 1881.

———. *Papers Relating to the Foreign Relations of the United States, 1914*. Washington, DC: U.S. Government Printing Office, 1928.

———. *Papers Relating to the Foreign Relations of the United States, 1914, Supplement, the World War*. Washington, DC: Government Printing Co., 1914.

van den Boogert, Maurits H. *The Capitulations and the Ottoman Legal System: Qadis, Consuls, and Beratlis in the 18th Century*. Leiden: Brill, 2005.

Vassilikou, Maria. "Post-Cosmopolitan Salonika—Jewish Politics in the Interwar Period." *Simon Dubnow Institute Yearbook* 2 (2003): 99–118.

Warburg, Felix Moritz. *Reports Received by the Joint Distribution Committee of Funds for Jewish War Sufferers*. Edited by Joint Distribution Committee. New York, 1916.

Weil, Patrick. *How to Be French: Nationality in the Making since 1789*. Translated by Catherine Porter. Durham: Duke University Press, 2008.

Westlake, John. *A Treatise on Private International Law, with Particular Reference to Its Practice in England*. London: Sweet & Maxwell, 1905.

Willoughby, Wester W. *Foreign Rights and Interests in China*. Baltimore: Johns Hopkins Press, 1920.

Yad Vashem. "Sebastián de Romero Radigales of Spain to Be Recognized as Righteous among the Nations." http://www.yadvashem.org/yv/en/pressroom/pressreleases/pr_details .asp?cid=890.

Yahil, Leni. *The Holocaust: The Fate of European Jewry, 1932–1945*. Translated by Ina Friedman and Haya Galai. Oxford: Oxford University Press, 1990.

Yeh, Wen-Hsin. *Shanghai Splendor: Economic Sentiments and the Making of Modern China, 1843–1949*. Berkeley: University of California Press, 2007.

Yellin, Shlomo. *Les Capitulations et la juridiction consulaire*. Beirut: Selim E. Mann, 1909.

Yerushalmi, Yosef. *From Spanish Court to Italian Ghetto: Isaac Cordoso, a Study in Seventeenth-Century Marranism and Jewish Apologetics*. New York: Columbia University Press, 1971.

Yosmaoğlu, Ipek. "Counting Bodies, Shaping Souls: The 1903 Census and National Identity in Ottoman Macedonia." *International Journal of Middle East Studies* 38, no. 1 (2006): 55–77.

Yudelowits, David. "Goley Erets Israel be-mitsrayim (be-yemei milhemet ha-'olam)." *Miyamim rishonim* 1, no. 7–12 (1934–35).

Yue, Meng. *Shanghai and the Edges of Empire*. Minneapolis: University of Minnesota Press, 2006.

Zuccotti, Susan. *The Italians and the Holocaust: Persecution, Rescue, and Survival*. New York: Basic Books, 1987.

INDEX

Abdülmecid I, 15
Abdülmecid II, 69, 186n2
Abravanel, Jacques, 48
Aciman, André, vii, 126–27, 128
ahdnameler. *See* capitulatory regimes
Ajaccio (refugee camp), 66, 67, 70
Akras, Alexander, 56–57
Aleppo, 17, 56, 59, 64, 89, 141n20, 147n61
Alexandria, 18, 19, 59–61, 62, 67
Algeria, 19, 50, 67, 69, 95, 145n43, 147n55, 168n7, 171n40
Algrante, Albert, 32, 33
Aliens Act (1914), 106
Aliens Restriction (Armenians, &c.) Order (1915), 88, 89, 90
Alliance israélite universelle (AIU): funds for burials, 71; honorability of individuals vouched for by, 81, 88, 171n29; influence on American Jewry, 93–94; leadership of, 63; Ottoman Jews supported by, 78, 81–82, 88; on policies regarding Jewish foreign nationals, 88; *protégés spéciaux,* 73; relations with French government, 77–79, 82, 88; relief aid, 62, 70, 71; schools of, 66, 94
allosemitism, 33, 88, 154n39
Alpes-Maritimes, Ottoman Jews in, 83

Amado, Abraham, 57
Amar family, 30, 31fig.1.1
American Jewry, 62, 76, 93–94, 96
Angola, 30–31, 32, 36, 46–47, 48, 49
Anticoni, Moise, 174n60
anti-Semitism, 15–16, 22, 25, 77, 144n35
Arab Jews, 111, 183n49
Arditti, David, 57
Arditti, Solomon/Salomão, 24, 34, 36, 42, 48, 157n64
Armenian genocide, 7, 12, 51, 52, 94, 161n7
Armenians, 7, 73, 77, 149n68
Ashkenazi brothers (Salomon, Abraham Haim, Israel), 50, 57, 66, 71
Ashkenazi Jews, 101, 118, 177n11
Asseo family, 146n46, 147n62
Association cultuelle orientale, 73, 81, 93–94, 170n26
Auschwitz (concentration camp), 121, 122, 125, 187n7
Austria-Hungary: and the abrogation of the capitulations, 54, 55; citizenship rights, 35, 43, 146n46, 147n62; imperial ambitions of, 10, 30; registrations of Salonican Jews, 33–34, 41, 151n8
Avrupa tüccarı, 147n61

Azose, Jacques, 73, 77–78, 80fig.3.1, 86, 93, 95–96

Baghdadi Jewish community of Shanghai: British policies toward, 99, 101–5, 178n16, 179n25; Indian residence of, 102–3, 116, 179n18; legal status of, 101, 103–4; marriage, 112–13; naturalization requests, 103–5; registration requests, 115–16; social status in, 107–8. *See also* Hardoon, Silas Aaron

Baghdadi Jews: acculturation of, 101, 177n12; advocacy on behalf of, 89; ambitions of, 100–102; British policies toward, 90, 92–93, 102–6, 113, 116, 174n62, 179n23, 180n31; defining, 100–101, 177n11; D. Sassoon and Company, 97, 102, 104, 106, 108, 176n3, 177n12; in India, 102–3, 116, 179n18; migration patterns of, 101, 105, 116; privileged treatment of, 108; protégé status of, 99; visibility of, 116

Balkan Wars, 17, 21–22, 24–26, 28, 30, 37, 77

Bastia (internment camp), 67

Bayonne, 5, 67, 138n7

Behar, Alberto, 123

Behar, Eugenia, 123

Behar-Menaham, Samuel, 18

Beja, Isaac, 37fig.1.2A, 38fig.1.2B, 39fig.1.2C

Beja, Julie, 37fig.1.2A, 39fig.1.2C

Belgian Congo, 81

Bene Israel (India), 102

Bentwich, Norman, 107, 113, 178n16, 181nn35–36, 184n60

Benveniste family, 45, 122

Ben-Yehuda, Eliezer, 163n20

berat (Ottoman grant of privilege), 13, 23, 141n20

Bergen-Belsen (concentration camp), 120–21, 187n7

Bigart, Jacques, 63

birth certificates, 74, 76, 91

birth place: in designation of British protected persons, 83–85, 89–91, 103, 110;

documentation of, 74, 76, 83, 84–85, 91, 101, 114; *jus soli,* 85, 171n40; Ottoman in designation of, 83–85, 89–91; subjecthood, 178n16

Blanzy (internment camp), 171n29

blood libels, 15–16, 144n35

Board of Deputies of British Jews, 62, 68, 88–90, 173n58

Borges family, 14, 28

Brazil, 42, 44, 45

British consular representatives: Baghdadi Jewish relations with, 99, 101–5, 115–16, 178n16; naturalization granted by, 22–23, 32, 103, 149n69; and Ottoman Jews in Great Britain, 87–88, 89; on Portuguese protection of Salonican Jews, 42; preferential treatment by, 64–65, 100, 107–11, 115; on protected persons status, 19–20, 87–88, 103–7, 115–16; protégé status granted by, 19–20; refugee aid by, 60, 64–65; restrictions on registration renewals by, 103–8; wartime service of, 56–57

British Foreign Office: Aliens Act (1914), 106; Baghdadi Jews' registration as British protected persons, 103–4; on Hardoon's subjecthood, 111–12; men's applications for naturalization papers denied by, 104–5, 179n25; on "Ottoman subjects of Jewish nationality," 75–76; protégé defined by, 116; subjecthood granted by, 108–11, 181n39, 182n41

British Home Office, 89–90, 91

British Nationality Act (1948), 102

British Nationality and Status of Aliens Act (1914), 88

British naturalization laws, 88, 89–90, 102, 110fig.4.2, 182n41, 182n45

British protected persons: Baghdadi Jews as, 99, 101–5, 113, 178n16; birth place in designation of, 83–85, 89–91, 103, 110; defining, 114, 115, 116, 117, 182n46, 183n52; denials of, 105, 106; domicile of choice in an extraterritorial community, 114,

naturalization: Baghdadi Jews' requests for,
102–6, 116, 180n31; bureaucratization in
Britain, 179n23; coercion, 58; commercial
possibilities of, 32–33; contestation of,
19–20, 97–99, 103–4, 110–11, 112, 182n46;
denial of, 22–23, 85, 104–5, 106, 110,
171n40, 179n25, 180n31; estate taxes, 110–
11, 182n41; of families, 34–35; flexibility
in awarding, 32–34; by gender, 84–85,
94–95, 104–5, 171n36, 179n25; of Jewish
merchants, 13–14, 26–34, 95, 101–2, 152n18,
153n25, 154n33; legislation, 28, 30–31, 33,
36, 76, 108–11, 115; negotiations for, 34–
35; personal narratives of, 106, 180n31;
provisional registrations, 35–36, 155n44;
social privilege, 108, 116, 181n39, 182n41;
strategies for, 25, 30, 34–35, 41–42, 105–6,
145n43, 180n31; in wartime, 41–42, 123
Nazi Germany, 120–26, 187n7
Nehama, Joseph, 29, 38–39, 41, 121, 152n19,
153n25, 156n49
New Christians, 5, 27, 67, 166n74
Nissim, Youda Leon, 76–77, 86
Noble Rescript of the Rose Chamber (Hatt-ı
Şerif of Gülhane), 15, 144n35

Ottoman consular representatives: citizenship granted by, 22–23, 30; legal jurisdiction over Ottoman subjects, 18, 147n62;
protected status granted by, 32
Ottoman Empire: abrogation of capitulatory
regime, 14–15, 17, 20–22, 27, 51, 53–57, 107,
143n28, 147n61, 162n20, 181n35; alliance
with Central Powers, 53; Allies declaration
of war on, 77; British consular representatives in, 19, 20; British relations with, 123,
174n65, 174n70; citizenship in, 21, 58–59,
147n61; Committee of Union and Progress
(CUP), 7, 17, 50, 51, 69, 186n2; erasure as
legal designation, 85–86; European public
law adopted by, 15; expulsions by, 50–51,
57, 163n31; identification as citizen of, 63;
identification of, 79; jihad used by, 51, 52,

69; Law of Nationality (1869), 21, 147n61;
millet system, 80–81; mixed court system,
126; Ottoman Jews in France, 79–81, 84,
87, 95–96; Public Debt Administration,
15; repatriation of Muslim protégés, 69;
Rhodesli Jews as protégé Italians in, 81, 85,
170n24; the Sublime Porte, 13, 69, 141n20,
144n35; supervision of protected subjects,
21, 147n62; Tanzimat (Ottoman reforms),
14–15; Treaty of Lausanne, 22, 119, 148n64.
See also capitulatory regimes; citizenship;
national identity
Ottoman Jews, 80fig.3.1; ancestry in
Bayonne, 67–68, 166n74; citizenship, 10,
22, 149n68; documentation of, 76–77;
in France, 73–84, 80, 80fig.3.1, 87–89,
94, 95–96, 123, 169n10, 171n29; in Great
Britain, 87–93, 102, 123, 172n46, 174n65,
174n70; *heimatlosen* status, 22, 149n67; migrations after World War I, 17; patriotism
of, 17–18, 89, 94; special protégés status,
75; in Tunisia, 82, 171n29; as Turkish
subjects by accident of birth, 89–90. *See
also* citizenship; documentation; protégé
status; Salonican Jewish community;
subjecthood
"Ottoman subjects of Jewish nationality,"
75–76, 87, 88, 91, 92fig.3.2

Padova, Salomon, 57
Palestine: Norman Bentwich in, 107, 113,
178n16, 181nn35–36; Christian community
in, 143n28; expulsion of foreign subjects,
50–51, 52, 57–58, 59, 63; French protégés
in, 70; Jewish community in, 16, 50, 57–58,
143n28, 160n2, 187n7; legal pluralism in,
53, 162n16; Occupied Enemy Territory
Administration, 71; reactions to the *irade*,
54, 162n16; repatriation to, 68, 71; treatment of Muslim protégés in, 69
Palmerston, Henry John Temple, 15–16
pan-Islamicism, 69
Paris Peace Treaty (1919), 15, 149n68